Making the Match

A Reader Confesses
by Kathi Appelt

I could tell you how much I loved
Black Beauty, and how I longed
to touch his silky skin, to pat his
neck when he was nothing more
than a street horse, "Oh Beauty,"
I would say, and stroke his
soft nose, his velvet ears,
and how it was that I wept for
his old stablemate Ginger.
I could tell you how horses
thundered through my dreams,
ran straight out of the pages
of Marguerite Henry and Will James
and Anna Sewell. I could say that
Misty and Smoky and Fury
were my best friends, and maybe
in some small sweet corner,
some dusty, yearning place
they still paw the ground,
swish their tails.

I could tell you all this,
but I'd rather say what books
are to me today, now that
those dreams of stallions and
mares and newborn foals
have passed to some other girl,
some other dreamer. Now that
my breasts sag and my
heart beats harder to coffee
than to Appaloosas and grays.

They didn't stop, the books.

They rest beside my bed,
the next to last thing I touch
before I mosey off to
sleep, my husband being
the last. They ride in my
purse on airplanes and ferries.
They come with me to
foreign countries and accompany
me to the dentist's office.

I share them with my closest
friends, feel connected through
our conversations of what we
loved, what we didn't, what
moved us, where we went.

They bind us, don't they,
these pages, these wandering
words, these stories that call
us to meet on a common street.

I could tell you about Black Beauty
and that girl who loved him.

But she wouldn't know to say
that it was the book that mattered,
not the horse.

May 26, 2003

Making the Match

The Right Book
for the Right Reader
at the Right Time,
Grades 4–12

Teri S. Lesesne

Stenhouse Publishers
Portland, Maine

Stenhouse Publishers
www.stenhouse.com

Library of Congress Cataloging-in-Publication Data
Lesesne, Teri S.
    Making the match : the right book for the right reader at the right time, grades 4–12 / Teri Lesesne.
        p. cm.
    Includes bibliographical references.
    ISBN 1-57110-381-3 (alk. paper)
    1. Teenagers—Books and reading—United States. 2. Preteens—Books and reading—United States. 3. High school students—Books and reading—United States. 4. Middle school students—Books and reading—United States. 5. Reading promotion—United States. 6. Young adult literature—Bibliography. I. Title.
Z1037.A1L47 2003
028.5′5—dc22   2003057392

Cover and interior design by Martha Drury
Cover illustration by Jon Berkeley/Getty Images

Manufactured in the United States of America on acid-free paper
09 08 07 06 05 04 9 8 7 6 5 4 3 2

This book is dedicated to the hundreds of students who have allowed me to talk incessantly about books, and to their teachers and librarians who continue to welcome me into their classrooms and libraries.

Author's Note

When I decided to write this book, I knew I wanted to include voices other than my own. I called upon some wonderfully talented authors of books for young adults and asked them to reflect on their reading during their youth. What were their memories of books and reading? What did they enjoy reading as young people? Why do they write for young adult readers? Why is reading so critical to the lives of our students?

Their eloquent contributions, placed between the chapters of this book, illuminate the power of books and reading in these authors' lives, and confirm the importance of encountering the right book at the right time.

Contributors
Kathi Appelt
T. A. Barron
Michael Cart
Sharon Creech
Chris Crowe
Chris Crutcher
Jack Gantos
Mel Glenn
Kimberly Willis Holt
Lee Bennett Hopkins
Jeanette Ingold
Paul Janeczko
Cynthia Leitich-Smith
Carolyn Meyer
Joan Lowery Nixon
John H. Ritter
Sonya Sones
Lori Aurelia Williams

Contents

Foreword

I once heard a parent ask a principal what type of child would not be successful at a particular magnet school. The principal, anticipating the more expected question of what type of child would be successful, had to pause and rethink his answer. He then began to list behaviors that would limit a child's chance of success at this particular school. I've always remembered that parent's way of forcing an answer that moved away from the expected—and therefore perhaps over-rehearsed—answer. I'll borrow that technique and start by describing who doesn't need to read *Making the Match*. If your students embrace reading with the passion we hoped they all would when we began teaching, then you don't need this book. If your students refuse to leave your classroom so that they can continue reading whatever novel you've most recently handed them, you don't need this book. If you don't have any trouble keeping up with young adult literature, you don't need this book. If you don't need to know any other ways to help connect kids to books, you don't need this book. But, if your kids are reluctant to read, if you find yourself wondering which books to recommend, if you need some powerful ways to motivate students to read, then *Making the Match* is the right match for you. While this book does all that, and more, its main goal is to help us guide our reluctant readers toward reading.

We see them every day—those students who sit in our classrooms unwilling to read for pleasure, for assignment, or for information. We can cajole, entreat, or demand that they read this book or that, and yet, despite (or sometimes it seems to spite) our best intentions, some students choose not to read. We hold up a book that we promise will offer intrigue, excitement, and page-turning suspense that they will love; they hold up their hands and ask if that will be on the test. We tell them about our favorite authors; they sink lower into their seats wondering who cares. We explain that reading a book is like creating a movie in our minds. They suggest that it's easier to just rent the video. We think about adopting their favorite gesture (a shrug) and their favorite answer ("I don't know") when considering what to do when kids won't read.

But then we pause and think of the consequences of aliteracy, the choice not to read. We quickly recognize the personal and societal issues that surround illiteracy. Such recognition has led to programs that help all students who struggle to read. However, less attention and therefore fewer dollars are given to the subtler problem of aliteracy. Reluctant readers often do their schoolwork well—or at least well enough that we shift our attention from students who are reluctant to read to those who can't read. They get by from year to year, becoming that invisible student when the conversation focuses on books they've supposedly read.

These reluctant readers vow that reading is "boring," a "do-nothing," a "waste of time," and "a thing so bad it almost hurts." They leave school— either at graduation or whenever they drop out—reporting that they'll never again read another book voluntarily. And then they have children and, keeping their vow, read to them occasionally, if at all. Those children enter first grade lacking the rich home reading experiences that, as explained by the landmark study *Becoming a Nation of Readers,* "prepare children for success in reading" (p. 57). These students come to school lacking a positive stance toward reading, having never experienced that aesthetic connection that Louise Rosenblatt, in *Literature as Exploration,* explained as critical to forge a connection with a text. Many of these students move through school adopting an aversion toward reading and the insidious cycle of aliteracy continues.

To break this cycle, teachers must recognize that a dislike of reading is an acquired taste. One isn't born with a love for or an aversion to reading. Experiences at school and at home with parents, peers, teachers, and a variety of texts all help form a student's reading attitude. By the time a child reaches middle or high school, teachers often believe that a negative reading attitude is set and the best that can be hoped for is a tolerance toward reading—or at least a passive acceptance of a particular book. But some teachers want more. Some teachers believe that when students are repeatedly given the right book they will come to embrace reading with a commitment that will turn their aversion into acceptance and their antipathy into passion. These teachers know that matching kids to books doesn't happen through happenstance. It happens when teachers know adolescents, know books, and know how to bring the two together. It happens when, in short, teachers know what Teri Lesesne knows about working with reluctant readers.

Those of us who know Teri know that she's best known by adolescents as "The Book Lady" and by colleagues as, well, "The Book Lady." Whether she's writing her young adult book column for *Voices from the Middle,* flying off to give a keynote speech at another conference, or visiting with a group of teachers at a National Council of Teachers of English annual conference, Teri is known for her willingness to tell anyone about yet another young adult literature book. Now, in *Making the Match,* Teri shows us how she's successfully connected countless reluctant readers to reading. Each time she's followed the same formula: know about kids, know about books, and know about ways to tell kids about books. And each time, kids discover that reading, whether informational texts or novels, can act as a mirror to teach them more about themselves or as a window to show them more about the world. They learn that a connection to literature isn't about passing another ten-item multiple choice test, but it is about measuring themselves against a character to see where they differ, where they match. They learn to sometimes resist the author and other times to applaud. They have the opportunity to consider our greatest dilemmas—good and evil, courage and fear, love and betrayal, greed and generosity—within the safe setting of the pages of a book.

Filled with essays about reading by young adult authors, hundreds of titles that teens always enjoy, tips on keeping up with what adolescents want to read, and practical suggestions for connecting kids to books, *Making the Match* informs and instructs as it entertains and enlightens.

Acknowledgments

Many people provided assistance, encouragement, and knowledge along the way, people whose influences helped to shape this book even before I began to write it. A book never comes simply from the mind of the person doing the writing. Well, maybe it does. However, my mind has been shaped by so many people and experiences. Without those influences, I would not be able to tell the stories in this book.

I am indebted to Dick Abrahamson. He has been teacher, friend, mentor, and colleague. He set the standard for those of us who sat in his classes. His knowledge of the field is extraordinary; his willingness to impart that knowledge is beyond generous. I can still hear Dick's lectures from the literature classes reverberate through my own. So much of what I know about this field comes from his wisdom. I was paid the ultimate compliment once by a student who had taken a class from Dick and then transferred to my university. She told me that I reminded her of Dr. Abrahamson. I strive for just that. Thanks, Dick, for teaching me about the wealth offered by young adult literature.

I am grateful that some folks thought I might have something to say in a book. Thanks, Janet Allen, Bill Varner, and Philippa Stratton, for telling me that I had words worth sharing with others. Janet would tell me every time she saw me that I needed to be writing it all down, that I had something worth sharing. She offered some valuable tips along the way. Bill Varner is one of the most talented editors I have had the good fortune to know. There was never any pressure placed on me, just gentle nudging when I needed it the most. I still wonder how he could sense, from thousands of miles away, that I needed a push toward the computer chair. He also knew when to tell me to walk away from it for a while to gain perspective. Philippa gave her all-important stamp of approval early in the writing. It spurred me to sit down in front of the computer. Thanks to all of you, also, for checking in with me without checking up on me, for reminding me that I needed to take time to write down what I was preaching.

I appreciate the encouragement from friends and colleagues. Mary Berry, boss and friend, not only encouraged me to take on this challenge but allowed me to adjust my schedule to make time for writing. Lois Buckman, friend, "sister," and librarian extraordinaire, provided me with stories and examples, helped me track down bibliographic information, and helped me complete the book lists in the appendixes. It is great to have a friend who is a librarian! Martha Magner, colleague, friend, and supportive shoulder: thanks for providing words of motivation when I most needed them. A special thanks to Kylene Beers for going first and then sharing the horror and the glory with me. Kylene would call and fill me with encouragement about what I was doing. She also gave me great advice and was kind enough to offer to write the foreword to this book despite her own hectic schedule. Kylene continues to be a model for me as a writer, an editor, and a teacher.

For the authors who took time from their own writing to contribute their own memories of reading, a thousand thank-yous are not enough. Their words capture so much of what I want to say about the importance of the right book at the right time for the right reader. Their eloquence speaks for itself in the pages of this book. Thanks, then, to Kathi Appelt, T. A. (Tom) Barron, Michael Cart, Sharon Creech, Chris Crowe, Chris Crutcher, Jack Gantos, Mel Glenn, Kimberly Willis Holt, Lee Bennett Hopkins, Jeanette Ingold, Paul Janeczko, Cynthia Leitich-Smith, Carolyn Meyer, Joan Lowery Nixon, John H. Ritter, Sonya Sones, and Lori Aurelia Williams. And a mighty special thanks to my pal Joan Bauer for her afterword for the book.

To my professional colleagues, especially my home base, ALAN (the Assembly on Literature for Adolescents of the National Council of Teachers of English), I owe more than I can ever repay. From Don Gallo, who was the first to invite me to share what little I knew about young adult literature at an ALAN workshop, to the countless leaders of this organization who have inspired and informed my writing, all I can say is thank you for allowing me to be a part of this august group. The Young Adult Library Services Association of the American Library Association welcomed me into that group despite my lack of experience in the field. I found a second home there thanks to Patty Campbell, Bonnie Kunzel, Mary Arnold, Ed Sullivan, and Michael Cart. The National Council of Teachers of English has always felt like home to me, even more so when the council added the middle-level section. I have been fortunate to work side by side with fabulous teachers in that group. Thanks, Kathie Ramsey, Barry Hoonan, Sandy Hayes, Virginia

Broz, Howard Miller, Tonya Perry, Suzanne Metcalfe, Ruth Lowrey, Linda Rief, and Kathy Egawa.

Finally, always, there is a huge debt owed to my family. To my sisters, Jo, Ruth, and Mary Pat, who bust their buttons over any small accomplishment in my professional career; to my mom, who has shared every piece I have ever written with unwitting guests to her home; and to my dad, who calls me "Doc" and smiles proudly over every accomplishment, thanks, guys. My grandchildren, Cali, Corrie, and Natalie, keep me grounded in reality. I am fortunate to have them close at hand. Their experiences continue to provide me with some of my best material. They were willing subjects in my grand experiment in raising readers. I hope this book reminds them of all they can accomplish through hard work with the assistance of family and friends. Thanks also to them for their permission to share some of their reading stories throughout the book. Finally, to Henry, thanks for giving me some important gifts: the freedom to grow professionally even though it meant time away from you and the kids, time by myself to write, and constant reassurance that I had this book in me. Thanks for helping me give birth to this work.

Introduction

For Christmas one year, I presented my then eleven-year-old grand-daughter Corrie with a new book in the Darren Shan vampire series she had been reading. She opened the small package less eagerly than she had the brightly colored boxes containing her new CD player and the CDs to accompany it. It was easy to tell from the shape of the package that it was, after all, just a book. However, when Corrie saw the title she burst into tears! "This is the best gift I ever got," she announced as she struggled to convey her pleasure. By the end of Christmas Day, Corrie had completed her first reading of the book. "Did you ever read a book that was perfect, one that you did not want to end?" she asked. As a lifetime reader, I knew exactly what Corrie meant. This book was the right book at the right time. In a few years, its memory would fade. Corrie might one day find it hard to explain why this book had meant so much to her. But, at the time, it was just the right book.

Okay, I can hear you saying, "But this was your granddaughter. Finding the right book at the right time for her was much easier than finding such books for all of my students." Of course, there is some truth in that. However, my making the match for Corrie and your making the matches for your students are not terribly different. Making the match between book and reader relies on knowledge in three areas: knowing the reader, knowing the book, and knowing the techniques and strategies for bringing book and reader together. Over the more than twenty-five years I have been teaching, I have learned as much as I could about teens, books, and teaching strategies. I have had the good fortune to find good books and pair them with less-than-enthusiastic readers.

My first fifteen years of teaching were spent teaching English and reading to middle school students. In that time I encountered thousands of students. Some were gifted students who were already avid readers. Making the match for them was a simple matter of defining their interests and locating books that met their stated preferences. Avid readers know how to ask for book suggestions. They also have friends who are readers and who can recommend new books. However, I have had more than my share of students who were unmotivated and unskilled readers, kids who threw down a verbal gauntlet on the first day of class: "I have never found a book I like, and I intend to keep this record going another year." Frankly, I love this challenge. It gets my juices flowing. Even after all these years, the faces of these gauntlet throwers come to me.

Peter was one of the most gifted students I have had the pleasure to teach. His challenge was a bit atypical. He had read all the good books out there (or so he told me). I thought he had me stumped until I paired him with S. E. Hinton's *The Outsiders*. Yes, Peter had read tons of books. However, he had missed a few along the way, most notably, the classics of young adult (YA) literature. Peter proceeded from Hinton, a "guy" who truly seemed to understand him, to Paul Zindel, and then to Robert Cormier. Rafael confided to me that he had never read a book completely for a school assignment. He would read just enough to do his book report and then turn on the TV. When I asked him what an author could write about that might be of interest, he replied, "Baseball." He finally discovered the joy of reading with Gary Soto's *Baseball in April and Other Stories*. Sean rejected many titles and fought me with all his might before succumbing to Bruce Brooks's *The Moves Make the Man*. I still remember the day he dropped the book casually on the desk and announced to me that I should not let the cover fool me; the book was about a whole lot more than basketball. Sean, Peter, and Rafael are the archetypes, it seems to me, for all the kids who came and went over those fifteen years of teaching middle school. Making the match was important for avid, reluctant, and nonreaders alike.

How did I begin this process of making matches between books and readers? I had help from some terrific teachers. Nancie Atwell's *In the Middle* (1987) clarified much of what I had been attempting to do with literature in the classroom. Running a reading workshop seemed easier once I had read Nancie's groundbreaking work. Graduate classes in literature for children and teens from Dick Abrahamson were an immense help as I struggled to find the right books at the right time for my students. Later in my teaching career, more books and teachers inspired and informed me. Janet Allen's books discussed how to make books come alive in the classroom. Harvey Daniels's concept of literature circles brought some organization to how we plan book discussion in classrooms. And even before literature circles, there was the writing of Terry Ley on Directed Individualized Reading. The work of Linda Rief informed me about various approaches as well, especially how to connect with classroom strategies. I sat in workshops and listened to my good friend and colleague Kylene Beers as she described quick activities for less-than-enthusiastic readers. I have had the great good fortune of a world of classrooms in which I could play student and teacher all in one fell swoop. The bottom line, though, is even more basic. I read tons of books and still do. You need to be a reader to even begin to make a match between a student and the perfect book.

While all the teachers and books became part of what I was doing in the classroom, there were a few elements missing, pieces that I needed to complete the process. The more reading I did, both of professional books and of YA books, the more tuned the process became for me. Over the past few years, as I honed my skills teaching at the university level, other events have refined my process.

- One of my former middle school students, now a doctoral student in education, recently attended an International Reading Association conference. As I introduced him to colleagues, he talked about the books and strategies I had used some twelve years earlier to help him find and read good books.
- Undergraduate and graduate students in my university classes write at the beginning of the semester about their fears of having to read so much in such a short time. By the end of the semester, they are amazed to see that they have managed not only to read what is required but have gone beyond the requirements and read even more. Many comment that their interest in reading has been renewed.
- As I go out into classrooms and libraries to talk to students about books, you can imagine how resistant the audience is at first. However, there is always a demand for the books "that lady told us about" after my visit is over.
- Recently, more than one thousand librarians packed a session on new books for teens. I receive requests to speak to kids and teachers each year about books and reading.

Clearly, the time had come for me to begin telling my story, the story of how I helped make the match between book and reader.

So, what is this book all about? How will it add to the wonderful professional texts already in the field? In a sentence, this is a book that describes how to make the match between reader and text. If you will take this journey with me, I will guide you to the books and activities and strategies and theories that will help you in your efforts to help students become lifelong readers, those of us who read because reading is such an ingrained part of who we are. Along the journey, I hope to answer several questions. Who are these beings we call young adults? Why is it important to find good books to motivate them to read? How does the content of this book fit into what you are already doing in your classes? What can you do to motivate reluctant readers? Which books work best with different types of readers? It is an ambitious travel plan, certainly. I hope you will pack snacks, find a comfortable seat, and fasten your seat belt as we embark on a voyage to discover how to find the right book at the right time for the right reader.

From the time I could decode a baseball box score in the morning paper, I've loved reading, especially reading with a purpose. But I've never been a so-called voracious reader. Call it the boredom factor, call it impatience, call it a lust for a certain music on the page, but from as far back as I can remember, I've been so picky about what I want from a book that, even today, I finish reading maybe one novel out of every one hundred I start. And it's not for lack of trying.

I love to read. In my early years, biographies topped my list. Wild and crazy Dizzy Dean, crazier still Jimmy Pearsall, and beer-sucking, hot dog-chomping, cigar-puffing Babe Ruth, to name a few. And every one was a character. By the time I was nine years old, I'd read all about their lives and a lot more.

My Life as a Reader in a Stolen Moment Talkin' Blues by John H. Ritter

And I had a reason. Convinced that some day I would be a pro ballplayer myself, I needed to know what each one was doing by age nine (when I was nine) and at age ten (when I turned ten), and so on, year by year, until well into my teens. I needed to know their tricks and jokes. I needed to know how wild I could be. At each turn and juncture, I needed to measure the progress of my dreams.

But with fiction I was more demanding. Where biographies and histories were like listening to the news, fiction was more like listening to music. Novels needed to sing to catch my attention. Fictional prose needed rhythm, melodic themes, subthemes, and harmonies. I looked for licks and lyrics, hooks and bridges, allegros and crescendos. On the page I craved la vida.

For a country boy who grew up dreaming, I needed novels that could fill my well with thirst-quenching stories, fill the fairground grandstands with characters of wild color, and the whole mountain sky with lies and folderol, sincerity and grace, with gumption and guilt. If Dizzy Dean could tell three straight reporters he was born in three different towns, and none of them the true one, then the novels should be able to people their pages with characters bigger than Babe and Dizzy and Jimmy combined. At least for my money. If Jimmy Pearsall could have a nervous breakdown in the middle of a ballgame and climb the screen behind home plate screaming at a mortified hometown crowd, then characters in novels should be able to jump through that screen and into the minds and lives of those living on the other side.

Ah, but dreams can change. And lucky thing. Because so did my ability to hit a left-handed curveball, coming at me about head high, making me duck and close my eyes just before it magically broke right over the plate. Somewhere around my junior year in high school, somewhere between the time a Charlie Company 1st Battalion 20th Infantry unit slaughtered some 350 unarmed villagers in the hamlet of My Lai and my senior prom, I realized that whatever gift I'd had for hitting a baseball—and the dreams tied to it—were no longer important enough or relevant enough for me to pursue.

It was right around that time when a certain black book fell from heaven into my hands and changed my life. An amazing book—full of crazy characters, of sadness and love, of desperation and revolution, of insight and morality. It was political and poetical, religious and surreptitious. It was a biography of the world and it was pure fiction. I was captivated by it, motivated by it, undressed, unblest, and depressed by it. All that summer, I'd been teaching myself primitive piano, had fancied myself a bluesy, outraged rock star or an actor maybe, or anyone with an audience, anyone with a voice. Then on this one particular hot, dry October afternoon, my older brother left for college and left behind his Bob Dylan songbook.

It was long, lean, shiny, and black, a paperback, over a hundred pages full of musical notes and chords and the most surprising poetry I'd ever read. All of a sudden I had a new dream. I tore the baffle off my electric organ, cranked up the tiny Sears and Roebuck mail order amp, and sang that raggedy book from cover to cover, memorizing beat street lyrics, adopting the wail of a moaning man of constant sorrow, a tambourine man, a weather man, only a pawn, only a hobo, but one more is gone. Leaving nobody to sing his sad song, and on and on. And I knew what I wanted to be.

I would be the storyteller, the historian, the biographer of mixed up, dreamed up characters like these, who push fake morals, insult, and stare, whose money doesn't talk, it swears. Or those who sing in the rat race choir, bent out of shape by society's pliers. Characters with eyes, with guts.

And so I wrote. Dear God, I wrote. I began carrying around a spiral notebook in my pocket, cover torn, metal spirals flattened from school desk seats, pages bent, half-ripped, but all filled with blue pen lines scribbled out, fast-paced, double-spaced, into crumbled civil rightist protest war love songs about jack the pauper who earns money now sellin' plants he grows around. Or, the welfare girl who lives next door, sleeps with poisons on her floor. Or, judy who cries to herself at night and gypsy harold looking bitter an' tight, machine gun hermits on a friday night, drinkin' in the backseat shot after shot, screamin' out the window, what hath god rot.

Stuff like that.

John Updike once said that of all the fine arts, writing is the most self-taught. I agree. You learn to write by reading what other thinkers have thought, what other writers have wrought, by studying the struggles and battles they've fought. You watch them riff, then you try it yourself.

Dylan's poems led me to Jack Kerouac's *On the Road,* then to John Steinbeck's *The Grapes of Wrath,* and back again somehow—with different eyes—to Mark Twain's *Roughing It.* All journey books, all the manic panic of romance and motion that a country boy needs.

A book may show you something new and amazing, or it may not. Depends on the words. Personally, I look for the ones that do. And I don't think finding one out of a hundred is all that unexpected or disappointing. But to this day, I cannot hear a Bob Dylan song without getting extra nervous.

For my money, that's what a book should do. It should tie you up, it should work you up, make you think, make you see, make you feel extra happy and sorrowful, extra nervous and bold. It must be dream laden, scheme sodden, soul shaking. And it must do all of this as mysteriously as a left-handed curveball coming at your head, twisting and spinning and making you duck until, at the very end, it magically crosses home plate, with such grace and command that it humbles, crumbles, and amazes you.

To paraphrase Tolstoy, "All normal families are like one another; each dysfunctional family is dysfunctional in its own way."

Without going into the pathology, without detailing in large font the idiosyncrasies of my family, where drama loomed larger than the black-and-white Hallmark specials of the '50s and '60s, reading was for me a magic Narnia portal back then, one that would fly me above and beyond the mean though tree-lined streets of Brooklyn.

Later on, I would make good my escape to the campuses of Indiana and the rain forests of Sierra Leone, but growing up, pre–double digits years, there was no escape from the battles that raged nightly over mandatory family dinners, a chronically sick sibling, or power struggles between my mother and my father. I was a prisoner of war before I knew what the term meant.

On Reading, or a Reader Grows in Brooklyn by Mel Glenn

I read to escape, pure and simple, and to breathe. Inside the pages of many books I could breathe rarefied air, far away from domestic turmoil. Reading provided an insulation against a house gone crazy. If Faulkner wrote about skeletons in the closet, I had a wardrobe. Monsters were much more manageable in print than in real life. Only later on did I learn, surprise (!), that many other families lived on the brink and maybe my dysfunctional family functioned better than some.

My first recollection of reading was of subway signs out of Brighton Beach, Brooklyn. I knew them all: Brighton Beach, Sheepshead Bay, Kings Highway, Newkirk Ave., Church Ave., Prospect Park, Seventh Ave., Atlantic Ave., Dekalb Ave., and then into the city of Manhattan. (Was I planning an escape route so early in life?)

I would read anything in print with my large "four eyes" glasses. I'd stack comic books (loved Donald Duck), newspapers, library books on a table near my chair, and swallow them hungrily as country music poured from the radio. (Was this the first mixed media approach to reading?)

At different ages, at different times, I read anything printed, from the backs of cereal boxes to the front of the sports pages, from catching *The Taxi That Hurried* [Lucy Mitchell], to losing myself in the adventures of Herbert, from the rebellion of Holden in *Catcher in the Rye* [J. D. Salinger], to the rebellion on *Animal Farm* [George

Orwell]. The book I remember most in high school was Neville Shute's *On the Beach* with its vision of thermonuclear war, a true horror story. Fantasy, fiction, true life, I devoured books whole like some myopic carnivore who sometimes retreated back to his cave blanket with flashlight to continue reading well into the a.m.

What else do I remember reading? Too numerous to name, but I do remember the Landmark series of books, which told about history as diverse as the Wright Brothers, the French Revolution, and the California Gold Rush. I could be standing at Kitty Hawk, the Bastille, or Sutter's Mill, far from the current events raging on at my house.

I remember reading newspapers from the back pages to the front because sports was another essential escape route. I found the front pages, too, with their faraway places. I'd collect datelines like some collected stamps: Ulan Bator, Kuala Lumpur, Marrakech, Rio de Janeiro, Geneva. These cities and more sang a siren song to me, making me wonder what lay on the other side of the ocean which was just blocks from my house, whose occupants often shook it to its foundations.

Years later, high school provided neither geography nor direction. To be sure, I felt more comfortable with Steinbeck than Shakespeare, Hemingway than Hawthorne. Dickens seemed too dense, and Wordsworth, well, too wordy. And in those Eisenhower years there were few books that contained teenage protagonists who in any way or form resembled me or my weird family.

I realized I was on a mission to find myself, define myself, and discovered relatively late as an adult, the only way I could do that was by writing about the kids I knew and taught. I taught for over thirty years in the same high school I went to as a kid, and though times change, certain teenage truths don't, and I saw in my students' faces some of the same joys and pains I had experienced years before.

I attempted to find myself through my fictional characters. As Nolan says, standing in front of a fun-house mirror, "Parents, teachers, friends, / shout advice from every corner of the park, / But all I hear is the same tinny music / Over and over again. / I wonder if I'll ever see / A clear image of myself." I am still looking for that clear image of myself as I check airline schedules and places I haven't seen to run far away from a childhood I never asked for.

Oh, by the way, I live on one of the nicest tree-lined streets in Brooklyn. I still read voraciously, fantasy, fiction, true life—and the newspapers, of course.

Knowing the Kids

The library in the small Pennsylvania town where I grew up was a single room, rather dark; books lined the walls with row upon row of shelves crammed in the open space between. When I stopped off there after school, dust motes danced in the late afternoon light. The only sounds were the creak of the old wooden floors and the clunk of the date stamp wielded by Mrs. Stuckenrath, the librarian, who also happened to be a member of my mother's bridge club.

A Literary Quest

by Carolyn Meyer

I knew those densely packed shelves held all kinds of knowledge, and the knowledge I sought most earnestly when I was a young teenager usually revolved around sex. Those were the days before sexual images smacked us in the eyeballs at the movies, on TV, on billboards along the highway, and thongs were the subject of the evening news. My mother subscribed to *Cosmopolitan* (well before the era of Helen Gurley Brown and the navel-baring magazine covers), and I devoured the short stories with illustrations of square-jawed men embracing women with eyelashes thick as toothbrushes—aware that more might be going on in those tales than was stated. Trying to tease out the details became my literary quest.

Mrs. Stuckenrath, however, was the lion who fiercely guarded the gates of the library; she also stood in loco parentis, protecting me and my curious friends from improper, if not evil, influences. If I learned anything at all about sex from a book, it was not going to be on her watch.

My friends and I had heard that Kathleen Winsor's *Forever Amber* might provide the missing clues; Erskine Caldwell's novel *Tobacco Road,* published a good twenty years before I began my quest, was alleged to be quite juicy. But there was no way I would have tried to get those books past Mrs. Stuckenrath, who would not only have refused to let me check them out but would have redirected my attention to something wholesome—she was partial to horse stories for adolescent girls—and then reported the incident to my mother over martinis at the next bridge club luncheon. My mother would have been appalled.

I read constantly all through my teens, and yet I don't remember a single one of those "wholesome" books thrust into my hands by the redoubtable Mrs. Stuckenrath.

Not one! You could put it down to a poor memory; I'm more likely to believe it's because the books I read didn't grab my imagination. Maybe that's the reason I began to write for YA readers—to do what I can to provide them with characters they'll remember and the kind of stories I might have found (almost) as interesting as sex.

CHAPTER 1

What Is a Young Adult?

Snapshot of a Reader: Cali, 16

Cali is sixteen years old. More accurately, she is sixteen going on twenty-six or going on six, depending on the situation, the time of day, the phases of the moon. In some ways, she is a typical adolescent. She chats on the phone and online every evening. She obsesses about how her hair and make-up will look to her peers. She grouses good-naturedly about curfews and other silly rules she has to obey. Cali is also an atypical teen in that she is an avid reader. That makes her unlike a good many of her friends who find time to read only what is assigned in school (and sometimes only the Cliff Notes or Spark Notes). Tonight she is absorbed in Alice Sebold's The Lovely Bones, *an adult novel with tremendous appeal to younger readers. She shuns phone calls so she can finish the last chapter. After she finishes the book, she moves on to her assigned novel, Conrad's* Heart of Darkness, *all the while complaining about how boring reading is.*

Although Cali is my very own teen, she is typical of many of the adolescents with whom I work in schools. Her emotions fluctuate from moment to moment. She can be incredibly mature at times. At other times she seems less mature than her age warrants. She enjoys reading those books she herself selects, books in which she is vested. School reading, in her vernacular, "bites."

However, using the terms *typical, average,* and even *normal* can be misleading when discussing young adults. It is tough to capture the essence of this group in run-of-the-mill adjectives. What is it that defines this age group? What are the common characteristics of this population? What do we know about this time in the lives of our students? Some background information on the nature of the young adult seems necessary at this point. Before we can make the match, we need to know who our readers are. So, what is a young adult?

Age

The answer very much depends upon who is being asked. For example, the Young Adult Library Services Association (YALSA) of the American Library Association (ALA) defines a young adult as someone between the ages of twelve and eighteen. Compare that age definition to the one used by most publishers, who label books for this group as ages twelve and up in most cases. Psychologists indicate the age range as children in their teen years. Some schools divide this population into segments as wide-ranging as fourth to twelfth grade. The Society for Adolescent Medicine suggests that adolescence includes ten- to twenty-six-year-olds. The MacArthur Foundation serves young adults up to the age of thirty. Recently, a graduate student in my young adult (YA) literature class defined adolescence as a time of "limbo between childhood and adulthood." Indeed, "young adult" may be a misleading label because these children are not miniature versions of adults.

For the purposes of this book, I use the term *young adult* or *adolescent* to indicate a reader ranging from ten to twenty years old. This rather broad definition allows me to talk about books for those readers in the fourth and fifth grades who are ready for more mature themes in their books. According to Edward Sullivan (2002), students in these intermediate grades dwell in a "no man's land." They are too old for children's books and not nearly ready for adult reading. It is also around these years that we begin to lose readers. Those eager beaver readers of the elementary school become less enthusiastic about reading. So, I make every effort to include these students in my definition. The broad definition of ages also allows inclusion of high school students in the eleventh and twelfth grades and even students entering college. While some may say it is too late to recapture readers once they pass the age of fifteen or sixteen, I believe it is never too late. At one time, YA literature was geared mostly for middle school and junior high school readers. Now the range of YA materials meets the needs of ten- to twenty-year-olds. As the audience for the literature has expanded, so must our discussion of that audience.

Just setting age boundaries is not sufficient for characterizing the young adult. Chapter 2 details areas other than age that need to be included in the portrait: the physical, mental, emotional, and social development of adolescence. Before proceeding any further, though, let's examine two other facets of this fascinating age group.

The Inner Child

Take a trip back in time with me to your own adolescence for a moment. What was it like? What are your standout memories of that time in your life? What emotions do you remember experiencing? How do you feel looking back at it now? And perhaps most important, what memories do you have about books and reading? How did teachers make you want to read or fail to excite you about books and reading? I think it is important to keep hold of your inner teen, so to speak, as the discussion proceeds.

It is also important to remember that even though we may be dealing with kids who are fourteen or eighteen, they still have traces of their younger selves within them. Just as you and I have our own inner child who lurks about and occasionally surfaces at odd moments, so do young adults have a strong inner child. In many ways, the inner child of an adolescent is stronger because childhood is a recent memory for most of the kids we teach.

As Cali's snapshot reminds us, young adults are a collection of all the experiences they have had before entering our classrooms. In the insightful short story "Eleven," Sandra Cisneros's narrator reminds us that we are not just the age we are now. Rather, inside us we keep all the years gone past. Cisneros likens it to the rings inside a tree: one year is yet another layer on top of the previous one. So, if you teach thirteen- and fourteen-year-olds, it is essential to remember that they have inside them all the emotions and experiences of one- and two- and three-year-olds they were as well as their current experiences and emotions.

In a moment, it is possible for adolescents to swing from behavior appropriate to their age to behavior more expected from a younger child. The mercurial nature of adolescents makes them challenging to teach but also makes the teaching more rewarding.

The YA Culture: What's Hot and What's *So* Last Year

Adolescents do not exist in a vacuum. The culture that surrounds and absorbs young adults plays a huge role in their lives. It also needs to play a significant role in how we approach this group and the books we offer them to read. Culture changes constantly; it also differs from place to place. I spent most of my childhood in a large inner city, Pittsburgh. I attended a Catholic school from first to eleventh grade. My freshman, sophomore, and junior years were in an all-girls Catholic school. Basically, I attended school with the same twenty-five or so kids from age five to age sixteen. However, my pivotal senior year meant change. I moved from Pittsburgh to southern California and to a public school. Then, the following year, my family moved to Houston, Texas. I was in culture shock for some time. As a result of those relocations, I think I have some insight into the strong role played by culture in the lives of our students. In order to effectively make a match between reader and book, we need to know more about these cultural aspects.

Music, Fashion, Media, Dialect, and Slang

Do you know who leads the current *Billboard* charts? What is No. 1 on TRL? Does it make any difference if you can at least hum a few bars from popular songs? Strangely enough, it does. If we want our students to believe that we can recommend a book they will like, it's downright important to demonstrate that we know their tastes in music. Do we need to personally share those tastes? Certainly not. On long car trips my adolescent kids and I argued about stations, CDs, and tapes. I am not a huge fan of rap. While I like some punk bands, others are not my cup of tea. But I do listen to music they like, watch MTV and CMT, and occasionally even buy a new CD or tape. Because I have shown my kids that I am open, they, in turn, are more open to my suggestions about music and about books. In addition, musical references may date books. Meg Cabot's *All American Girl,* a humorous novel about a girl who saves the life of the President and falls in love with his son, refers to Gwen Stefani and her group No Doubt. While teens today will recognize and even appreciate the reference, the inclusion of a currently popular singer could cause the book to have limited shelf life. When No Doubt's time on the music stage is past, so is the reference to them lost to another generation of readers.

What does fashion have to do with creating readers? Fair question. Take a look at a book that has been in print for a while, and I think the importance of fashion becomes more apparent. S. E. Hinton's *The Outsiders* has been popular with adolescents for several generations. In the course of its more than twenty-five years of publication, the book's cover has undergone quite a few changes. How the characters are portrayed on the cover has

Some Questions to Ask About Adolescents' Preferences

- What TV shows are your favorites?
- What is the last movie you saw at a theater and liked?
- What type of story do you prefer?
- What kind of music is your favorite, and why?
- Where do you shop?
- Where do you and your friends like to go and hang out, and why?
- What do you like to do in your spare time, and why?
- When you read outside of school, what do you like to read?
- What kind of reading material do you have around your house?
- Do you read things other than books, such as magazines, newspapers, comic books?
- Do you read in bed? in front of the TV? lying down on the couch? sitting up straight at your desk?
- About how much time do you spend getting ready for school in the morning?
- If you could change one rule at this school, what would it be, and why?
- If you could add a rule to the class or to the school, what would it be, and why?
- What is your favorite subject in school? the one you like least?
- Who are the good readers in your class? How do you know?
- What kind of a reader are you?
- What is the best book you can remember reading? the worst?
- What type of book would you never pick up, and why?
- What is the best way to let someone know about a good book you have read?
- Where do you go to find out about good books to read, and why?
- What could a teacher or librarian do to make you want to read more?
- What do teachers and librarians do that makes you want to stop reading?

much to do with fashion. Since the cover is one of the first impressions a book can make, characters that appear outmoded on the cover would put readers off from even picking up the book and giving it a chance. (There is, however, an advantage in using a book that has several different editions or covers; see Chapter 10.)

Likewise, I keep an ear open to the latest slang or dialect of adolescents. There is no sense offering young adult readers a book in which the language will be dated and thus inaccessible. Some of the founders of YA literature knew enough to avoid using language that might become outdated. *The Outsiders* seems as vibrant and relevant today as it did more than twenty-five years ago, when it was first written. While there may be no "Socs" or "Greasers" in your school, readers will recognize the reincarnation of those two groups in their own communities: the haves and the have-nots. However, there are countless other books that show their age less well.

"Teenspeak" is in constant flux. Words such as *groovy* or *phat* may cause eyeballs to roll and readers to reject a book when those terms go out of current lingo.

Finally, being aware of the media preferences of this group is essential. What are the popular movies, TV shows, radio stations? These may be as fleeting as the changes in language, fashion, and music, but we do need to keep up. I once overheard a fifteen-year-old put down a TV show I thought was popular among her peers by saying with derision, "That is *so* seventh-grade." So, not only do we need to keep our fingers on the pulse of the media, we need to know which portions of our students like which shows and stations and movies. Hey, if this were an easy job, we would not be making the big bucks, right?

Your Mission, Should You Choose to Accept It

So, take some time to acquaint yourself with these curious creatures we call adolescents. Learn what you can about their lives outside of school. Listen to their music. Watch their movies and favorite TV shows (this will come in handy later, when we talk about censorship issues). Eavesdrop on conversations around you. Hang out at the local mall eating area and watch how they interact with one another. Observe their fashion trends. Ask these kids about their interests and preferences. What you learn can help you when you make the match between your students and books.

Like a lot of kids, when I went to the librarian for advice on what to read I was given a list of Newbery books. I read through a good bit of those—*The Witch of Blackbird Pond* by Elizabeth George Speare, *Johnny Tremain* by Esther Forbes, and *Island of the Blue Dolphins* by Scott O'Dell. And these were satisfying, but I didn't feel much kinship with the characters. I was after more contemporary literature and rooted around for it, but didn't know where to look.

At school we read the classics, which was fine with me. The writing was so involving. Dickens was spellbinding to me, and the rest of the English Lit canon was pretty good, but at least Dickens had young characters to bond with, and George Orwell had characters that captured me with their utopian and political ideas. Jack London and John Steinbeck were two of my American favorites. I loved Camus, too. When I read *The Plague* and *The Stranger* I was hooked. I was sixteen when I read Hinton's *The Outsiders* and thought that was pretty hip. Then I read *Catcher in the Rye* by J. D. Salinger and knew that was a world apart. I told my teacher I liked that one, and she told me to read Frank Conroy's *Stop-Time*. I did, and that sent me

Exploring Feelings and Desires in Books

by Jack Gantos

reeling. When I read them I knew there was a lot more world to experience beyond my house and high school, and a lot more of me that hadn't yet been revealed. The words in books often gave shape to feelings or partial thoughts I had only stumbled across, and at moments when I gained some insight into myself through reading it was as if a secret part of me was stepping forward. It seemed then that I began to find my way from historical fiction that was engaging, to contemporary fiction that began to open doors within me—to make me explore my own feelings and desires and put them into words, and write my own books.

I didn't have much direction or encouragement to read young adult literature but instead read mostly adult literature when I was a teen. Ironically, as an adult I read a lot of young adult work, and find it entirely fulfilling—fulfilling because so many fine writers have been writing for young adult readers. When I wrote *Desire Lines* and *Hole in My Life* I clearly recall making a decision to write these books for young adults rather than for the adult market. Both books contain mature subjects and could have been adult books, and yet I felt that the stories would have more impact with young adults. Perhaps some of my words will give shape to their unspoken thoughts.

CHAPTER 2

Adolescent Development: Physical, Mental, Emotional, Social

Snapshot of a Reader: Corrie, 11

Corrie is a girl on the verge of adolescence. Her body is changing, much to her chagrin. She favors baggy shirts and pants to camouflage the changes. On the other hand, she is taking more of an interest in beauty products. She uses flowery shower gel and shampoos; she wants to use the same face products as her older sister. While she is embarrassed to be seen reading books about growing up and puberty, they are carefully shelved next to her copies of J. K. Rowling's Harry Potter *books and Darren Shan's* Cirque Du Freak *books. She talks on the phone for hours about "nothing"; sometimes she and her friends simply listen to the same TV show in the background and talk only during commercials. She still enjoys hugs but does not want to be seen in public holding hands with her grandmother. Right now she is reading the* Goosebumps *books for her assigned reading in school. When she gets done, though, she plunges back into the world of Philip Pullman's* His Dark Materials *series.*

Corrie is a 'tween. This term, coined by writers looking for some way to describe children caught between childhood and adolescence, seems a perfect description of her. She is between so many things in her life. She is between sleeping with her stuffed animals and pajama parties; she is between thinking boys are vile, disgusting creatures and thinking boys are too cute; she is between Nickelodeon and MTV. Most of all, Corrie is caught between books for young readers and more mature YA literature. She presents just one of the challenges we face in our classrooms. We have to discover what is going on in her body and mind so that we can hope to discover books to meet her needs and interests. We need to do the same with her older counterparts, too.

So, what is going on in the minds and hearts and bodies of this population? How do adolescents develop physically, intellectually, emotionally, and socially? To answer this complex question, we need to return to the psychology class most of us took as we prepared to become teachers. I admit that I learned little about the true nature of adolescence as I was taking classes toward my undergraduate degree. I recall mostly theorists like Piaget, Maslow, and Kohlberg, and wondered how in the world their work would inform my teaching. In addition, experts in young adult literature, such as Donelson and Nilsen (1999), Bushman and Bushman (1997), and Brown and Stephens (1995), show how various psychological, physical, and social models inform us in our work with students. Now that I have the benefit of years of classroom experience, I can see how such theories are essential guides to working with young adults. Revisit that Psych 101 classroom for a moment and see how some of these theories can assist us in working more effectively with our students.

Physical Development

Let's work from the outside in. During puberty and adolescence, children begin to change physically. Often, growth spurts occur. Unfortunately, not all adolescents develop at the same time. More often than not, girls' development can proceed faster than that of their male counterparts. So, in a typical seventh-grade classroom, girls may tower over the boys. To add insult to injury, physical growth may appear first in the limbs and appendages.

Think of adolescents like that little German shepherd puppy: cute and cuddly with enormous paws that cause it to run sideways when it is exuberantly happy to see you approach. Adolescents are much like that. There was a running joke in our house as Cali bloomed from her 5'2" to 5'9" in the period of a few years. When we heard a thud somewhere in the house, one of us called out "wall." Why? Well, in Cali's case (and she is not atypical here), her feet grew from children's to women's sizes. She seemed to be constantly smacking into walls and doors and corners and furniture. It is a wonder that her legs are not permanently scarred. Now, it is nine-year-old Natalie who always seems to be sporting a bruise from where something jumped out and hit her legs and feet and hands and arms. Her shoes, only a month old, are already too small. Pants look like capris within weeks, or so it seems.

Stand Tall by Joan Bauer boasts a character with whom Cali and Corrie and Natalie can readily identify. Tree is only in seventh grade and yet stands head and shoulders above his peers, hence the nickname. What Tree eventually determines is that his height can be a blessing. In fact, there are more than a few novels in which the main characters are coming to terms with their physical bodies. Part of adolescence is this intense period of physical development.

Of course, also growing during adolescence are those other secondary sexual characteristics. The appearance of hair in funny places (at least from the pubescent child's perspective), the deepening of the male voice, and the development of breasts are all part of this phase. Phyllis Reynolds Naylor captures the angst of this time and combines it with great good humor in *Alice in April*. In this book, part of Naylor's series following the life of a young girl through her adolescence, Alice discovers that boys in her school are giving nicknames to the girls. Suddenly, girls are being referred to, instead of by name, by different states. One girl is Colorado; another is Oklahoma. Alice soon learns that the nicknames are a result of how the boys determine the development of the chest region of the girls. Girls who are well endowed are given names of mountainous states. Alice is torn between two feelings: anxiety about her own nickname and anger that the boys have reduced her to body parts.

Mental Development

Contrary to what some outside the profession might think, adolescence is a time of growth in mental ability as well as physical development. One of the biggest changes is the movement from what Piaget termed concrete to more formal operational thinking (Piaget and Inhelder 1969). During this time, adolescents develop the ability to think more and more in the abstract. Remember the classic Piagetian test of where students are? Take two identical containers of liquid (I use a can of Coke and a can of Sprite for this experiment). Pour the liquid from one container into a tall thin beaker or cylinder. Pour the liquid from the second container into a short, squat beaker or cylinder. Now ask students which has more liquid. Of course, the kids who can think abstractly know that both containers have an equal amount of liquid still. However, the students who have not yet made this transition will assert that the tall thin container has more liquid. (Note: You need to do this one-on-one or have kids write down their answers and pass them in to you without comment in order for the experiment to be effective.) Why is this change of interest to those of us who want to connect kids to books?

The types of questions we ask students as they are transitioning between these two stages of thinking should reflect what we know about their ability to perform abstract functions. For example, questions that examine the symbolic nature of a story might better be left to those students who are better able to think in the abstract. Students who are more concrete thinkers will fare better with more concrete questions (questions where the text itself provides answers). That does not mean we cannot ask good, thoughtful questions of concrete thinkers. It does mean, however, that we may need to guide them as they think through their answers. Here are a few sets of questions that should serve to illustrate the difference between the questions or activities appropriate for concrete thinkers and for abstract thinkers.

Concrete: *As you are reading* The Moves Make the Man *by Bruce Brooks, keep a chart with two columns. In the first column, note any reference made to light (for instance, the Spin Light, the lantern Jerome and Bix use on the court). In the second column, note any references to dark (for instance, what major events occur at night in the story?).*

Abstract: *Light and dark play a symbolic role in the novel* The Moves Make the Man *by Bruce Brooks. What is the purpose of this juxtaposition of light and dark? What is the author hoping to accomplish?*

Concrete: *Where is the novel* Slake's Limbo *by Felice Holman set? Could this story take place in a different location? Why, or why not?*

Abstract: *Why is* Slake's Limbo *by Felice Holman set where it is?*

Concrete: *The title of Robert Cormier's book* The Chocolate War *contains an oxymoron. Here are two words,* chocolate *and* war, *that are not normally placed together because they tend to have opposite kinds of meanings and emotions associated with them. Think of another oxymoron that might serve as a title for this novel.*

Abstract: *The title* The Chocolate War *has two levels of meaning: literal and symbolic. What is the literal meaning of the title? What could be a more symbolic meaning?*

Notice that these examples do not ask significantly different questions. However, the questions are posed differently. Sometimes, the more concrete questions have some prompts to guide responses that require abstraction. Asking different questions is only one way in which you can use the Piaget's analysis to guide you in the classroom. Care should also be taken in the selection of the reading material itself. In a typical tenth-grade classroom, some students may be ready for a challenging read such as Chris Lynch's *Freewill*. However, if you have kids who are still fairly concrete thinkers, this book will fail abysmally. The second-person voice and the nonlinear narrative will defeat them despite the fact that the readability level of the book is below 4.0. Likewise, *The Giver* by Lois Lowry is written on approximately a fifth-grade level. The content of the book, though, is beyond many fifth-graders (and even sixth- and seventh-graders). This futuristic novel deals with a Utopian society that has disturbing elements just beneath its very civilized surface. The concepts students will be asked to read about and discuss are too abstract for most readers at the intermediate age range. So it is important to know where your students are in terms of their Piagetian development as you select materials for them to read. There are some other important factors to consider as well, such as emotional and social development.

Emotional Development

Adolescence can be a time of tremendous emotional swings. Remember, chemicals are being released into a body that heretofore has not experienced this rush of hormones. In the course of a day (or even in the course of an hour), students can move from joyous to downcast. Emotions are strong and seemingly close to the surface. Many adolescents are struggling to learn how to control these outbursts of feelings and reactions. So, how can we help our students deal with their own emotions and with the emotional needs of their peers?

Books can serve as portals to help students see others struggling with similar emotions and feelings and reactions. In Avi's *The True Confessions of Charlotte Doyle,* readers can see a young girl become involved in a mutiny aboard a sailing ship in the eighteenth century. Why does Charlotte become a mutineer? It is her strong reaction to the way she sees the captain of her sailing vessel mistreating those under his command. Charlotte's initial response is to approach the captain in an attempt to have him soften his dictatorial command. When that fails, Charlotte joins in the mutiny aboard ship. She acts on her sense of outrage. I can hear you wondering, Is she seriously saying that we ought to encourage kids to act on their emotions? In this example, I would be thrilled if readers took Charlotte's actions to heart. Here is a young woman who puts aside fear to fight for what is morally right. I think Charlotte is an excellent role model of the socially conscious people we hope our students are or will become.

Books that deal with emotions too close to the surface to be controlled include *Breathing Underwater* by Alex Flinn, *Stotan!* and *Ironman* by Chris Crutcher, and *Dog Eat Dog* by Chris Lynch. *Dreamland* by Sarah Dessen explores the feelings and thoughts and reactions of a young girl whose boyfriend is abusing her. "Eleven," a short story in *Woman Hollering Creek and Other Stories* by Sandra Cisneros, encapsulates the world of emotions beautifully. Many YA books show how characters learn to deal with strong emotional reactions. Authors who write for this age group know how strong feelings can affect the world of the adolescent.

Another way in which the emotional development of our readers plays a role in book selection is a bit tougher to delineate. Perhaps a few examples will illustrate the point I am trying to make. Several years ago, the students in my children's literature class clamored for me to include Robert Munsch's *Love You Forever.* Here is the story of a young boy whose mother picks him up every night and rocks him, singing a song about her eternal love for her son. The boy gets older, and as he ages, readers see the mother creep into her son's room on all fours. She peers over the edge of his bed, and if he is asleep, gathers him in her arms and sings her song. She does this even after her son is grown and married and living across town. At the end of the story, the roles of parent and child have reversed. It is now the son who gently rocks his mother in a chair and sings of his love for her.

It is a real tearjerker in the college classroom. However, this book does not play as well with younger children, the ones we assume to be the intended readership of a picture book. Kids think the behavior of the mother is rather bizarre; she uses a ladder at one point to get into his bedroom window at night. This book strikes a chord with adults because we are more emotionally mature. We know now that our parents love us unconditionally and that they will not always be with us. Younger readers are not yet at this stage in emotional development.

Another example comes from a high school reading list. Recently, a young friend of mine confided that she had received a D on a paper analyzing Joseph Conrad's *Heart of Darkness*. The teacher's comment on the paper was that she (the teacher) did not think that the reader had understood the character's motivation and emotions in the book. This comment piqued my curiosity enough for me to pick up the book and read a few chapters. Well, of course, the teen had not comprehended the character of this novel. One reason was that the main character was a different gender. The bigger reason, though, was that the main character was well beyond this sixteen-year-old's development. Conrad's characters live in a world that is evil and corrupt. Many display a fatalistic attitude toward life in general. How many teens fall into this category? So, how can we expect a high school students to "get" it?

This idea that a novel must be developmentally appropriate for a reader's maturity level is not new. It is part and parcel of the reason why many high school students reject the books forced upon them by the curriculum. When readers cannot grasp the character's motivation, the story becomes one they label boring or dumb or stupid. What they are saying is that as readers they cannot identify with the story. As teachers, we can offer our readers stories in which the main characters are accessible: characters who are close to their age or a bit older, characters who are going through many of the same trials and tribulations as our students, characters who speak to our readers.

Social Development

How adolescents develop as moral creatures in society is also an important area of concern for educators. Kohlberg's (1987) theory of moral development is one model that can provide us with information. Basically, Kohlberg suggests there are three levels of moral development: preconventional, conventional, and postconventional. At the preconventional level of moral development, we make decisions based upon reward and punishment. Conventional morality follows a code of what is right and wrong. That code can be secular or religious. At this level of moral development, we obey laws. The postconventional level of moral development recognizes that sometimes laws and social rules conflict with what is "right." How does Kohlberg's theory affect our teaching of YA literature?

We all want to share books with readers that present characters "doing the right thing." Literature presents readers with all kinds of options for living. Books offer readers the chance to see heroes of their own age in action. In fiction and in nonfiction, we can expose students to characters and people who lead heroic lives, whether facing down racists (*Stotan!* by Chris Crutcher) or standing up for who they are despite the fact that they may be ostracized (*Annie on My Mind* by Nancy Garden) or becoming social activists (*Freedom's Children* by Ellen Levine). We want to share biographies of heroic people, too, people like Martin Luther King, Jr., and César Chávez and Susan

B. Anthony. What we want to do is noble. However, we need to keep in mind that sometimes the models we extend to our students are people operating at the postconventional level of morality.

Havighurst's Theory of Developmental Tasks

In 1972, Richard Havighurst defined the developmental tasks that healthy individuals should be able to accomplish. One set of tasks is specific to adolescent development and to the ability to find appropriate materials for our classrooms. The tasks are neither good nor bad, positive or negative. They simply *are*. What we can do as teachers is help our students who are struggling with various tasks by suggesting books in which the main characters also struggle to achieve that task. So, here are the tasks as defined by Havighurst. Appendix T suggests some books to accompany each of the following tasks.

Adolescents need to learn how to get along with peers. Negotiation, compromise, working cooperatively in groups, accepting differences: all of these are components of getting along with peers. Additionally, there are some significant changes in how relationships and friendships are forged during adolescence. When our students were younger, chances are their friends were the children who lived nearby. Friendships often develop during youth as a function of proximity. During adolescence, however, friendships become based on shared interests and preferences. It is possible for two friends to separate during their teen years as their interests and preferences diverge. What makes this even tougher is that kids go through this developmental task at different times. So it is possible for one friend suddenly to reject the other. This can be a time of high emotion.

Adolescents undergo changing relationships with parents. Since adolescence is a time of gaining independence, pulling away from parents and from their authority is not unusual. In many YA novels, parents are completely absent. When parents are present, they may be able to help their teen deal with life's tragedies.

Adolescents need to develop an easy relationship with the opposite sex. As a veteran of the middle school, I was able to watch students transition through this task. They were able to have friends of the opposite gender without sex becoming a factor in the relationship. Remember having to explain to your friends that you had a friend who was a boy (or girl) but he (or she) was not your boyfriend (or girlfriend)?

Adolescents must develop morals and values. This is a time of weighing one's morals and values, of rejecting some and gaining others. During adolescence, teens begin to put the morals and values they observe at home and at school to the test. Do the rules set forth by others apply to those making the rules? Does Mom avoid telling lies? Does Dad call when he is going to be late? Is the school dress code enforced fairly? Teens question the disconnect between the actions they see and what the rules say they should be.

Adolescents have to adapt to their physical bodies. Recall our earlier discussion about the changing nature of the physical body during puberty and adolescence.

Adolescents must define their appropriate sex roles (sometime as dictated by society). Negotiating the expectations of what it means to be a young man or a young woman in our society can be difficult. Sometimes a teen does not fit comfortably into the well-defined boxes that society makes for him or her. What exactly is expected of a young man or woman in terms of appearance, interests, attitudes, and behaviors? What does this mean to the hapless teen who does not meet these expectations? As a middle school teacher, I saw young people struggle with societal expectations. For instance, more than a handful of students took dance lessons as children; some continued as teens. For girls this interest in dancing was expected and encouraged, but for boys it was not. Likewise, an interest in football was acceptable for boys but not for girls. Some students whose interests clashed with societal expectations had to struggle to pursue their individual desires.

Adolescents need to work for pay. How well I recall watching this development in my sixteen-year-old granddaughter, Cali. As a child, she loved to help around the house. Her favorite job, oddly enough, was scrubbing out the toilets. We never could understand why, but it was lovely for a time to have our toilets always pristine. Then, at some point during her adolescence, Cali was less and less eager to help. She began to ask for an allowance, to ask when she could start babysitting. Here was the developmental task in action right in front of us. Cali wanted some measure of independence. Making money to buy her own music or some of her own clothes was part of her declaration of independence. Finding that first job was important.

Adolescents should find a vocation. This task goes a bit beyond working for pay. It is not so much about finding a job as about deciding upon a career. What do I want to be when I grow up? is a question considered more seriously during adolescence. Gone are the dreams of childhood. More realistic plans are coming into the picture.

Development of Lifetime Readers

Readers are not born; they develop. From research, we know that there are certain experiences lifetime readers have that schooltime (only) readers do not. Carlsen and Sherrill, in *Voices of Readers: How We Come to Love Books* (1988), discuss some of those common experiences of lifetime readers. They include having teachers and parents read aloud to them (see Chapters 8 and 9), having teachers and parents who themselves read continually, and being able to select reading materials on their own.

Donelson and Nilsen (1999) describe this progression toward a lifetime of reading using the analogy of a birthday cake. Each layer represents a different stage in the development of a reader. Although these stages do not occur in a lockstep order, they do tend to build one upon the other. Basically, there are five stages in the development of a lifetime reader. Early (1960) and later Carlsen (1974) building on Early's work, identify the stages that are part of the Donelson and Nilsen analogy. The stages in the development of a lifetime readers are as follows.

- Reading for unconscious delight
- Reading autobiographically
- Reading for vicarious experiences
- Reading for philosophical speculation
- Reading for aesthetic experience

How does each of these stages play into the types of literature we share with classes? What sorts of activities and strategies are best at each of these stages? Answers to those questions may be found in Chapter 10. Before we can guide students to a lifetime of reading, we must know more about the adolescents themselves. Chapter 3 examines what YA readers tell us about books, reading, and teachers.

Finally . . .

Complicated, isn't it? There are so many factors to consider when working with this age group. Selecting the right book for the right reader becomes a matter of taking all the preceding into consideration. We must ponder physical, mental, emotional, social, and psychological facets of the reader in order to make more knowledgeable recommendations. If we are to be successful in making the match, we need to know the readers thoroughly.

When I started talking about my writing with students in schools around the country I usually included the fact that, in high school, I read only one book of fiction cover to cover. I'm a little embarrassed to admit that I was at one time proud of the fact that I cheated (there's no other word for it) on almost all my book reports and yet was able to go on and write a number of fairly well-received novels. Truth is, I probably cheated myself out of ten years of being a writer while I caught up, and also out of the sublime intimacy that comes from connection with a literary character real enough to be a true friend. Through all my defenses against doing what I was told, came Scout Finch in *To Kill a Mockingbird,* who captured my heart and my imagination in the first pages and hasn't yet let me go. As a teen I fought against all literature that had no immediate meaning to me, and probably lost some great stuff in that wide dragnet, yet Harper Lee prevailed.

Finding the Meaning Myself
by Chris Crutcher

I came to love reading just as soon as people stopped trying to make me read. I had always loved stories and always been fascinated by words. When the pressure from others was off, I turned it on for myself.

I wouldn't say I write for young adults. I'm interested in adolescence for a number of reasons, so that's what I write about. Beyond that, I welcome as wide an audience as I can find.

My memories of reading as a child and adolescent vary. In elementary school I was encouraged to read whatever I wanted to read and found a lot of books to love, books I felt spoke to me. I loved Dr. Seuss as a young kid and, as I got into upper elementary school, fell in love with a series of books about famous people when they were young. Because of these books I have always preferred Will Clark over Meriwether Lewis, Lou Gehrig over Babe Ruth; and I discovered one of my all-time favorite heroes, Tecumseh. I was also captivated by the Chip Hilton series, about a high school athlete who had lost his father. But in junior high and high school I ran into a lot more required reading and along with that came teachers telling me what each story meant, a huge turnoff because they had different meanings for me, and I often ended up feeling stupid. That almost killed reading for me, and I didn't begin enjoying it again until after college.

CHAPTER 3

What Young Adults Tell Us About Books, Reading, and Educators

Snapshot of a Reader: Crystal, 13

Crystal was clearly frustrated. "How can I find a book to read? Look at all of these books!" She gestured around the well-stocked library. It was clear to me that Crystal was overwhelmed by the wide selection of books. For someone like me who loves to read, browsing in a large library or bookstore is a rare and wonderful treat. However, as Kylene Beers points out in When Kids Can't Read, What Teachers Can Do *(2002), kids who are not avid readers often feel the same frustrations as Crystal. There are simply too many books from which to select. "Which one is right for me?" Crystal asked. Good question. I turned it right back to her. "So, if an author could write a book just for you, what would it be like?" As Crystal described the perfect book, talking about plot and characters and setting, I began to mentally compile titles to recommend. Crystal wanted a book about someone like her (so a female main character seemed appropriate, and one close to her age or a little older), preferably a book that had some suspense to it (as it turned out, she wanted a mystery) without being too scary (so eliminate the gory ones) and one she would not solve until the end (so a bit of a complex plot with maybe a red herring or two to throw the reader off track). Crystal and I walked around the shelves for several minutes, and I did impromptu booktalks about some novels I thought would match Crystal's stated criteria. After a few minutes, Crystal left with the "perfect" book tucked into her backpack. Nowadays, as budgets are being slashed in schools, too often the school librarian is one of the first casualties. How can we expect kids like Crystal to find a book without someone who knows the questions to ask and the books to recommend?*

More than a dozen years ago, my friend Lois Buckman and I embarked on what we thought would be a short-term research project. We were interested in seeing if we could come up with some unique ways of motivating the students at her middle school to read. Lois and I had taught English classes in the same school for years. Then, when I moved on to the university, she completed her librarian certification and entered a middle school/high school library. The two buildings, housing grades 7 through 12, were joined in one spot: the library. What a unique opportunity to examine readers over a long period of time.

Lois and I had some ideas, a small budget of $1,500, and a very cooperative principal. What began as a semester-long study evolved into a longitudinal one looking at the effects of electronic mentoring (middle school students were mentored via e-mail by my university students; see Chapter 10) and other intervention techniques with middle schoolers. Since these middle school students progressed to the high school on the same campus, we had the unique opportunity to follow them for another four years. What can we say about leading readers to a lifelong love of books and reading after all these years?

Perhaps the most important thing we have learned in all our work with these students is that there is no one template for a reader. Think about this statement for a moment; it makes perfect sense. There is no typical librarian, no typical teen, no typical YA book. Likewise, there is no typical YA reader. Prepackaged programs loudly proclaim that they can make all kids want to read. That is simply not the case. It is a matter of one size not fitting all; one program cannot be successful with every student. However, there are certain strategies and activities that can be used successfully in each classroom (see Chapter 10).

There are as well certain observations that I can now make about this population that can assist teachers to make decisions about classroom materials and activities and strategies. These observations come from my more than a dozen years of research and from my nearly thirty years as an educator. Some of the observations come from the students themselves. I have grouped the findings into three categories: observations about books, observations about readers, and observations about educators.

Observations About Books

So, what qualities do middle school students look for in books? The results of our long-term study may seem surprising, but if you really want to know what kids want, all you have to do is ask them. In addition to watching kids as they navigated their school library, I distributed surveys and questionnaires to students in the study each year (see Chapter 4). I asked them to tell me about the types of books they might consider reading as well as how they went about choosing books to read. What do these kids want?

Kids Want Mysteries

Students prefer books with heightened suspense and excitement. Good mysteries fit the bill here. Mystery is one genre that has cross-gender appeal. It is liked and read almost equally by boys and girls, especially at the middle school and high school levels. One of the most popular authors with the students we have worked with the past several years is Joan Lowery Nixon. She is a four-time winner of the Edgar Allen Poe Award for her juvenile mysteries. Nixon's books circulate well among both reluctant and avid readers. Her *Whispers from the Dead* is one of the books most often requested. Other popular authors of mysteries include Caroline Cooney, Jay Bennett, Avi, Lois Duncan, Mel Glenn, and Nancy Werlin. (See Appendix K for a list of popular mysteries for YA readers.) Visit the Web site of the Mystery Writers of America for a complete listing of the juvenile and YA books that have been nominated for or have won the Edgar Allan Poe Award for mystery: www.mysterywriters.org/awards.html.

Kids Want Humor

For some students, books with humor are important. It appears to us that books for the middle school reader tend to get more and more serious in nature. Sometimes these kids enjoy a good laugh. Gordon and Bernice Korman's *The D- Poems of Jeremy Bloom* and *The Last Place Sports Poems of Jeremy Bloom* offer quips and puns along with a nice dose of poetry. They have become quite popular, also, because they are thin, though the length of the book is not always a factor in how students select books. Actually, many of Korman's books are popular with middle and high school students.

No More Dead Dogs makes an excellent and funny read-aloud as does *Son of the Mob*. Another popular humorous choice recently has been Rob Thomas's *Green Thumb*. Thomas's books for older YA readers include *Rats Saw God, Slave Day, Satellite Down*, and *Doing Time: Notes from the Undergrad*. (See Appendix J for a list of good humorous books for YA readers.)

Kids Want Nonfiction

An often neglected genre that has wide appeal with at-risk readers is nonfiction. As we were establishing the core of the books we would offer students in our initial study, we chose books by Janet Bode, in particular, *Hard Time* and *Heartbreak and Roses*. The first book recounts the stories of juveniles who are incarcerated for serious crimes, including murder and armed robbery. The latter is a collection of stories about kids in the throes and the aftermath of love. Bode allows the voices of the kids she interviews to dominate the books. Students seemed to respond to the reality of the situations dealt with in the books. Here are kids like themselves, kids in trouble and kids with troubles. Other good choices for nonfiction books for young adults are Phillip Hoose, Laurence Pringle, Milton Meltzer, James Cross Giblin, and Susan Kuklin. (Appendix N lists some nonfiction and informational books.)

Kids Judge a Book by Its Cover

Finally, students expressed some preference for book selection based on book covers. While length, book flap summaries, and blurbs did not seem to make much of a difference, students did indicate that they selected books (and rejected them) based on the covers. This observation is important, I think. The best book in the world will not circulate if the cover appears "dorky" to your kids.

Examine the covers of the books you think will appeal to readers. Do the jacket illustrations appeal as well? If not, what can you do to lure kids into those books? One answer is to team up with classroom teachers and ask them to make new covers for the books that lack teen appeal. Ask the art teacher to assist kids in designing the new cover illustrations. Ask the English teachers to have students write the book flap summaries. Ask social studies teachers to strengthen research skills by having students find out information about the authors of the books from a variety of sources. This interdisciplinary approach is a winner for everyone concerned.

Take this one step further and have students create new covers for their favorite books. A good book cover has five sections: a front flap, a back flap, the front cover, the back cover, and the spine. Have students examine a variety of covers to determine what type of information goes where. The front flap generally gives the reader a glimpse into the plot of the book. It should be written to gain the attention of the reader. It certainly never gives away too much of the story. The back flap generally has information about the author of the book. Front covers are composed of illustration plus title and author. Back covers vary. Some have reviews or blurbs about the book. Occasionally, the back cover is a continuation from the front illustration. Finally, the spine has author, title, and publisher. Think of all the skills and objectives you can cover with this simple activity. The range of skills includes writing summaries, using research tools (and not just the Internet), using proper punctuation, representing material using symbols or graphics (important in this age of Web sites and billboards and nonstop ads), and writing for purpose and audience.

Students can construct new covers for their books using various art supplies. Once the covers are completed, have them laminated. Then, ask the school librarian to create a display of the books for which the new covers have been constructed. Placing these newly created covers on the books accomplishes two things. First, it provides an outlet for the work of your students. Second, it serves as yet another way to motivate readers via the book display. Killing two birds with one stone is rare and a real plus with this simple activity.

Observations About Young Adult Readers

As suggested before, there is no typical YA reader, whether avid or reluctant. Some are reluctant to read because they have some problems with reading such as decoding and comprehension. In addition to instruction designed to strengthen areas of weakness, these kids need access to interesting, developmentally appropriate books that are a bit simpler to read. Did you know that *Fallen Angels* by Walter Dean Myers is written at the fourth-grade level? Here is a book powerful enough to entice readers and yet easy enough for them to read independently. There are plenty of engrossing YA novels and nonfiction books that are accessible in terms of readability (see Appendix I, Easy Reading). Additionally, the National Council of Teachers of English publishes annotated book lists in *High Interest—Easy Reading*. The Quick Picks lists from the American Library Association's Young Adult Library Services Association (YALSA) are another good resource for Hi-Lo books. (See Appendix X, which also lists selected awards for YA and children's literature.

Other kids fail to read because they are unmotivated. The unmotivated readers often find themselves in a dilemma. Like most middle school students, they turn to one another for advice: advice on girlfriends and boyfriends and advice about books. Consider the following scenario in which Sam and Joe are both unmotivated readers.

Sam: I'm looking for something to read for my next book report.
Joe: Yeah, me, too.
Sam: So, have you read anything good lately?
Joe: Nah, have you?
Sam: Nope.
Joe: Wish I knew some good books to read.
Sam: But how do you find them?
Joe: Beats me.

Okay, this is not an actual conversation, but you catch the drift. Kids who are not eager readers want to know where all the good books are being kept. What I have learned from research is that these unmotivated kids want a personal introduction to books. They are more likely to select a book from a narrowed choice. So, let me suggest how to narrow their selection and ensure better success for these reluctant readers. First, take a cart of books into the classroom. Give booktalks on all the titles and allow kids to check out books on the spot. Even better, ask your school librarian to join you in this endeavor. Chances are, he or she is well trained in booktalking (see Chapter 9). Inform the kids that the cart will be kept in the hall outside the librarian's office and may only be used by your class.

When Lois Buckman and I did this some time ago, we got a real thrill when we watched one of the seventh-graders motion over a ninth-grade friend. "Here is where she keeps the good books," he hissed conspiratorially, "but I'd better check one out for you. She only lets *us* read these books." Here was a former reluctant reader talking to another student about a good book.

Some YA readers are what Kylene Beers (1990) calls dormant readers. There is simply too much going on in their lives right now, so reading takes a back seat for a while. All of us go through periods of time in our lives when things are too hectic to do much reading. The only thing I love about flying to a conference or meeting is that I get uninterrupted time for reading. Perhaps we need to offer these harried kids some time to read at school if it is not already in place. Allowing kids to come into the library before and after school and during lunch may give them just enough time to settle in and read for a while. Even better is allowing time in class to read daily. It does not have to be much: ten minutes will suffice at the start. I began my classes after lunch with time for quiet reading and was amazed at how the students clamored for just a few more minutes after they became accustomed to the break in their schedule.

Books on tape come in handy here. Many of the students I work with spend thirty to forty-five minutes on the bus to and from school each day. I took some grant money and purchased plenty of cassette players and headphones, which Lois now checks out of her library along with the books on tape. Over the course of a week, kids can generally finish listening to a book (see Chapter 8 and Appendix D). Finding other ways to give kids time to read should be a priority.

Observations About Educators

Finally, let me offer some tips for working with these students. The following bits of advice come from the students themselves. I asked them, "What advice would you give a teacher or librarian who was trying to get you to read?" Here are some of their answers.

Accept Our Interests

In other words, give kids what they want when they ask for a book. It is too tempting to continually push kids into longer and tougher books as they grow older and more confident as readers. Sometimes we are too quick to say, "That's too easy a book for you. Try this one instead." I have heard parents brag about their precocious children who read Harry Potter books in second grade. I think, "What will be available for this child in fifth grade, then, that he or she has not already read?" I also worry about the other books children who are prodded into older books might miss along the way. Sometimes we need to stand back and allow kids the chance to read easy and enjoyable texts. We call some of their leisure reading material trashy. We know it is not easy to see kids pick up one series book after another. However, instead of immediately trying to change the reading material, meet these kids halfway. Kids are impressed when I talk about the most recent book in A Series of Unfortunate Events or Left Behind or Babysitters' Club. They quickly become engaged when they know I understand their reading tastes. They are then more likely to accept a gentle nudge the next time I recommend a book. My friend and colleague Bob Seney read two to three Sweet Valley High books at the peak of their popularity. All the girls in his class thought Bob was the coolest teacher. He slowly began to encourage them to read beyond the series but still in the romance/school story genres. Kids accepted his recommendations because he first accepted theirs.

This is what the kids request: Don't try to change our tastes; let us read the books that interest us. Of course, it also reminds us that we need, as teachers, to read widely. I call it reading beyond my comfort zone. If I can model that as a teacher, I can have some expectation of seeing this behavior in my students later.

Let Us Keep the Books as Long as We Want

Kids did not feel that they could finish the reading in the traditional two-week checkout period from the library. Even though they were told they could check the book out again, they wanted a more open-ended checkout. I know from research that ownership plays an important role in reading motivation (see the success of programs such as Reading Is Fundamental, for example), so in my classroom library, books can stay out as long as kids need them (yes, I do occasionally remind students to bring them back). Lois and I decided to allow the students to simply take books from the cart without formally going through the library circulation desk. Kids can keep the books as long as they like. Some opt to keep the books. We allow that as well because it generally means that a book has touched the student deeply. We simply add to the stock of books on the cart as needed.

We Want to Meet the Author

Kids want to know more about the person behind the books. To facilitate this, we have arranged teleconferences with Joan Lowery Nixon on three separate occasions. This gracious lady answered every single question the kids asked in lengthy interviews. We recorded and transcribed and edited the interviews, which have appeared in two national publications. Can you imagine how proud these at-risk kids were when their names appeared in print for the first time? We have also arranged to have authors visit the school. Gary Paulsen, Carolyn Meyer, Chris Crutcher, Bruce Brooks, and Mel Glenn have all been visiting authors. More are scheduled for this coming school year. We try to provide each student in the program with his or her own copy of the book for autographing. We have seen kids eager to have an autograph, eager to get a photograph, eager to have a moment to share with an author they admire. (See Appendix Y for some tips about author visits.)

We Want to Hear the Book Read Aloud

This should not be a confounding idea. Kids have been telling us they enjoy read-aloud time for decades. We have known the value of reading aloud as well thanks to the efforts of folks like Jim Trelease in *The New Read-Aloud*

Handbook (2002) and Mem Fox's *Reading Magic* (2001). Mary Lee Hahn's *Reconsidering Read-Aloud* (2002) reminds us of the richness of this simple activity. Read-aloud has given way in the past few years to an emphasis on test scores. However, we should not lose sight of the fact that reading aloud can positively affect test scores. The work of researchers like Stephen Krashen reminds us that this is a valuable tool in our crusade to raise reading scores. I continue the practice of beginning each of my classes at the university with a read-aloud. My students seem to enjoy that time as much as my middle school kids came to love it years ago. (See Chapter 8.) Do not overlook the value of books on tape, either. For the past four years, I have used audiobooks with reluctant readers with great success. We purchased unabridged versions of good books (see Appendix D), headphones, and tape players with funds from several small grants. (See Appendix Y for grant sources.) Students were permitted to check out books and players together. They reported "reading" more than they expected. I spend a great deal of time in commuting and rely on audiobooks as well. Family vacations are made more bearable in the car with the addition of audiobooks the entire family can enjoy.

We Want to Hear More About Good Books

It should come as no surprise that having role models is important in the process of creating lifetime readers. Most of us are lifetime readers because we had many models in our development. We had parents who read aloud to us and teachers who read books to us. We saw folks reading in the home and at school. Think about how that may have changed for some of our students. Nowadays, when both parents work, they may not see adults reading at home. Indeed, many of the students I have interviewed about books and reading in the past ten years tell me there are no books in their homes other than the telephone book and the Bible. They do not see parents reading the newspaper (honestly, I cannot recall the last time I read the newspaper) or pick up a book. At school, teachers are harried. They have skills to cover and tests to prepare for. How many times recently have you found the time at school to pick up a book and read? We need to make time daily for reading so that we can share our passion for books with our students. I spend at least three to four days each month visiting classrooms and libraries and telling kids about good books they might want to read. After sessions of booktalks and read-alouds, circulation picks up tremendously. Kids simply want us to tell them about books they might find interesting (see Chapter 9).

Finally . . .

We remain committed to these at-risk students. Thanks to grants from Sam Houston State University, the Texas Council of Teachers of English, the Texas State Reading Association, the Texas Education Agency, the Young Adult Library Services Association of the American Library Association, Voice of Youth Advocates, and the Adolescent Literature Assembly of the National Council of Teachers of English, we have enough funds to continue the project year after year. Though each grant was relatively small, we have managed to purchase books, tapes, cassette players, and the various supplies needed for the project. Publishers and authors have also been kind enough to contribute books and tapes when they hear the stories of the kids whose lives have been changed through the program we call STOMP, for Student Teacher Online Mentoring Program (see Chapter 10). With the vast network of computers, it is much easier to reach out; we are no longer confined by classroom walls, by geography. The reaching out has been rewarding; the success stories keep us committed to the project. Now the program is being replicated across the United States. Imagine the possibilities of hundreds and thousands of at-risk kids discovering the joy of the right book at the right time. We witness that miracle each and every year. It keeps us going.

Recently the film department of the University of South Carolina gave me a video of outtakes from the archives of Fox Movietone News, showing little Joan Lowery, age 3 years and 1 month, sitting on her mother's lap, performing for the cameraman by reading aloud from a first-grade reader.

At the time, the activity may have seemed unusual enough for a short newsreel feature story, but to me there was nothing unusual about it. Reading was a normal, necessary, integral part of my life. It still is.

Along the way books played an important part in my life. When I read *Little Women,* I devotedly picked Jo March as my role model. Jo was a writer, and I would be one, too.

The Gift of Reading by Joan Lowery Nixon

When I was seven or eight, during one of my family's weekly trips to our neighborhood branch library, I found a mystery novel for children. I don't remember the name of the book or the author. I only remember that I was entranced by the scary moments of suspense and the challenge to solve the mystery before the main character did. What a wonderful way to tell a story! I became firmly hooked on mysteries.

When I was twelve, the librarian allowed me to cross the aisle from the children's room into the main library. There was no middle ground, no books written for teens at that time. I was considered to be an adult, and I reveled in the stacks and stacks of books which I could now explore.

It felt as if I were standing before an enormous buffet of delicious food. I could pick and choose at will. Tasting a little of everything, I read popular novels, Shakespeare, Elizabeth Barrett Browning's romantic poetry, and the biting verse of Sara Teasdale and Edna St. Vincent Millay. I dipped into history, biography, and nonfiction best sellers.

Although the librarian raised an eyebrow at a few of my choices, when I was thirteen she objected outright to a book I was checking out: Jan Valdin's *Out of the Night,* a book exposing many of Hitler's horrors.

"I don't think you should read this," she said. "It's very graphic."

"But I need to know what is going on in the world," I complained. "It's important to read it and find out."

The librarian had been right. After all these years little ghosts from that book still occasionally pop up in my mind, haunting me. Yet the world in trouble was my world, too, and I did need to know.

My main interest in reading was still the mystery novel. Through my teen years I delighted in the cozies of Agatha Christie and Ngaio Marsh, shivered at the terrifying suspense in Mary Roberts Rinehart's novels, and didn't miss a single hardboiled detective story written by Raymond Chandler (whose stories were set in my hometown of Los Angeles) or Dashiell Hammett (whose characters inhabited my second favorite city, San Francisco). The mystery novels of all five writers were strong in plotting, suspense techniques, and characterization, and I loved Chandler's and Hammett's use of metaphors. As I read, I learned.

I have vivid memories of my teen years, with their insecurities, tears, concerns, excitements, and moments of pure joy. This is probably why I enjoy writing for teens. The problems teens come up against change from generation to generation, but the emotions experienced remain the same, so I write through my emotions.

Certain books and authors have given direction to my life, and in turn my books have done the same for many teenagers. I love the letters that begin, "I didn't like to read, but then a friend gave me one of your books, and now I love to read." The ninth-grade author of one of the letters I received wrote, "Thank you for the gift of reading." I couldn't have received a better reward than this.

CHAPTER 4

Getting to Know You: Using Surveys and Questionnaires

Snapshot of a Reader: Gay, 30

Gay was a fellow teacher. A few years after I left my school to teach at the university, I was invited back to the district to do some in-service presentations on books for middle school students. Teachers from all disciplines were present. Some were interested in the presentation. Others wondered how good books would help them in their classes. Gay was a physical education teacher and a coach. She was one who seemed to wonder why attending my presentation was important. I decided to highlight some books with strong sports connections, knowing her love for athletics. I ran into Gay a few months later at a social event. She pulled me aside to confess that she had read some of the books I recommended for her students. "These are good books," she enthused. "Where were these books when I was in school? Are there some other books you could recommend?" It is never too late, I thought, to capture the interest of a nonreader.

Before we can successfully make the match between reader and book, we have to know the three elements involved in the process. First, we need to know the readers. In Chapters 1–3 I discuss the development and needs and interests of the YA population in a general way. However, my experiences with middle and high school kids in different parts of Texas may not mirror the more specific needs and interests of your students across the country. We can certainly make some general assumptions about the YA population. But making the match will be more successful if you know the needs and interests and preferences and habits of the kids in your own classroom. So this chapter includes some ideas for getting to know *your* students.

Of course, the best way to get to know your students is to talk to them one-on-one. At the beginning of the school year, though, there may be little time for this. I know very little about my students at the outset of each semester, but I do learn more about them as the weeks progress and we begin class discussions of the books we are reading. I do take some time on the first day of class to gather some general information about the needs, interests, habits, and preferences of my students. As teachers, we need to use an instrument to gather information quickly. Several professional books offer ready-made surveys for students. Nancie Atwell's *In the Middle* (1987) offers a reading inventory of sorts with dozens of questions for students to answer. I opt for a survey that takes little time to complete and yet yields some basic information for me as a teacher. It is simple enough to design a short survey to help in the information-gathering process.

Questions About the Students

The first part of a good survey about books and reading should contain basic questions about the students: age, gender, grade level (if, like me, you have cross-grade classes). I would encourage you to make these surveys anonymous. It is not necessary at this point to have information about the individual students in the class. That is better left to the one-on-one interviews we conduct later in the school year. For now, gather general information about the class as a whole.

Included in this first part of the survey should be some items about how students assess their own reading ability, preferences, habits, interests, and needs. Items asking students to select their favorite (and least favorite) books of various types also can provide important information as you decide about books the class will read together. Ask students how they go about selecting books to read on their own. What book qualities are important to them? To whom do they turn for advice on books? Who gives them recommendations on what to read? Finally, I insert some questions about popular culture: movies, TV, music, and the like. The answers to these queries help me understand teen culture and also give me a handle on the maturity level of the students (I can also use this information if the need arises in a censorship situation; see Appendix Y.)

Survey—Part I

Age: 10   11   12   13   14   15   16   17   18
Grade: 5   6   7   8   9   10   11   12
Gender: M   F

How well do you think you read? Check one answer that best describes you.
___ I am a poor reader.   ___ I read OK.
___ I am a good reader.   ___ I am an excellent reader.

How often do you read for pleasure at home each week?
1 hour or less   2 hours   3 hours   4 hours   5+ hours

How may books have you read on your own in the past month?
0   1   2   3   4   5   6   7   8   9   10+

How many books would you estimate that you own?
0   1–5   6–10   11–15   16–20   21–25   25+

What are your favorite types of books to read? Check all that describe your reading tastes:
___ Mystery   ___ Humor   ___ Science fiction   ___ Fantasy
___ Poetry   ___ Biography   ___ Autobiography   ___ Short stories
___ Art books   ___ Comics   ___ Magazines   ___ Series
___ Horror   ___ Suspense   ___ Sports stories   ___ Romance
___ Drawing books   ___ Trivia books   ___ Science books
___ Historical fiction ___ History books   ___ Sports books
___ Plays/drama   ___ Other (specify) _____

What books are your least favorite? Check all that describe your reading tastes:
___ Mystery   ___ Humor   ___ Science fiction   ___ Fantasy
___ Poetry   ___ Biography   ___ Autobiography   ___ Short stories
___ Art books   ___ Comics   ___ Magazines   ___ Series
___ Horror   ___ Suspense   ___ Sports stories   ___ Romance
___ Drawing books   ___ Trivia books   ___ Science books
___ Historical fiction ___ History books   ___ Sports books
___ Plays/drama   ___ Other (specify) _____

Which of the following do you use when selecting a book? Check all that apply:
___ Cover art   ___ Title   ___ Author
___ Length   ___ Reviews   ___ Summary on cover flap
___ Genre/type of book   ___ Other (explain) _____

Whom do you trust to recommend a good book for you to read? Check all that apply:
___ Parents   ___ Friends   ___ Teacher
___ Librarian   ___ Browse a bookstore ___ Browse in the library
___ Web site   ___ Other (explain) _____

Survey—Part I (continued)

What type of music do you listen to on the radio or on CD? Check all that apply:

___ Rock   ___ Country   ___ Classical
___ Oldies   ___ Dance music   ___ Hip-hop/Rap
___ Alternative   ___ Other (explain) _____

What are your favorite TV shows?

What is the best movie you ever saw?

If an author could write a book just for you to read, what would it be about?

Are there any particular books or authors you would like to see in our classroom library?

Questions About Attitudes Toward Books and Reading

A second part of a good survey measures students' attitudes toward books and reading. There are several attitudinal measures that are reliable and valid with this age group. I have used the Estes Scale to Measure Attitude Toward Reading (1971). This attitudinal measure contains twenty items and asks students to use a Likert-type scale for their responses. Statements are both positive and negative, as the following examples suggest.

Books make good presents.
Free reading is something I can do without.

Responses to the statements range from "strongly agree" to "strongly disagree." Responses that strongly agree to a positive statement receive five points, and responses that strongly disagree with a negative statement also receive five points. Thus, answers to these twenty statements can yield a score ranging from 20 to 100. The higher the score, the more positive the attitude toward books and reading.

Why is this information important? Simply, if we have students who score in the 80–100 range, we already have motivated readers. Students whose scores are in the 20–40 range, on the other hand, lack positive attitudes toward books and reading. Our approaches with these two groups of students are by necessity different. Motivated readers need us only to point them in the direction of good books; they readily accept our recommendations. These kids are active readers, members of what Frank Smith calls the "reading club." The students who do not see the value of books and reading, on the other hand, need more guidance. For many of these students, school reading has been a chore. Books are "boring." Reading is not a preferred activity. These students need more personal introductions to books. As teachers, we need to ensure that we find drop-dead good books for this population and that we take the books directly to them. Chapters 8 and 9 discuss strategies for connecting these kids to books, including reading aloud and booktalking.

Taking This Information to Heart

The more we know about our students, the better able we are to forge connections between readers and books. When I am booktalking to a group of kids I do not know well, I use sort of a scattershot approach. I talk about as wide a variety of books as I can, hoping one will hit a target somewhere. However, if I have the chance to talk to the kids before I begin the booktalks, I can ask questions about interests and preferences and use that information to guide the booktalks. If I know kids are big fans of *Buffy*, the TV show, I will include some vampire books. If I have fans of the Harry Potter books, I will be sure to include *Artemis Fowl* by Eoin Colfer and *Summerland* by Michael Chabon and other books that have some of the same appeal. As teachers, once you know your students' interests, it will be much simpler to find those good books they will want to read.

I was only five or six years old when we lived there, but I still remember the address: 415 E. Taylor Street.

That was our two-story stucco house in Bloomington, Illinois. It sat on the corner of two tree lined brick streets in a residential neighborhood just a few blocks from downtown.

On evenings when I wasn't in trouble for breaking a window, tearing my pants, or bloodying someone's nose, or if my brothers and I weren't outside playing whatever sport was in season, I'd sit on the front porch steps waiting for Dad to get home from his job at Osco's Drug Store. Sometimes he'd have nickel candy bars in his pockets, sometimes he'd play catch with us in the backyard, and sometimes, if he wasn't too tired and if we weren't too wild, he'd read to us while Mom got supper ready.

What Reading Means to Me by Chris Crowe

Before Dad could even sit on the davenport in the living room, Mike, Bill, and I would be angling for a place on his lap. Unless he intervened, the losers had to settle for snuggling on each side of him while the lap-sitter perched on dad's ample abdomen, nestled his head under Dad's chin, and held the book as Dad read.

No particular evening stands out in my memory, but lots of general details remain: the prickly stubble on Dad's cheeks, the aroma of his Old Spice mixed with cigarette smoke, the gentle rhythm of his low reading voice. I always looked forward to being close to Dad as he read to us, I felt warm. Safe. Loved.

I can now recall only a few of the books Dad read to us—*Mike Mulligan and His Steam Shovel, Danny and the Dinosaur, The Cat in the Hat,* but it wasn't the stories that mattered. What mattered was that connection with my father, the feeling that Dad cared enough about me to share a few minutes with me at the end of a long day.

Fast-forward twenty-five years.

One of our family albums contains a photo of the adult me, flat on my back on the floor in the hallway between my son's and daughter's rooms, unconscious. My arms are limp at my sides, my mouth is agape, and a children's book lies open across my chest. Christy and Jonathan are on their hands and knees, peeking out of their bedrooms, grinning at the photographer.

This photograph documents a popular family joke—I rarely survived the nightly bedtime reading. Most evenings, the kids amused themselves by watching me struggle to read while at the same time battling to withstand the truckloads of sleepy dust the Sandman was dumping on my head. Almost always before storytime was over, Mr. Sandman would win: the book and my eyes drooped, my speech slurred, and I slowly slid into slumber land on the hallway floor.

For some reason, my storytime narcolepsy always delighted my children.

But my sleep attacks weren't the only attraction. Over the years, I did stay awake long enough each night to have read shelf loads of books to my kids: *There Are Rocks in My Socks! Said the Ox to the Fox* [Patricia Thomas], *Charlotte's Web* [E. B. White], The Boxcar Children series [Gertrude C. Warner], *A Wrinkle in Time* [Madeleine L'Engle], all of the Little House on the Prairie series, *To Kill a Mockingbird* [Harper Lee], and many more books that my children and I have since forgotten. But it wasn't the stories that mattered—what mattered more was the time we spent together every evening, talking, wrestling, laughing, and eventually, reading. Memories of those warm and fuzzy moments with my kids are even more important to me now that all my children are nearly grown up and on their own.

So what does reading mean to me? In addition to all the more obvious educational and entertainment benefits, reading has provided me with opportunities to build relationships with my family, and when everything else has crumbled into dust, when I'm old, alone, and forgotten, it will be the relationships I have had with the people I love that I'll treasure most. As a child—and as a father—books have given me priceless opportunities for important, intimate family time, time that I will never forget, time that I can never recapture.

Now that my father is dead and my children are nearly grown up, I realize just how important those intimate moments were, and I will always be grateful that my father found the time and the energy to read to me, and that somehow I found the time and the energy to read to my own children.

Maybe that's why reading—and writing—books is so important to me. When I settle into a comfortable chair with a good book, I'm not just enjoying the story at hand, I'm also savoring the warm feelings I have always associated with reading. When I'm reading a good story, that transaction stirs all sorts of pleasant memories. But in addition to reviving family memories, reading has also taught me that the people I share this world with are as important as members of my own family. Good stories remind me of people I have known and loved, help me understand people whose lives are different from mine, and introduce me to people and places I've never seen. Without books, I'd be ignorant of many of the people who inhabit the world I live in. I am as grateful for those reading lessons and memories as I am for the very personal family memories that reading has provided.

It's a big wish, but as a writer of books for teenagers, I can only hope that my books will provide readers with the same sorts of connections to others that I've enjoyed from a lifetime of reading.

Let me tell you about an ever-changing stack of books. Sometimes it's five books high and sometimes it's fifteen; sometimes it's a tower on my nightstand and sometimes it's an untidy heap in a basket or on a shelf in my study. It's the richness of books I want to read next and after that and after that. It's pleasure and surprise waiting, and it's a family-and-friends affair.

I hope you grew up with a parent who read to you. If you did, you were blessed, but you were also blessed if you had a parent like my mother, who *found* books for me. She started my book stack and kept it going until I went off on my own, and the books she put in it both made me a reader and started me on my way to writing.

The Richness

of Books

by Jeanette Ingold

Not that she read them all herself. In fact, I don't remember her reading much at all back then. That was a luxury she reserved for after she was done raising my brother and me.

No, my father was the parent I saw reading. His glasses pushed up on his head and a book held out at arm's length, Dad would read an encyclopedia volume article by article, and when he'd get to a topic he wanted to learn more about—tree farming or cattle breeds or advances in some technology—he'd tell Mom, and she'd put it on her library list.

And then she'd start her search: in town first, and then on to a couple of Long Island's bigger libraries, and then—the final resort—into Manhattan to the stone lions and great holdings of the New York Public Library. She liked the hunt, and her face would light up with pleasure at Dad's delight over what she found.

Keeping me in books must have been a harder job, because I rarely told my mother what I wanted. I myself usually didn't know. At one time or another, though—and somehow, almost always at the *right* time—the Little House books joined the stack of Nancy Drews and Cherry Ameses in my room, as did whole series of biographies, and Mark Twain's books and Charles Dickens's and Jane Austen's. Only a few—*The Adventures of Tom Sawyer, Little Women, The Swiss Family Robinson*—held semipermanent places in the stack. (And I still think wistfully about riding an ostrich and living in a tree house.)

I suppose Mom must have gotten some guidance from librarians and my teachers, but her selection process was largely instinctive, a product of what she remembered from her own childhood and what she saw and hoped for in mine. That was the key to it, of course: The changing book selection worked because it was maintained by someone who valued books, loved a child, and wanted to bring them together.

In the years since, thousands of books have moved through that stack Mom started for me. There've been times when all it's held has been spy adventure or historical fiction or Southern writers. Times when I wouldn't give space to any author who wouldn't make me laugh the way James Thurber and P. G. Wodehouse, Ferrol Sams, Carl Hiaasen, and Mark Childress do. Like Mom, I've learned to trust my instincts about reading, just as I've learned to trust my instincts about what I need to write next, and in what form and voice. Not that I don't listen to friends—writer buddies, my editor, my favorite bookseller, some great librarians and teachers—whose recommendations rarely disappoint.

At times the stack has shrunk perilously low, but someone always stepped in to keep it from disappearing. One of the nicest Christmas presents I ever received was one my husband gave me early in our marriage. Overwhelmed by the demands of work and housekeeping, I'd pretty much let reading go by the wayside. But that Christmas morning I opened a gift-wrapped library book, Kenneth Roberts's *Oliver Wiswell,* and a note promising me time to read it.

Right now the stack is an eclectic mix that includes several new young adult novels suggested by colleagues who think, as I do, that some of the most exciting writing being done today is being done for young adults. The stack also includes a local history, Jimmy Carter's *An Hour Before Daylight,* and Sandra Cisneros's *Caramelo.* There's a computer book and a book on nineteenth-century cooking. A memoir my daughter gave me to read called *Stolen Lives: Twenty Years in a Desert Jail,* by Malika Oufkir and Michèle Fitoussi, and Hemingway's *A Moveable Feast,* which my son suggested. Those last two are there because my kids, grown now, understand all about book stacks, their own and others'.

I think my mom would be pleased with what she started. Or maybe she was just carrying on something her mother began? Or maybe a tradition that one of her grandparents initiated? I don't know—I never thought to ask—but as I said, book stacks are a family-and-friends affair.

Although on a good day in grammar school I was a mediocre student, I did have the good fortune in fifth grade to run into two brothers who showed me all the excitement that reading offered. The boys were Frank and Joe Hardy. Until I met them, my reading was limited largely to baseball magazines, the daily sports page, and the backs of baseball cards.

The Hardy Boys Made Me Do It by Paul Janeczko

All that changed one rainy Saturday afternoon in the summer—too rainy for my younger brother and me to play ball—when we went with our parents to Frankie's Market, a huge indoor flea market. While my parents browsed for "house things," John and I wandered by booths offering jigsaw puzzles, license plates, dinnerware, and Lionel trains. We stopped in front of a booth selling used books, his attention snagged by issues of *Life* magazine with black-and-white pictures of World War II battle scenes. When he disappeared down the magazine aisle, I drifted over to the books. Don't ask me why, but I was drawn to several shelves of uniform books with light brown covers that bore names like *The Tower Treasure, The Sinister Signpost,* and *The Shore Road Mystery* and had a silhouette of the two boys with a lightning bolt crossing behind them. I eased *The Tower Treasure* from the shelf.

When I read the opening pages of that novel, I knew that I was onto something. It was as if my teachers had been teaching me to read by looking through the wrong end of a telescope. But when I read the beginning of my first Hardy Boys book, it was as if Frank and Joe had turned the telescope around and said, "Here, chum. Try it this way." I did. And wow!

The Tower Treasure had it all. Two brothers who wanted to be detectives out for a Saturday ride on their motorcycles. Good start. I read on. What's this? Some idiot is trying to run them off the road! What was going to happen to Frank and Joe (I was already on a first-name basis with them)? I read through the final paragraphs of the first chapter right there in the store. When John joined me, I shoved the book at him and said, "You gotta read this." He had the good sense to listen to his big brother.

We looked up and saw the shop owner. We never knew his name, so he became the Used Book Guy. He with the black mustache and curly hair, with that yellow pencil tucked behind his ear. The same pencil that scrawled 25¢ in the corner of the end paper of every Hardy Boys book. He smiled at us. I guess he knew he'd made a sale. (I wonder if he knew he'd made new friends.)

Any money I could make from delivering papers, running errands, and pitching nickels behind the candy store went into my Hardy Boys fund, which my brother and I made sure we carried the next time we visited the Used Book Guy. When he left Frankie's Market for a store front, we continued to buy Hardy Boys books from him. Years later, I continued stop in to see him whenever I came home from college. Of course, I always walked out of the shop with a book or two (or three).

Is it too dramatic to say that the Hardy Boys changed my life? Perhaps, but not by much. From the Hardy Boys books I went on to paperbacks and read my way through several phases—gangster books being the most notable—as grammar school slowly turned into high school. My parents became alarmed that I could recite all pertinent dates in the rise and fall of Al Capone but could not remember when William Shakespeare was born. (I have since learned Shakespeare's dates.) Even some of the stuff I had to read in high school and college couldn't stop me. I'd become a reader.

I suspect that some of my grammar school teachers would be surprised—okay, shocked—that I went on to become a reader, let alone a writer. Some of them might be tempted to take credit for it. Which is okay with me. But I know the truth: the credit really goes to two brothers I met in a used book shop on a rainy Saturday afternoon many summers ago.

CHAPTER 5

What Makes a Book "Good"?

Snapshot of a Reader: Kathy, 25

The in-service presentation had gone well. I was finishing up and allowing some time for questions and answers before starting the long drive back home when a teacher raised her hand tentatively. She looked barely old enough to be in the front of a classroom herself. "How do you find all these good books?" she asked. "I try to keep up, but there are just so many books. Is there somewhere I can look to help me find out what books I should be reading?" The murmuring in the background let me know that Kathy had hit a nerve. Her colleagues, too, wanted to know where to find those elusive good books. "It's all well and good to wait for you to come and talk to us every year," someone commented, "but I'd like some ideas about how you pick the books you talk about. Where can we go on our own to get information?"

Hundreds of books are published for adolescents each year. How can we determine which of those books to purchase for our classroom libraries? Which might be good for classroom study? Do we have to read all the books to find the ones most suited to our needs, or are there resources to help us narrow the choices?

Selecting the best books for our students takes time and effort, but the payoff is impressive: students who clamor for more books and time to read them. What follows is a discussion of some of the defining characteristics of the best YA literature. Included are some resources for locating those good books to share with your students.

A Definition

It may be a little late in the game, but now seems a good point to pause and define what I mean by the term *YA literature.* Professionals disagree somewhat over the term and its definition. For the purposes of this book, I define this field of literature broadly as "books either written for or read by YA readers." That lets all kinds of books to fall under the YA umbrella. Since we are including students from fourth grade and up, that means we include the books directly marketed for this group as well as those books they pick up on their own.

Notice that already I have mentioned books as wide-ranging as *The Lovely Bones* (Sebold) and *Woman Hollering Creek and Other Stories* (Cisneros), both adult novels popular with many high school students, and *The Outsiders* (Hinton), which many would consider a more typical YA novel. Later, I'll also talk about books such as *The Bad Beginning,* the first book in the Series of Unfortunate Events books by Lemony Snicket, a book that many might call a children's book. However, in making the match, the key is the right book for the right reader at the right time. That "right" book might be a children's book, a YA book, or an adult book. Hence, the definition remains broad.

Narrowing the Field

To help narrow the number of books a teacher might be required to read in any given year, let's consider how we can make the task more manageable. Several suggestions follow.

Read the Review Journals

I think this is a must. Ask to see the current issues of the review journals the school librarian uses in purchasing decisions. The most common include *Booklist, Horn Book, School Library Journal (SLJ),* and *Voice of Youth Advocates (VOYA).* Begin by looking at the reviews of the books that have received the highest rating (stars in *SLJ* and *Horn Book* and *Booklist;* 5Q [for quality] and 5P [for popularity] in *VOYA*). Determine from the reviews which of those books might meet the needs of some of your students. You can ask that the librarian keep a running list of the books you find of interest and add them to the school collection as budget allows. Remember, the one person in the building with a fluid budget during the year is generally the school librarian. Also, use the other review journals in English and reading. The *English Journal* (National Council of Teachers of English) and the *Journal of*

Adolescent and Adult Literacy (International Reading Association) review YA books regularly. A review of YA books by middle school students along with a YA review column may be found in each issue of *Voices from the Middle* (NCTE). The *ALAN Review* (Assembly on Literature for Adolescents) not only reviews YA books but includes lots of articles about YA literature in general.

Consult the Awards Lists

Many awards are given for YA and children's literature each year (see Appendix X).

The American Library Association (ALA) presents annual awards for distinguished achievement in literature for children and young adults. The Newbery medal is given for children's literature, but many of the titles from the past decade or so are appropriate for YA readers. A list of all the winners from 1922 to the present is available at ALA's Web site.

The Michael Printz Award is presented for achievement in YA literature by the Young Adult Library Services Association (YALSA) of the ALA. Additionally, this group prepares an annual list of Best Books for Young Adults (BBYA) and Quick Picks for Reluctant Readers.

The International Reading Association publishes two lists each year through their Choices programs. The Teachers' Choices list contains thirty books of interest to teachers of various content areas. These are books that might be useful in lessons throughout the curriculum. The Young Adult Choices list contains books voted on by YA readers as their favorites.

There are other award lists that may be of interest to you. The Pura Belpre recognizes the contributions of Hispanic authors and illustrators in the field of children's literature. The Coretta Scott King Award recognizes the work of African-Americans in the field. For more information about the various awards presented in the field, visit the Children's Literature Web Guide at www.acs.ucalgary.ca/.

Don't overlook the award or recommended reading lists from your state organizations. In Texas, we have the 2 x 2 List for Pre-K and early elementary grades, the Bluebonnet Master Reading List for grades 3–6, the Lone Star List for grades 6–8, and the TAYSHAS List for grades 8–12. All lists are prepared by committees of the Texas Library Association. Similar lists are available in many states.

See What Sells

Look at the *New York Times* bestseller list (or the list of teen bestsellers at Amazon.com or another online bookstore) to see what YA readers are buying and reading. Surely, these are books we should know as well. As I write this chapter, high on the bestseller lists are J. R. R. Tolkien's *The Lord of the Rings* trilogy and *Holes* by Louis Sachar. Not new, I know. However, the movie versions of these books have moved them back to bestseller status. Also on the list are the Series of Unfortunate Events books (five in the top ten) by Lemony Snicket, and the Harry Potter books along with Natalie Babbitt's *Tuck Everlasting* (also recently released in movie version) and *Chicken Soup for the Teenage Soul.*

Characteristics of Good Books

The YA literature guru Ted Hipple (1991) once offered some criteria that are useful in ferreting out the best in this field. Three of them can be applied to narrowing your choices of books:

- The book beats others at the common games: vocabulary, character development, and moral concern.
- The book has classroom usefulness.
- The book reflects real life and has artistry in detail.

Basically, what makes a book good does not differ much from age group to age group. Sure, you look for more illustrative qualities in picture books for younger readers, but the characteristics of YA literature are similar to those for adult books. Here are some qualities to consider as you are making additions to the classroom and school libraries.

Plot

Is the plot unique or predictable? Do not discount a book simply because it is predictable, however, as some kids enjoy reading books that make it easy for them to predict the outcome. This is the attraction of series books for many readers. As an adult fan of books by Stephen King, I know what to expect from his stories. I read all of his works because of their predictable nature. It's not that there will not be surprises in the novel. It is simply that I know how the story will unfold as a narrative. Better yet, I search for novels that present a unique take on the more mundane stories. *Dancing with an Alien* by Mary Logue, Louise Plummer's *The Unlikely Romance of Kate Bjorkman,* and *Too Much T. J.* by Jacqueline Shannon, for example, all take on the romance genre and present it in new light.

Dancing with an Alien presents dual narrators, Tonia and Branko. Branko is an alien come to earth to find a young woman willing to return to his planet with him. Branko's planet has been devastated by a virus that killed most of the women. Hence, the population is gradually dying out. Branko must convince a woman to go with him. Enter Tonia, a young woman who is strangely attracted to Branko. The two begin a relationship that deepens into love. Tonia agrees to leave her home and planet behind and follow Branko. Branko has second thoughts about uprooting the woman he loves and exiling her to a planet where she will become not much more than an incubator of babies. The alternating voices and the unusual twist on a familiar genre make this book an example of how the familiar can become strange.

Louise Plummer's book is actually a story within a story. Kate aspires to be a writer. She knows the rules of writing romance novels. As a matter of fact, she has the *Romance Writer's Handbook* near her trusty computer. She knows kisses should be paragraphs long, that the hero has to have a masculine-sounding name, and that the heroine should have long, silky legs. She tells readers that she is in love and plans to write of that romance. If she does not have long, silky legs, she can at least have kisses lasting paragraphs. This wonderfully warm, intimate, and humorous tone draws readers in. At the end of several chapters, Kate makes notes about what she should revise in future drafts. What a terrific model to bring into writing class!

Is the plot linear, or does it employ techniques such as flashback, dual time narratives, foreshadowing, and the like? If you are looking for some novels to share in an English classroom, you may want to consider books that challenge readers by using more mature literary devices such as flashback and dual narratives. *Slake's Limbo* by Felice Holman, *Shattering Glass* by Gail Giles, *Rats Saw God* by Rob Thomas, and Paul Zindel's *The Pigman* are all excellent examples of how to employ unique plot structures to tell a story.

Both *Slake's Limbo* and *The Pigman* utilize dual narrators. This device allows the author to provide a more complete picture of the story world to the readers. Rather than writing in the third person, the author is able to use two distinctive first-person accounts so that readers can see how perceptions color stories. *Rats Saw God* and *Shattering Glass* use two distinctive time frames within the same story. *Rats Saw God* moves back and forth between Steve's senior and sophomore years of high school. *Shattering Glass* tells the story in real time. However, each chapter opens with part of a statement given by the young men involved in the murder of Simon Glass, an event that has yet to occur in the story line. These sophisticated plot devices demonstrate that YA books can be challenging and worthy of study in the classroom.

Conflict

Conflict is basically the problem that lies at the core of the story. The main character or protagonist can be placed in conflict with another person or even him/herself, pitted against nature, or confronted with a societal issue. Of course, conflict is not that cut-and-dried. Generally, there are facets of more than one conflict in the best of stories. In *Hatchet* by Gary Paulsen, Brian Robeson must battle against the forces of nature to survive. Along the way, he also wrestles with how to deal with his parents' divorce and his mother's new relationship. He has to find his own strength, the will to live, so to speak. The same is true for Walter Dean Myers's *Fallen Angels*. Set during the Vietnam War, this novel follows a platoon of African-American soldiers, most of them teens, into jungle combat. Obviously, part of the conflict is physical, literally man against man. However, each of the soldiers in the unit is facing his own personal demons. Thus, we have man against himself. Nature plays a role in the conflict, and certainly the views of society about this war will also come into play before the novel ends. Therefore, various facets of conflict are present in some novels. Teachers might ask students to keep a log of each chapter in the novel and which conflict is paramount in that chapter. An interesting piece of writing might arise from asking students, Which conflict is the most important one in this novel, and why? Another potentially good discussion point about conflict is how characters are drawn into the conflict.

Characters

Characters are the heart and soul of any story. How the author creates memorable characters is part of what draws readers into the novel. Some questions to keep in mind when examining character include

Are the characters richly developed or stereotyped?

Do the stereotypes serve a purpose?

What about archetypes?

How does the author reveal character?

Do the characters behave in an adolescent fashion, or are they wise beyond their years?

In serial fiction, often stereotypes are present. As someone who grew up reading Nancy Drew, Cherry Ames, Sue Barton, and the Bobbsey Twins books, I liked the stereotyping. I knew exactly what to expect from George and Sue and Nancy and Cherry and their nemeses. They did not grow and change; they remained static. The unchanging nature of the characters in these books is in direct antithesis to what is going on in real life and may be part of the comfort, too.

In nonserial reading, however, stereotyping disappoints. How about a not-so-perky cheerleader once in a while? Cynthia Voigt's *Izzy, Willy-Nilly* presents the story of what happens when a cheerleader loses her leg as the result of a car accident. Suddenly, the world of athletics and cheerleading is over. Just relearning how to walk is a challenge for Izzy. How can she redefine herself now that her life has changed so drastically? What about an athlete struggling with feelings of depression and self-doubt? *Damage* by A. M. Jenkins covers this formerly uncharted territory: Austin Reid is clinically depressed. He has seemingly nowhere to turn for help. Here, then, is the self-assured jock turned upside down and inside out, creating a fresh slant and a riveting character.

Sometimes archetypes are present in YA literature. Remember the archetypal characters from the world of fairy tales: the wiser, older mentor; the young impulsive child; the seemingly powerless who becomes the most powerful? All of those may be found in contemporary fiction as well as in fantasy, a genre that draws from those more traditional roots of fairy tales. Chris Crutcher's books often feature an older, wiser person who is there to assist the protagonist. Mr. Nak in *Ironman* is key to helping Bo Brewster find a way to control and channel his temper. Likewise, Joan Bauer's *Hope Was Here* and *Rules of the Road* both feature older, wiser women who serve both as a role model and a mentor/guide for the central characters.

The details an author brings to her or his characters are also essential features of good YA books. There are various means of developing and revealing character. Characterization may include information about the physical nature of the characters. Richard Peck describes Grandma Dowdel of *A Long Way from Chicago* and *A Year Down Yonder* in such painstaking detail that it is simple to form a mental image of this formidable force. Priscilla Roseberry, Monk Klutter, and Melvin Detweiler in Peck's classic short story "Priscilla and the Wimps" likewise come to life thanks to the author's close attention to small details: Monk's clothes and boots, Grandma's affinity for sensible shoes. And finally, there is the chilling description of the "other" mother in Neil Gaiman's *Coraline* replete with long sharpened fingernails and shiny black button eyes. These and other details in the spooky book caused ten-year-old Natalie to bury the book in the bottom of her toy chest each night as she solemnly informed me, "Not at night, Nana." It was Gaiman's attention to detail that causes such strong reactions in his readers.

Authors let readers know about characters through speech patterns, mannerisms, habits, and gestures. The hallmark of Brian Jacques's animal fantasies is his differentiation of characters through their speech patterns. Martin speaks in a different pattern and accent than his fellow inhabitants of Redwall Abbey. Joey Pigza's "Can I get back to you on that?" is a trademark response made when he does not want to consider the circumstances in which he finds himself. Karen Hesse manages to make eleven voices distinct in *Witness*. Each character speaks with a clear and unique voice as they relate, from their own perspectives, the events that unfold when the Klan moves into a town in Vermont at the turn of the century. In a similar vein, Paul Fleischman uses multiple voices to describe the personal toll of the Civil War in *Bull Run*. Of course, who can forget John and Lorraine, the dynamic duo of teens in Paul Zindel's classic *The Pigman*?

However, in addition to describing hair color, height, gestures, and mannerisms, an author must also be able to reveal the inner character. How does each character think and feel? How might they respond in any given situation? What other distinctive qualities are part and parcel of the characters? Of course, the answers to these questions have to come indirectly. How characters think and feel about each other and how they interact also help to reveal the inner workings of the cast of the story.

Gary Paulsen's use of the first person in *Nightjohn* serves as one example of how masterfully an author brings a character to life. From the opening paragraph, readers come to know Sarney, a young slave girl who has not yet reached maturity. Her speech pattern is distinctive. From her own words, we come to know how day-to-day life is for Sarney and the other slaves. *You Don't Know Me* by David Klass also provides readers with insights into the inner workings of the main character through John's sustained monologues about playing the tuba, about his stepfather-to-be, and about his new interest in girls. Janie finds her true self in the blues music of the past in Han Nolan's *Born Blue*. Surely she was meant to sing the blues; surely this is why her life has been so brutal? Alex Flinn gives readers a glimpse into the inner turmoil of Nick, a young man accused of being physically abusive of his girlfriend in *Breathing Underwater*.

The reactions and interactions of other characters can also reveal character effectively. *Sisterhood of the Traveling Pants* by Ann Brashares and its sequel, *The Second Summer of the Sisterhood,* in part show Lena, Tibby, Bridget, and Carmen as singular personalities. Though all four girls share the magic of the pants, they are very different people underneath. In *Fighting Ruben Wolfe* by Markus Zusak, two brothers share an evening ritual: an argument over who has to get out of bed to turn out the light. Their conversations and arguments tell readers a great deal about their true characters.

On the other hand, in *The Gospel According to Larry,* Janet Tashjian's central character, Larry, is unseen by those around him. He is the brains behind a Web site that urges teens to fight the way advertisers attempt to sway them into purchases. The only clues to Larry's true identity for those who visit his Web site are obscure photos of his few possessions. Even in Larry's real world of school and friends, few are allowed to glimpse the real person behind the persona. In *Up on Cloud Nine*, Anne Fine creates a character who remains in a comalike state throughout most of the novel. Most of what readers learn about him is through the recollections of his best friend.

Theme

The theme of the book is the message left to the reader once the story ends. Individual readers may perceive different themes or different aspects of the same theme depending on their development and life experiences. For example, someone who has survived a tragedy or surmounted an obstacle might see the theme of *The Chocolate War* by Cormier as ultimately realistic. The good guys do not always win; sometimes you can't beat the system. On the other hand, readers who have not witnessed as much in their lives might see the theme in a different light. To them, the theme might be darker: do not try to beat the system because you will be defeated.

When evaluating the theme of a story, it is important to consider several questions: Is the theme of substance/value to the reader? Is the theme delivered in such a way as to avoid being didactic? Are multiple themes possible and accessible to the reader? The very best that YA literature has to offer readers comprises those books that present themes applicable to readers' own lives. Even though Gary Paulsen's evocative *Nightjohn* is set in the past, the story of how a young slave named Sarney frees herself from ignorance through learning is still valid and relevant to contemporary readers. *Dealing with Dragons* by Patricia Wrede, though a fantasy, still imparts a clear message about following dreams in order to make them a reality. Many of our students will never find themselves in the situation Melinda faces in Laurie Halse Anderson's *Speak*. Yet, reading this remarkable novel might assist readers in understanding how a person has to speak out about rape in order to begin the healing process.

Of course, the best YA literature offers readers themes subtly. Early on in *Words by Heart* by Ouida Sebestyen, Lena's father tells her that something always comes along to fill the empty spaces. This simple but wise remark becomes a recurring theme in the story of how a young girl has to face prejudice because of the color of her skin. Lena experiences many losses; however, as her father notes, something comes along to fill the spaces. Bruce Brooks's *The Moves Make the Man* deals partly with a similar theme. However, there are multiple themes that play out over the course of the story of an unlikely friendship between Bix Rivers and Jerome Foxworth. The title itself suggests one of the central themes for this novel.

Setting

Occasionally, setting plays an important role in the reading. Fantasy and historical fiction, for example, require detailed settings. Retellings of traditional stories (fairy tales) and some realistic fiction may need only a generic or backdrop type of setting. They could take place anywhere and anytime. Felice Holman's *Slake's Limbo* takes place in New York City. The setting here is relatively crucial as Aremis Slake, to escape from a gang of bullies, flees into the subway system. There he lives for weeks, eking out an existence actually a bit better than in his former foster home. Obviously, a city with a subterranean system is needed for this story to work. However, a story such as *We All Fall Down* by Robert Cormier, about teens vandalizing a home by trashing the furniture and destroying valuables, could happen in any town.

In stories where setting is essential, the author must weave the details of the setting into the story carefully. Action and character still must take precedence over setting if the reader is to be engaged in the book. An example can be found in the opening chapter of *Sarah, Plain and Tall* by Patricia MacLachlan.

Style

Simply put, style is the way an author chooses and uses language. Style encompasses so many different elements that it is sometimes tough to define succinctly for students. Those of us who read widely know the hallmark elements of the style of our favorite authors. We know, for example, what makes a Stephen King book a Stephen King book, what makes a Tom Clancy a Tom Clancy, what makes a Hemingway a Hemingway. The same is true for many authors in the field of YA literature. Authors have their own signature styles.

We know a Gary Paulsen book when we see one, and not just from the author's name on the cover of the book. We know what to expect from Paulsen, from Avi, from Joan Bauer, from Christopher Paul Curtis, from Jack Gantos. Even when these authors are working in a variety of genres and writing with different voices, their signature styles are plain to see.

So, what elements of style can we impart to our students? How can we help them see those signatures authors place within the pages of their books? I would suggest the following elements of style as those we can most easily teach students to identify within books.

Sentence patterns.   Who can forget the opening sentences of a Charles Dickens novel? While Dickens favored long, complex, compound structures for his writing, someone like Gary Paulsen eschews them in favor of the more staccato rhythm produced by shorter sentences. Like Hemingway, Paulsen's narrative style seems to drive the story forward relentlessly. This is especially true of books such as *Soldier's Heart,* a novel many termed spare because of its construction. Bruce Brooks's *The Moves Make the Man* has a unique narrative style in that the dialogue is related in stream-of-consciousness manner. This makes for somewhat complicated scenes between the main characters. It might be an interesting assignment from time to time to have students select random passages from the novel and examine the sentence structures and patterns to see if an author has a signature style in this area.

Vocabulary or word choice. A hallmark of the Lemony Snicket series is the use of incredibly complex language. What Snicket does so admirably is define these words in context to make the text continuously accessible for readers. Should he elect to describe someone as "morose," he will often in the following sentence indicate the meaning of the word as "quite sad and distressed." Nonfiction is an excellent example of how word choice can be essential to a book. The terminology of a particular subject matter is key to understanding it. Therefore, in nonfiction the presence of glossaries and dictionaries is important. David Macaulay's *The Way Things Work* has a glossary that covers terms from AC/DC to worm, a type of screw. Janet Allen's *Words, Words, Words* (1999) offers many interesting and instructional strategies for developing vocabulary. Using some of Allen's techniques such as the word wall may be valuable in helping students see how authors make word choices.

Figurative language. What always strikes me when I read a Robert Cormier book, especially *The Chocolate War,* is the use of simile and metaphor. Cormier's descriptions of actions and settings and characters is made all the more vivid through his use of figurative language. The act of mailing a letter is likened to placing an item in a hot oven; it is easy for the reader to envision the care with which this letter is mailed. There are many other uses of figurative language. Paulsen uses hyperbole to heighten the hilarity of books such as *The Schernoff Discoveries* and *How Angel Peterson Got His Name*. This same use of hyperbole also works well in Christopher Paul Curtis's *Bud, Not Buddy*.

Other Considerations

Once you have managed to narrow the choices of books, it is time to consider how best to spend your book funds. The average hardcover book for

YA readers costs about $17. Before committing to a hardcover purchase, I take some time to consider a few questions.

Is this a book that addresses a timeless topic, a book that will not become dated quickly? The fact that Tolkien and Cormier and Hinton continue to sell books long after their original issue dates is a testament to the staying power of a timeless book. Coming of age, facing down challenges, completing a quest are all themes that seem never to age.

Is this a book that discusses a topic of the moment or deals with an issue that may become dated in a short time? Occasionally, we see a spate of books about a particular topic. For instance, after the success of the Harry Potter books, it was not unusual to see other books about wizardry and magic. The covers all proclaimed that they were the next Harry Potter (sadly, most of them were not). Topics for novels wax and wane in popularity as well. Depending on what is going on in society, we may see a sudden spike in the number of books dealing with drugs, suicide, war, sexuality, or violence.

Are there cultural references in the book that will hasten its becoming outdated? For instance, a YA novel that makes reference to actual musical groups or songs will become hopelessly dated much too quickly. A book that refers to the President of the United States by name will suffer much the same fate unless it is a historical novel.

Is this a book that will find a wide audience or is it a book that will appeal to a small segment of the readers I know? There are those books that seemingly everyone will read or has read (shades of Harry Potter). Books with wide appeal are best purchased in hardcover as they will have to survive at the hands of many readers. There are other books, though, that will have a much more limited appeal. I think of those handful of readers over the years who became what I call specialists. They read all the books in a genre or by one particular author. These books might not have found many other readers, but they were of special interest to a small group of kids.

While we have discussed some of the criteria against which we can judge books, there are some other criteria, more specific to different genres, that may also prove valuable as we develop our classroom collections. The next chapter provides some guidance for those specific genres.

It was marketed, I think, as a middle-grade novel, but *The Witch of Blackbird Pond* by Elizabeth George Speare had a teen protagonist, and it may well be my favorite book of all time. I read it every couple of years or so. The appeal was the protagonist, Kit, who like me was a reader, a romantic, and felt she didn't particularly fit in.

I also was one of the girls from the original Judy Blume generation. Both *Forever* and *Tiger Eyes* were favorites. I'm sure that Blume's affection for the first person has been a tremendous influence on me as a writer today.

But I didn't just read trade fiction. I also went through a genre phase of Stephen King and V. C. Andrews. It's too bad horror YA wasn't at its popular peak when I was that age because I adored that genre. I liked my teen fiction with an edge, and I still do.

A Reader, a Romantic by Cynthia Leitich-Smith

My father was a big reader of genre fiction, the James Bond and Tarzan series in particular, and I wanted very much to be like him. My mama thought I should be reading books that would improve my mind, and so she picked up *The Britannica Junior* encyclopedias one volume at a time at the grocery store. They weren't perhaps the most sparkling introduction to nonfiction, but I read all of them, cover to cover.

When I was in elementary school, Mama also took me to our local public library every Saturday morning. It was the perfect activity for a shy, only child whose family lived on a mac-and-cheese budget. As I grew older and moved to a new district, the school library became my safe place. It was there that I could belong, despite being a gangly foot taller than everyone else (they eventually grew; I didn't).

I became enamored of the Newbery books. It was the 1980s, an era too aware of brands and logos. Never taking the time to really study it, I assumed that the awards sticker was a logo, that the books were published by Newbery Books, Inc., which, in my opinion, did very good work.

In addition, I read comic books and a variety of TV/movie tie-in books. I had a great affection for fandom, particularly *Star Wars, Quantum Leap,* and *Battlestar Galactica*. One of my most prized possessions is a 1984 movie novelization of *Supergirl* by Norma Fox Mazer.

So, I guess I came to love reading through exposure, parental and librarian involvement, and the sanctuary that was the book world.

I am a YA reader. "Teen literature" describes my favorite books, and teens make the most sense to me. At heart, I'll probably be fourteen forever. I have such strong memories of my teen years, such vivid recollections for inspiration.

I remember: being elected to student congress; being dumped for a girl who "put out"; being one of three girls in honors classes; being white in Kansas City and Indian in Oklahoma; serving popcorn to an "Indiana Jones" crowd; and getting drunk for the first time at my best friend's big brother's fraternity house. I also remember when some of my friends "came out," and a few of the jocks on the bus making fun of the Indian students when we rode past Haskell Indian school, and when a boy died at my feet of a congenital heart defect at the finish line of a cross-country meet. I remember crying in the bathroom. I remember being mortified by my parents and seeking solace in the company of my grandparents.

My great-grandma Bessie lived well into her nineties. At sixteen, she was a young, proudly Mohawk woman leaving home by covered wagon to marry an RLDS [Reorganized Latter Day Saints] minister. At that same age, I was a mixed-blood girl, quiet about her heritage, dating my first boyfriend and working on a school report about Harry S. Truman.

I was a girl. But some of the woman she'd been lived in my teenage soul.

Young adults are partly adult, partly child, and all about transition. That's fascinating, and so are the stories they inspire.

As a third-grader, I tried to find a book about Sacajawea for a school report and came up fairly empty-handed at both my public and school libraries. Of course, nowadays, Sacajawea is featured in many biographies, and finding ones about any other Native woman is the big challenge. It's understandable to bemoan the rate of progress, but the improvements in multiculturalism since I was a kid have been dramatic.

I remember being "booktalked," though I have no idea if they called it that back then, by a school librarian who then wanted to know what I thought of each title. She made me feel important, like my opinion actually mattered.

But what I remember most vividly is a story the night my parents left me home alone when they went out to dinner. I was a young teen, and they'd just begun to allow some unsupervised time. Thrilled, I crawled into bed with a horror novel. With the noise of the storm and how engrossed I was in the story, I never heard them return. But a few moments later, my ornery daddy pounces through my doorway with a really cheesy, dad-style "boo!" I simultaneously jumped, screamed, and tossed the book up to the ceiling, recovering seconds later in a fit of laughter, amazed at how convincingly the story had bled into my reality.

Now, that's effective fiction.

CHAPTER 6

Fiction Genres for Adolescents

Snapshot of several readers: Henry, Ruth, Peter, Michaela, Lakeesha

> *Henry reads science fiction, history, historical fiction, and books about religions; Ruth eschews almost everything save biographies and autobiographies. Peter thinks Robert Cormier is the best author in the world and is unwilling to give other writers a try. Michaela is more eclectic in her tastes, sampling poetry, realistic fiction, and anything recommended by her friends. Lakeesha favors short story collections.*

Most of us have a range of students' reading tastes and preferences in our classrooms. As each semester opens, I begin class with a sharing session. Students volunteer (and occasionally I help them to volunteer) to talk about the books they are reading for pleasure. Generally, a wide variety of books is discussed. Students present informal booktalks (see Chapter 9) to one another for the first ten to fifteen minutes of class. What becomes readily apparent from watching the expressions on the students' faces is that not everyone likes the same book or the same kind of book. We need to be sure that our collections feature the best that these various genres have to offer. This chapter and Chapter 7 present information about the different genres and formats available to contemporary readers.

In addition to knowing how to judge books for adolescents in general (see Chapter 5), we need to understand that different types of literature (genres) possess special features and characteristics. This chapter explores briefly several of the formats authors may use in writing fiction as well as the defining characteristics of the different genres, and it offers some suggestions for evaluating books from this range of material.

Poetry

I can already hear some of you grumbling, "But kids do not like poetry. Why bother?" Indeed, poems in literary anthologies often cause adverse reactions in students. It is almost as if they have developed some sort of allergy to poetry. Kids break out in a sweat; they roll their eyes; they gag.

One summer I decided to take my grandchildren on a trip from Georgia (where they were living at the time) to Texas (my home). So, I loaded suitcases and a car seat and an infant seat in the rental car and headed off on the thousand-mile trip with a seven-year-old, a two-year-old, and a one-year-old. Along the way, the kids got bored, of course, so we began to play the Wee Song and Play tapes with nursery rhymes. Natalie's favorite became "Twinkle, Twinkle, Little Star." Her sisters cooed it to her when she became fussy; we sang it at the top of our lungs as we drove into the night. Is it any wonder that Natalie loved poetry as a child? However, she announced quite loudly at an in-service meeting one day that she thought poetry was boring. She was nine years old at the time. I wondered what had happened to diminish her love of the genre. Her answer was the same as the one I get from my university students who also seem to have an aversion to poetry: the poems they were reading in class were "boring." Translation: the poems were not accessible to them.

Here is what I think happens. Young children become immersed in poetry. From nursery rhymes to finger plays to lullabies, children learn to love the rhythm of language. As they grow older and head off to school, the poetry is still enjoyable. However, there seems to be some sort of protective barrier that screens out effective poetry with kids beginning in intermediate grades in many cases. Suddenly gone are Shel Silverstein and Jack Prelutsky and Arnold Lobel and J. Patrick Lewis and David McCord. They are replaced with "the classics." I think this sudden transition is akin to asking kids to jump over a giant crevasse. We lose too many readers of poetry in the process. Instead, I suggest building a bridge between Shel Silverstein and Robert Frost, between David McCord and Emily Dickinson, between Arnold Lobel and John Keats. Using children's and YA poetry can help build such a bridge. Knowing how to select poems appropriate for adolescents is a necessary tool in the construction. C. Ann Terry's (1974) research into the poetry preferences of children, and Karen Kutiper's (1985) research with young adult poetry preferences, provides us with some suggestions for using poetry more effectively with our students.

Accessibility

First, to be effective, a poem has to be within the experience of the reader. The topic has to be something with which the reader is familiar. Think of the poems we see frequently within our anthologies: poems about war, daffodils, searching for the Holy Grail, adult love, death, and other topics not germane to the lives of the typical teen.

Instead, poems about getting a driver's license, passing tests, friendships, crushes, and life outside of school might be just the ticket to building that bridge. Appendix O lists books of poetry that will be of interest to middle and high school students. Here are a few quick titles, though. "Sick" by Shel Silverstein is a perennial favorite; it tells the story of a young girl who is so ill that she cannot possibly survive much longer. Of course, once she learns that it is Saturday, her recovery is rapid. In coming back to Silverstein, a favorite poet from my students' childhood, I am exploring a way to move kids comfortably to more sophisticated verse (although I do not consider Silverstein a poet solely for young children). In Kathi Appelt's *Poems from Homeroom,* a poem entitled "Apply Yourself" speaks loud and clear to any teen whose parents have uttered that phrase about school. Appelt also has a poem about a driver's license, sure to resonate with many readers. Mel Glenn's *Class Dismissed!* contains some terrific poems about new cars, English teachers, and other subjects accessible and interesting to readers. My particular favorite is "Paul Hewitt," in which a young man asks his teacher for books other than *Moby Dick* and *The Grapes of Wrath.* Instead, asks Paul, give him books about how to pick up girls. Then he might be interested. "Got any books that deal with real life?" Paul asks at the end of the poem. These words, I think, demonstrate that Glenn knows what adolescents are searching for in books, even in books of poetry. It also shows how the bridge between the world of poetry for younger readers and poetry for older readers is built. We go from Silverstein to Appelt to Glenn (and perhaps to some of "the classics").

Rhythm

Good poetry, of course, must have a rhythm. Different poetic forms have different rhythms. Shakespeare favored iambic pentameter. Edward Lear worked in anapestic meter. However, to begin a discussion of poetry with these vocabulary terms would not be a good idea. Rather, we should seek out poems with different rhythms and have students clap them out or tap their feet or nod their heads in time to the rhythm. (I taught for ten years in an open concept classroom, and we did a great deal more head nodding or finger snapping than clapping, to keep the sound down.)

I generally begin with poems such as "Lasagna" by X. J. Kennedy. It is a four-line poem, one I teach in about thirty seconds. Once it is committed to memory, we take another minute to snap out the rhythm of the poem and talk about its pattern. The next day in class, we once again recite "Lasagna" and snap its rhythm. Then I might share one of Arnold Lobel's "Pigericks," limericks about pigs. The rhythm here is distinctly different from "Lasagna." Now we have a basis for a discussion of how a poet accomplishes a rhythmic pattern in a poem. A superb picture book of poetry for teaching about rhythm is Jane Yolen's *Dinosaur Dances*. The poems range from waltz pattern to flamenco to disco. Of course, Bruce Degen's illustrations just add to the fun of reading this book. My personal favorite in the collection is entitled "Square Dance." Here is another example of building bridges, as we move from children's poetry to works by classic poets like Robert Frost.

Recently, I read on a listserv that "Stopping by Woods on a Snowy Evening" can be sung to the tune of "Hernando's Hideaway." For my students, the song "Hernando's Hideaway" might not be familiar. However, a remix titled "Let's Dance the Night Away" is. So, we sing Frost's immortal poem to the tune of that song and talk about rhythm for a third time in class. Since rhythm is essential to song, kids can begin to forge the connection.

Rhyme

Yes, I know a poem does not need to rhyme. But I also know that kids' ears grow accustomed to hearing the rhyme of poetry during those early years when all their poems do rhyme. So, we need to slowly wean them from rhymed verse, not yank it all away at once. Let's begin with "Lasagna" once again. Here is a poem that rhymes. However, look at the interesting way in which Kennedy has to maneuver language in order to achieve a rhyme between lasagna and "onya." This is, of course, an example of poetic license. At this point, I distribute some art supplies and we make poetic licenses. I place the students' photos on them (I can use a digital camera and print some off quickly) and then they are laminated. Poetic licenses are tucked away and can be brought out any time we want to play around with not only rhyme but language.

I search for poems that use rhyme in unusual ways. *The Happy Hippopotami* by Bill Martin Jr. is a picture book I generally use for this lesson in unusual rhyme. In the book-length poem, Martin tells of a day at the beach with some hippopotami. He creates rhymes with invented words, such as hippopotomamas and hippopotopilots. Lynne Cherry's *The Armadillo from Amarillo* is also useful for teaching about inventive rhymes. The book is a perfect example of poetic license. Also, take a look at Alice Shertle's *Advice for a Frog,* a lovely picture book of poems about unusual animals. We can bridge from these children's books of poetry to the rhymes of Ogden Nash, someone who took great poetic license in his light verse.

Figurative Language

Another hallmark of excellent poetry for adolescents is the use of figurative language such as simile, metaphor, personification, and hyperbole. Such use, though, still has to be within the experience of the reader. It does little good to share, "My love is like a red red rose that's newly sprung in spring," with students who have not yet experienced that depth of mature life. Think of simile and metaphor as equations: readers need to understand both sides of the equation in order to understand the simile or metaphor. In "Apply Yourself," Kathi Appelt likens applying yourself, using your gray matter, to spreading peanut butter on toast. In her novel told in verse, *Locomotion,* Jacqueline Woodson's main character describes a sky as the gray of aluminum foil, a Reynolds Wrap sky. These similes and metaphors work because they use images within the range of experience of the reader.

One terrific book for teaching readers about simile and metaphor is Audrey and Don Wood's *I'm as Quick as a Cricket.* On each page, an exuberant youth describes himself in terms of how he is like a particular animal (busy as a bee, tame as a poodle, brave as a tiger). Each page, then, contains a simile well within the range of experience of even young readers. Another good poetry collection is *Hailstones and Halibut Bones* by Mary O'Neill. The poems in this collection describe various colors in terms of the moods and images they conjure. Red is a show-off; black is kind, because it covers up the things we do not wish to see; purple is the great-grandmother of pink. Again, here are uses of figurative language that are completely accessible to our students. They will serve as planks in that bridge that helps our students move from children's verse to adolescent poetry more easily and confidently.

Imagery

Good poetry for our students should affect their senses. It can either create mental images or cause us to smell, taste, hear, or feel something while reading. The classic "Sarah Cynthia Sylvia Stout" is a prime example. Through Shel Silverstein's descriptions of all the garbage piling up, we should perhaps begin to wrinkle our noses in distaste. Sour cottage cheese, green baloney, and other nasty bits are all roiled together in one huge heap. It is too easy to imagine exactly how that would look and smell. That is what makes this particular poem a favorite of readers of all ages. Naomi Nye creates some startling images in her poems in *19 Varieties of Gazelle: Poems of the Middle East* as she describes the colorful decor of an elementary classroom here in the United States. She then compares that image to a classroom in the Middle East, allowing readers to visualize the contrast.

A Final Thought About Poetry

Remember, part of what makes a poem a poem is its shape on the page. Students are readily able to distinguish between prose and poetry because of poetry's distinctive appearance. Poets, then, make some decisions about text differently than authors of other genres. An interesting exercise that puts students in a poet's mind-set is to give them a piece of prose and ask them to make it look like a poem. For instance, take the Preamble to the Constitution, the Gettysburg Address, a news story, a paragraph from a science textbook, or a passage explaining adjectives from your language arts textbook. Ask students to make the prose appear as if it were a poem. I guarantee that if you have thirty warm bodies in your classroom, you will receive thirty different-looking "poems." I also guarantee that some of these attempts at making text look poetic might actually approximate a very real poem. This exercise ingrains two concepts into kids: first, poets have to give some thought to how to make the poem look, and second, the words poets use are essentially like the words that any other writer uses. What differs is how the words are arranged rhythmically.

Drama

When it comes to this particular genre, literature anthologies tend to have few selections from which to choose. Additionally, there is little out there in YA literature to supplement the textbook (Brown and Stephens 1995). There are, I think, some salient points to be made here. The first is that drama was meant to be performed, not read. Shakespeare did not envision the school children of the twenty-first century sitting around reading his plays. He lived to see them performed at the Globe Theater. Likewise, contemporary playwrights wish to see their name in lights on Broadway, not in the table of contents of a secondary literature textbook.

The problem remains, then, how to give kids access to drama of interest and relevance to their needs and desires. To that end, I make two suggestions: use Readers Theater (RT) in the classroom, and ensure that the plays being shared with students could be performed or viewed in some manner. Here are some essential resources for accomplishing these goals.

One of the best sites out there for Readers Theater is maintained and operated by Aaron Shepard at www.aaronshep.com/. Shepard not only provides tips about using RT in the classroom; he provides actual RT scripts that can be downloaded and used in the classroom. The scripts range from slapstick and humorous to ironic and satiric and tragic. Scripts based on traditional folktales and award-winning novels along with classics coexist at this site. Additionally, Shepard has demonstrated how teachers can take any novel or story and show students how to transform it into an RT script.

Two play collections are among the best available. One is *Center Stage*, edited by Donald R. Gallo, a collection of one-act plays by writers of YA literature such as Alden Carter and Walter Dean Myers. The plays require little or no costuming, props, and scenery. The topics of the plays range from the warmly humorous tale of a young man who has once again failed his driving exam (this time before he actually left the driveway of the motor vehicle registry) to the chilling "Cages," in which young people talk about the cages they are kept in by society's prejudices. Another good collection, especially for performance, is *Acting Natural* by Peg Kehret. This is a collection of monologues, dialogues, and playlets for teens to produce with little time and effort. They would work equally well as Readers Theater productions. Two girls argue about the mundane in "The Worst Hair in the World." Other plays deal with ecological disasters and drunk driving. Both of these play anthologies would make excellent additions to the offerings of the typical textbook. They also serve to get students up and performing in the classroom.

In Texas, we have a suggested reading list for middle school known as the Lone Star List. Twenty books intended for grades 6–8 are on the list each school year as a statewide reading motivation program. One of the teachers working in a local middle school uses Readers Theater for other purposes in her classroom. She assigns groups of students to work on RT scripts based on their favorite Lone Star book. She videotapes the performances of these short plays. The video is then played on the school's TV station and in the library to attract other readers to these books. Think of some of the different applications you could make using RT in your classroom. You could have the advanced class do RT teasers for the class sets of novels from which students select their reading over the course of the school year. Your classes could do RT performances for the local intermediate and elementary schools on books suitable for those audiences. A real payoff is all the skills students acquire through the preparation and performance of RT pieces.

Finally, don't overlook these books containing plays from other cultures: *¡Aplauso! Hispanic Children's Theater*, edited by Joe Rosenberg; *Novio Boy: A Play* by Gary Soto; *You're On! Seven Plays in English and Spanish*, selected by Lori Marie Carlson; and *Pushing up the Sky: And Other Native American Plays* by Joseph Bruchac.

Short Stories

Each of the fifteen years I spent as a middle school English teacher, I began the literature study with a unit on short stories. After a few years, even I had a difficult time cranking up enthusiasm for the same short stories year after year. Thankfully, along came Don Gallo and changed my approach to this unit forever. Gallo's first collection of short stories, *Sixteen,* provided us with short stories that spoke to my eighth- and seventh-graders. This first collection contained sixteen stories by YA authors such as Richard Peck and Ouida Sebestyen. The stories were arranged into four rather broad themes, making this a perfect choice for classroom use. I purchased a class set of the books and distributed them to the class. Their instructions were to read two stories from one of the four themes. They could select these stories in any way: length, author, title, whimsy. We came together at the end of the week prepared to talk about a variety of reading experiences.

What I discovered through this discussion is that students responded to the stories enthusiastically. By the time everyone in the class had shared their favorite stories, it became apparent that there was a story to suit virtually each member of the class. What was fascinating is that some students argued vehemently if someone else indicated a story was *not* one of their favorites. That moved the class discussion up a level. Students were discussing the stories beyond the plot; they were making evaluative judgments about the style and format of the stories along with the plot and characters. That first unit of study, then, set the tone for all that was to follow.

What was it about this book that inspired students to go beyond themselves and beyond the text? I think that three key elements were at work. First, I gave students some control by allowing them choice in their reading material. They only had to read two stories and not all of them (many students reported they had read them all anyway). Second, students knew many of the authors whose works appeared in this collection from their free reading time and from the titles I had shared with them in booktalks and read-alouds. Finally, they were reading stories about topics of interest to them. "Priscilla and the Wimps" by Richard Peck is a perennial favorite of students from this collection. In this brief story (it takes about seven minutes to read the story aloud), Priscilla Roseberry takes on Monk Klutter, the "head honcho" of the school. At the end of the story, Monk is thrown into a locker as the students file out for the day. A blizzard strikes the town, and school closes for a week. This O. Henry ending allowed a perfect segue to *The Ransom of Red Chief* when I decided to dip into the literature text. I could teach all the elements of plot and story readily through this and any other story in the collection.

Over the years, other Gallo story collections have become part of the landscape of YA literature. Other editors have also produce collections for this audience. Michael Cart's *Tomorrowland* examines life at the brink of a new millennium; his *Necessary Noise* focuses on families and all the different permutations that compose modern family life. David Rice's *Crazy Loco* looks at Hispanic life in the Rio Grande Valley. Vivian Vande Velde explores new ways to tell old tales in *Tales from the Brothers Grimm and the Sisters Weird*. Another favorite of mine for reading aloud is *Scary Stories to Tell in the Dark* and its sequels by folklorist Alvin Schwartz. A bibliography of short story collections may be found in Appendix L.

Folktales and Variants

Generally, when we think of folktales, we think of those bedtime stories of our youth. Tales of princesses and streets paved in gold are memories of childhood. However, there are quite a few variations of this popular genre available for adolescents today. In addition to tapping into that precious childhood cache of memories, traditional literature can be useful for teaching kids about stereotypes, archetypes, motifs, and other literary devices and terminology.

It all began with *The True Story of the Three Little Pigs* by Jon Scieszka. Suddenly, folktales provided fertile ground for picture books targeting older readers. Here is the story of the three pigs told from the point of view of Al T. Wolf. Hey, he was only trying to borrow some sugar to make a cake for his granny. All the rest of the story is simply misreported. Scieszka followed up on the success of *The True Story of the Three Little Pigs* with more twisted tales, including *The Frog Prince Continued* (in which we learn that the frog turned prince did not live happily ever after), *The Book That Jack Wrote* (which twists the familiar cumulative tale of *The House That Jack Built* with plenty of references to other pieces of literature for the careful reader), *Squids Will Be Squids* (in which Aesop's fables take a direct comic hit), and *The Stinky Cheese Man and Other Fairly Stupid Tales* (which would make an excellent introduction to the various parts of a book, such as table of contents and dedication page).

The Three Pigs by David Wiesner picks up where *The True Story of the Three Little Pigs* leaves off, so to speak. Here is a story that begins very traditionally and then veers off course midway through the book as the pigs escape the wolf and sail away on a paper airplane (fashioned, of course, from the book in which they are star performers) and sail to Mother Goose Land and in and out of various tales (including Wiesner's *Tuesday*) before living happily ever after with a dragon to guard them and their home. Of course, as a contrast for readers, you might select Trivizas's *The Three Little Wolves and the Big Bad Pig.*

Other books followed in this format of picture books that require more skilled, mature, experienced readers. Alma Flor Ada's *Dear Peter Rabbit* combines several stories from childhood as the story is told in letters exchanged between Goldilocks, Peter Rabbit, a Big Bad Wolf, and other assorted characters. *The Jolly Postman* by Janet Ahlberg combines fairy tale elements, epistolary format, and pop-up details to provide a challenging read with plenty of humor for intermediate students. Sue Denim's *The Dumb Bunnies* and its sequels are also loaded with humor as we meet some dumb bunnies who live in a log cabin made of bricks. In the first installment, the Dumb Bunnies encounter Little Red Goldilocks (though readers will more likely identify her as Snow White early in the reading). Pairing this book with Marilyn Tolhurst's *Somebody and the Three Blairs* and Heidi Petach's *Goldilocks and the Three Hares* makes another fine choice for a text set, books to compare and contrast.

Judy Sierra's *Monster Goose* presents nursery rhymes never conceived by the gentle Mother Goose. Instead, Humpty Dumpty neglects to use sunscreen and ends up hard-boiled; Little Bo Creep replaces Little Bo Peep; and Monster Goose writes using a laptop computer. A possible pairing might be with Bruce Lansky's *The New Adventures of Mother Goose: Gentle Rhymes for Happy Times,* a collection that seeks to remove any of the violence or sadness from the original rhymes. Using *The Annotated Mother Goose* by William Baring Gould will provide students with a unique perspective about the origin of some of the popular rhymes of their childhood. The tale of Daedalus and Icarus gets new life in Christopher Myers's incredibly riveting *Wings.* *The Three Questions* by Jon Muth is a retelling of a Tolstoy fable. A list of picture books for older readers may be found in Appendix H.

The possibilities for using picture book variations in the English classroom are virtually limitless. One of my favorites is based on an assignment given me by Dick Abrahamson in my graduate class in children's literature. Dick asked us to compare and contrast three versions of the same tale. We were to include in our analysis plot, main characters, setting, theme, motif, and illustration. I now use a variation of that activity with my students. First I provide information to them about the various categories, especially motif, the one term with which they may not be familiar. Motif is a recurring pattern and includes such things as magic numbers (3, 7, 12), magic objects (wand, lamp), magical transformations (from frog to prince with a kiss), and simple rhymes (fee, fi, fo, fum). We brainstorm examples of these motifs in some of the fairy tales we know. Now, they are ready for the activity.

I place on tables the different versions of "Cinderella" that I have collected over the years. The range includes Marcia Brown's romantically illustrated *Cinderella*; John Steptoe's African version, *Mufaro's Beautiful Daughters*; and some humorous takes, such as Helen Ketteman's *Bubba the Cowboy Prince* (a clever Texas version), *Prince Cinders* by Babette Cole, and William Wegman's astonishing *Cinderella*, in which his dogs dress the parts. Students form groups of three to five and select two different versions of the story to compare and contrast. They produce a chart like Dick Abrahamson used when I took his children's literature class (see Table 6.1). After this part of the assignment is complete, students present their charts to the whole class, thus sharing with everyone other versions of the Cinderella story.

This assignment may be taken further. Students could illustrate the charts and hang them on the walls. It is also a simple step from the chart to a written assignment in which students can compare and contrast the stories in paragraph form. They already have used an advanced organizer and

Table 6.1

	Plot	Characters	Theme	Motif
David Wiesner, *The Three Pigs*	To escape the wolf, three pigs make a paper airplane and sail out of the story to a new land where a dragon protects them from harm.	wolf pigs dragon	Creativity can solve seemingly insurmountable problems.	3—pigs houses simple rhyme
Jon Scieszka, *The True Story of the Three Little Pigs*	A wolf wants to make a cake for his granny and visits the pigs, who refuse to share.	wolf pigs	Sometimes there is more than one way to tell a story.	3—pigs houses simple rhyme
Eugene Trivizas, *The Three Little Wolves and the Big Bad Pig*	Wolves try to keep a pig from eating them.	wolves pig	The best way to thwart someone's anger is through love.	3—wolves houses simple rhyme

have their word banks ready on the chart, so writing should be easy. If time constraints exist (and they frequently do), I vary this assignment by having each student read a different version of the story (you can check out versions from the school and public library if you do not have this assortment) and then meet with a group to share the version read. Each group has to decide on its favorite version. Then, I put two groups together and repeat the process until one large group comes up with the class's favorite. Discussion is fierce, and still everyone has an idea of the variety of versions of this familiar tale from childhood.

Contemporary Realistic Fiction

Basically, in contemporary realistic novels, the story is entirely possible. Everything in the story—plot, characters, setting—is consistent with life in the real world. In the pages of this genre readers can experience life as it is even if it is not so in their own lives. YA literature was born in the pages of realistic novels. Early novels such as *The Pigman, The Outsiders,* and *The Chocolate War* all presented realities for contemporary readers. What separates these and other classics (or will-be classics) from novels simply set in contemporary times? How can we tell what stories will stand the test of time?

Good realistic novels must meet criteria beyond the generic ones discussed in Chapter 5. They should provide readers not only with a satisfying reading experience but with insight into their own worlds (Norton 2003, p. 371). Students may not face the Vigils, as Jerry does in *The Chocolate War.* However, peer pressure is an omnipresent factor in adolescent life. Readers can judge Jerry's attempts to deal with Archie and the Vigils and Brother Leon and Emil Janza. They can test themselves within the safe confines of the book and ask, How would I react in a situation like this? Students may not find themselves befriending a senior citizen, as John and Lorraine do in *The Pigman.* However, many of them will be placed in situations where they have to make tough decisions, decisions that will affect others besides themselves. Similarly, students may not be from the "wrong side of the tracks" like the Greasers, but many have felt like outsiders from time to time.

Good realistic novels must also show readers that people are more alike than they are different, that we are all connected in some way. At some point, everyone's parents are embarrassing in public. Most of us can recall trying to persuade our parents with, "But everyone else is allowed to," to little avail, of course. Adolescence is frequently a time of feeling isolated from others, of feeling like no one else has had these same thoughts and feelings before. YA novels assure readers that is not the case. Witness Jess's reactions to the sudden death of his best friend Leslie in the haunting *Bridge to Terabithia* by Katherine Paterson, or how Melinda reacts when she enters high school in *Speak,* or even how Wallace reacts to the failing grade given him for his honest appraisal of a book he has been forced to read for English class in Gordon Korman's hilarious *No More Dead Dogs*. All these characters have at their core some piece of human nature that is present in us all. Whether it is Jess's relationship with his bratty sister, or Melinda's fractured friendship with someone she has known most of her life, or Wallace's less-than-tactful way of dealing with people and events, readers will recognize something of themselves in these books.

Finally, the very best realistic novels show incomplete growth toward adulthood. Do not look for all happy endings and complete stories here. Remember that we all encounter many trials and tribulations as well as joys and successes along the path from childhood to adulthood. Adolescence is not completed in one fell swoop or at any one given moment. It is a gradual change in our lives, and the literature we share with kids needs to reflect this. When we reach the end of Bruce Brooks's *The Moves Make the Man*, we are still unsure about the whereabouts of Bix Rivers. We know that Bix has learned an important lesson in the book. However, he still has some way to go to reach manhood. *The Boy Who Saved Baseball* by John H. Ritter leaves us with many questions about the future of the main characters, even though we know that the town's future is more secure. Jack Gantos brings Jocy Pigza back for two sequels to *Joey Pigza Swallowed the Key* to show readers how Joey must continue to grow and to take charge of his own destiny. However, *What Would Joey Do?,* the third book in the Joey saga, still leaves Joey not completely matured into an adult. That is the mark of a good realistic novel. Not all problems can be solved neatly at the end of the novel.

These books offer readers a chance to see some of what life has to offer. They open a window on the world, so to speak, a window through which readers can have many experiences, all within the safe confines of the pages of a book. Several appendixes suggest contemporary realistic novels for YA readers.

Fantasy and Science Fiction

For many years, fantasy and science fiction have been designated escape literature. The fanciful ideas and settings and plots can mislead some to think of this genre as having little to do with the real world. However, rather than being purely escapist, fantasy and science fiction offer readers a unique perspective on the times in which they live. This genre can also assist us in the classroom as we teach the elements of literature.

Fantasy has its roots in the oral tradition. Those fanciful tales of princesses and fairies and goblins were the foundation for modern fantasy. So, when we examine fantasy and science fiction, it should be no surprise to see the common features the genres share. Perhaps one way of introducing fantasy to adolescents is to use some of the more traditional folktales mentioned in a previous section of this chapter. Knowing about motifs and archetypes can heighten students' appreciation for the elements of modern fantasy.

So, what are the elements of modern fantasy? One important ingredient for good fantasy for YA readers is that the theme be a universal one (Norton 2003, p. 274). In other words, the message the author wishes to impart needs to apply in the real world, not just in the fantasy world of the book. *The Giver* by Lois Lowry, though set in a chilling future, examines themes accessible to contemporary readers. As Jonas learns about the evil lurking beneath the veneer of his utopian society, readers can learn that they must look beyond the surface and see the motivation behind the actions of people and government. E. B. White's *Charlotte's Web* explores the topic of friendship and lets readers know that friendship involves both taking and giving in return. Tolkien's books about Middle Earth and Philip Pullman's His Dark Materials trilogy explore the nature of evil and ultimately demonstrate that even the seemingly small and defenseless can combat the larger evils of the world if they are willing to do so. In *Others See Us,* William Sleator examines how people really think about others inside their heads. On the outside, someone might be nice and charming. Inside, though, they may harbor all sorts of thoughts, even homicidal ones. Sometimes, it is best not to be able to see inside.

Fantasy, in order to be enjoyed, requires "a willing suspension of disbelief" from readers. If we are unwilling to suspend disbelief and allow Charlotte to spin words into her web to save the life of her friend Wilbur, then *Charlotte's Web* is not a story we will enjoy. To say to yourself as you are reading *Dancing with an Alien* that there is no intelligent life beyond our planet is to guarantee a dreadful reading experience. If, however, we can suppress that niggle of disbelief and let the story take us in, then we can fully appreciate the futuristic world created by Lois Lowry in *The Giver* and *Gathering Blue;* we can travel to Narnia and Middle Earth and Prydain.

To help facilitate this suspension of disbelief, authors employ various techniques. One way to assist readers in entering the world of the fantasy is by creating and developing characters who grow to be real to them. One of my students' chief responses to reading *Eva* by Peter Dickinson is that they would never allow the scientific experimentation Eva's mother consents to in order to save the life of her child following a near-fatal accident. They have accepted the possibility of transplanting the neurons of a girl into the brain and body of a chimp—suspended disbelief—and take up the debate as if it concerned real issues. Eva becomes real to the readers, so real that they demonstrate concern about her future as a hybrid animal/human. The same is true for other fantasies. The characters become real to us. We love to pity Wilbur from *Charlotte's Web*. We weep along with Winnie in *Tuck Everlasting* as she makes her difficult decision not to drink from the Fountain of Youth and join the Tuck family. We fear for Vivian's safety in the chillingly sensual *Blood and Chocolate* by Annette Curtis Klause. Authors create these memorable characters to keep us turning the pages to see what will happen to them next.

Some authors fashion wholly realized secondary worlds in which they place their characters. Even before the big screen brought it to life, we knew what Middle Earth looked like because of the meticulous details of Tolkien's *The Hobbit* and its companion books. From the sleepy town where Bilbo and Frodo led rather ordinary existences through the darkness of the land surrounding the Tower to the dank depths of Gollum's world, we could see in our mind's eye the flora and fauna, the sky and ground, the heavens and the depths. Lloyd Alexander's Prydain, the land in which young Taran the pig keeper must find his destiny, is familiar landscape to readers. Lyra and Will travel into multiple worlds all made real by Pullman in His Dark Materials trilogy. The same is true for C. S. Lewis's land of Narnia and J. K. Rowling's Hogwarts School of Wizardry.

Fantasy permits readers to travel to faraway worlds, to fight alongside hobbits and dwarves and elves, to face down the ultimate evil and survive. In some ways, I think, this literature is quite empowering. Because even small and insignificant creatures can endure, perhaps there is hope for us all, hope we can survive the evils of this world, hope we can confront wrong and try to make it right.

It might surprise you, but I read nothing of the kind of mythic quests that I write now. Instead, I read lots of two kinds of books: biographies and nature writing. In the former group, Carl Sandburg's biography of Abraham Lincoln was (and still is) a great favorite; in the latter, books by Henry David Thoreau, Rachel Carson, and John Muir ranked at the top (and still do). You can see the influence of these two themes on my writing today: my fascination with heroes, and my love of nature. That is why, for example, Kate Gordon strives to save a great redwood tree in *The Ancient One.* And why that boy who washes ashore at the start of *The Lost Years of Merlin,* on his way to becoming the greatest wizard of all time, discovers that nature is his best mentor.

Writing to Make One Fall from Trees

by T. A. Barron

Then, after I left my Colorado ranch to go to college, I came across a marvelous writer by the name of J. R. R. Tolkien. And I was hooked! After *The Lord of the Rings,* I read (and reread and reread) T. H. White's *Once and Future King.* Now, I still enjoyed biography and historical epics, which is why I loved Leon Uris's *Exodus.* But the time had come for me to drink deeply of writers who create rich new worlds. So after Tolkien and T. H. White, I read lots of Madeleine L'Engle, Lloyd Alexander, and Ursula Le Guin.

I read my first books up in the branches of a tree, an old ponderosa pine on our Colorado ranch. And I guess you could say I have never come down. The unseen influence here was my parents, especially my mother. She was (and still is, bless her) the model of a well-read person. At age 89, she is still sending me clippings of scientific articles on how snowflakes are formed, or newly discovered poems by Emily Dickinson. By her example, I learned that reading could be fun—exciting, really—and a great way to travel. We had terrific, wide-ranging conversations around the dinner table about books, politics, and religion . . . made possible in part by the fact that we hardly ever watched any television.

Why do I write for young adult readers? For starters, there is no more critical time of life. Young adults are absolutely on the cusp between childhood and adulthood (or you could say, between asking all the questions and knowing all the answers). The are openhearted enough to want to probe and explore life for all it's worth, yet sophisticated enough to want the raw truth and nothing but the truth. It's an incredibly powerful, highly charged time of life, full of potential and ideals and dreams. That is why all the heroic characters in my books are young adults. Anything is possible at that stage. And although they may not realize it themselves, they have enormous possibilities—indeed, magic—down inside of themselves.

What memories do I have about reading? Once I actually fell out of that old ponderosa pine tree while reading a book of Thoreau's essays. When I say that Thoreau's writing packs a punch, I mean physically as well as spiritually! When I was in fifth or sixth grade, I started my own little humor magazine. It was ridiculously silly, but it did give me a chance to explore the fun and power of words. It also kept me largely out of trouble, which is why my language arts teacher supported the project. The closest to disaster I came was when I wrote a fictional exposé about the secret life of teachers . . . which came a bit too close to the truth!

CHAPTER 7

Moving from Fiction to Informational Books

Snapshot of a Reader: Trish, 15

Trish eschews most fiction, preferring to read historical novels, biographies, and how-to books. She is disappointed with the narrow range of materials in her English classes. Most of what the teacher assigns for common reading is fiction. About the only nonfiction reading required is essays by Thoreau and others of his generation. Strangely, the state-mandated testing tends to favor expository reading, so some time is spent examining how to approach this type of text. What Trish would love to see, though, is the presence of more choices in the nonfiction area on the reading lists at school. She is not alone in her desires. An interest in nonfiction begins early in one's reading life, perhaps as early as kindergarten, according to research. Still, nonfiction, especially informational literature, is lacking in classroom reading materials. On her own, Trish has read biographies not only of her favorite media stars but of women in leadership roles, collective biographies of Hispanics in American history, and several how-to books in the area of art and drawing, one of her passions. What we need to be aware of as teachers is that there is a wide array of reading materials outside of fiction. We need to add those genres to the classroom library so that students like Trish can find something of interest to them when they are browsing for that next book.

For some readers, perhaps for all of us from time to time, there is a need for reading material other than pure fiction. I know that many of you read professional books and journals and articles. Some of you perhaps select informational literature about hobbies and interests you have. I am a sucker for a biography or autobiography about someone I admire. When Chris Crutcher's autobiography, *King of the Mild Frontier,* fell into my hands at a conference, I holed up in my room for an entire afternoon and read it from cover to cover. I do the same with any new book from Janet Allen or Linda Rief or Kylene Beers. Sometimes, I only want to read nonfiction.

I did not come to nonfiction early, though. As a classically trained teacher of English, I read more than my fair share of fiction. When it came to teaching, I could tackle poetry, drama, or the novel with no fear. However, give me a piece of nonfiction, and I was at a loss. It was not until I read Carter and Abrahamson's *Nonfiction for Young Adults: From Delight to Wisdom* (1990) that I understood the power of nonfiction in the development of lifetime readers.

This chapter, then, presents genres that move from fiction to informational literature. As we journey from historical fiction to biography to informational books, the landscape begins to change a bit. It may be unfamiliar territory from some of you and for some of your readers. It is, though, fertile ground in which to nurture and grow lifetime readers.

Historical Fiction

The task of writers of historical novels is, in one sense, more difficult than that of writers of fiction set in contemporary milieus. The historical novelist has to re-create a time and place, and transport readers there. This is no mean feat in a society where adolescents are usually focused on the here and now and on themselves. How can an author fashion a historical novel that engages contemporary readers? Why should we even care whether kids read historical fiction?

Before answering those questions, though, it is important to point out that because historical fiction is any story set in the past, there may be some disagreement about which books can be designated historical. For example, I overheard two seventh-grade students talking about *The Watsons Go to Birmingham—1963* as a good book set in the "olden days." Well, when I read this book, I never once thought it was set in the olden days. I was ten years old when the church bombings in Alabama and elsewhere were happening. This was not a story set in the past for me. It was real and immediate. However, this bit of eavesdropping did make me think about how our students define the past. For younger readers, the past might be something that happened earlier this same day. As we grow older, our definition of the past changes. I might, for instance, label a book set in the Depression as historical; my parents would not. Even an event like the 2003 war in Iraq may one day be considered history by the kids in our classes. So remember that the past is something our students may not have a complete handle on now. Historical fiction can help them see that there is much more to the past than what is in their memories.

Historical fiction gives kids a sense of how we are all connected through time, that even though times change, the needs we have as people remain unchanged. The opening of *Sarah, Plain and Tall* by Patricia MacLachlan is a perfect example of this connection across time. As the novel opens, Anna and Caleb are talking about their mother. Caleb asks about Mama because he was an infant when she died. What Caleb and, secretly, Anna want more than anything else is for someone to come and sing to them like Mama did. When their father sends off for a mail-order bride, Sarah arrives. Though she is plain and tall she is also exactly what this family needs. Students who read this novel can see that the needs of family and love are constant over time. We may not have mail-order brides or live on farms, but we all share the need for someone to love us; we share the needs of Caleb and Anna and Jacob and Sarah.

Historical fiction offers readers a chance to experience vicariously what it was like to live in the past (Norton 2003, p. 412). When I read *The Moves Make the Man* by Bruce Brooks, I can witness what it was like to be the only African-American in a school of white students. I can experience, along with Jerome, the incredible racism and prejudice on display. I can see the unfair treatment given to Jerome by peers and by adults. In a sense, this provides a better lesson than any textbook. There is no objectivity here: emotions are raw and at the surface. As I travel along with the Watson family in Christopher Paul Curtis's *The Watsons Go to Birmingham—1963*, I can see how attitudes change as the family travels from Michigan to Alabama. I feel I have lived a little of this era.

Historical fiction gives a human face to history. Gary Paulsen's *Nightjohn* is a novel set during slavery in the South. It tells the story of a young girl named Sarny and how she is taught to read by another slave. Because Paulsen brings Sarny to life as a character, as a reader I grow to care about her and her fate. I cringe when John is beaten. I cry as Sarny experiences tragedy in her life. I rage against the injustice of the master. We recently discussed this book in my YA literature class. Student after student remarked to me that they really had never thought much about the mistreatment of the slaves. Sure, they had read about it in textbooks over the years, but somehow this novel made them *feel* and not just think about the time period and the treatment of slaves. One student commented that she was exhausted after reading the book because she had been with Sarny and had experienced all the pain and sorrow. She was drained emotionally and physically by the end of the novel. Ellie Rosen in Lois Lowry's *Number the Stars* puts a face on the Holocaust. Sarny puts a face on slavery. Jerome and the Watson family put a face on racism. That is one of the important benefits of reading historical fiction.

Historical fiction allows readers to see and judge the mistakes of the past. Following the bombing of Pearl Harbor during World War II, people of Japanese ancestry were rounded up. Property was seized; families were separated. Many were sent to relocation centers or internment camps. Fifty years later, the U.S. government offered compensation for this mistake. Contemporary readers can learn about these and other events through books. *Under the Blood Red Sun* by Graham Salisbury offers readers some insight into the suspicion faced by those of Japanese ancestry following the bombing of Pearl Harbor. *Bat 6* by Virginia Euwer Wolff examines the same sort of situation but from a different perspective. *Under the Blood Red Sun* concerns a family who had come from Japan to settle in Hawaii. Grandfather's habit of waving a Japanese flag is seen as eccentric until the bombings. Suddenly, the family is viewed as perhaps anti-American. Tomi, born in Hawaii, is still viewed with suspicion because his family is from Japan and just might have some involvement in the horrific events of Pearl Harbor. Is the flag-waving some sort of signal? Tomi has to negotiate his way with friends who are suddenly questioning the loyalty of their pal. In *Bat 6*, a story told from the viewpoints of the girls on two competing teams in a softball tournament, racism comes into play. Shazam, whose father was killed in the war, deliberately runs into Aki, a Japanese player who has spent some time in an internment camp. The story is told in flashbacks and reveals, a piece at a time, the attitudes of all the girls playing in this game.

So, how do we evaluate these stories? One hallmark of compelling historical fiction is that the story has to be interesting. If the story does not engage, whether through interesting characters, involved plots, or intriguing mysteries, then the reader is perhaps better off reading about the time and place in a history textbook. Therefore, while setting is essential to a work of historical fiction, setting cannot take precedence over action. An author has to involve the reader immediately. Curtis's *The Watsons Go to Birmingham—1963* is a perfect example of how an author lets readers know the time and place of the story without interfering with the actual story. In

Chapter 1, we meet the weird Watson family (well, weird from ten-year-old Kenny Watson's perspective). Byron gets into trouble at school, and the family decides it is time for Byron to become acquainted with his grandmother, who lives in Birmingham. Since it is the dead of winter and the Watsons live in Michigan, a trip south is more than a little appealing. Before the family can depart, however, the car windows must be scraped. In a scene that still brings a smile to my face, Byron manages to get adhered to the sideview mirror of the car. How he is released from this frosty prison is a fabulous read-aloud. It is also, though, a prime example of how the story must engage the reader before adding details about the time and place.

Sarah, Plain and Tall by Patricia MacLachlan, a Newbery award–winning piece of historical fiction, opens with a conversation between two children, Caleb and Anna. As the conversation progresses, small details allow the reader to see a different time and place. What is essential to this opening scene, however, is the focus on the family and their thoughts and feelings. Contemporary readers may identify either with Anna, who is losing patience with her pesky younger brother, or with Caleb, who does not remember his mother, who died shortly after giving birth to him. Both children long for someone to come and fill the empty space left vacant by their mother's death.

Of course, no matter how engaging the story, the facts of the historical period have to be accurate and authentic. That means the language, the manner of dress, the architecture, and the entire social milieu have to conform to the time period in which the story is set. Not being a student of history myself, I have had to find resources that offer that historical evaluation for me. Each year, a list of Notable Social Studies Books for Young People is published through a cooperative venture of the Children's Book Council and the National Council for the Social Studies (see Appendix X). The annotated list addresses the ten key concepts of social studies education and provides titles for a wide range of readers and historical periods. Ann Turner's *Abe Lincoln Remembers* offers a fictional look at the life of a great leader of the past. Sonia Levitin's *Clem's Chances* examines life during the Gold Rush, and *In the Shadow of the Alamo* by Sherry Garland looks at what it was like at this pivotal moment in Texas history. *Of Sound Mind* and *Spellbound* are two novels that examine contemporary issues. Jean Ferris's novel *Of Sound Mind* looks at the world through the eyes of a young man who is the only hearing member of his family. He sometimes resents having to be the one who serves as the chief communicator for his family. *Spellbound* by Janet McDonald deals with the life of a teen who has dropped out of school to care for her infant. While not historical fiction, these can be used quite easily in a history class examining contemporary issues and current events. This list would make an excellent resource for anyone seeking to use literature about different historical periods and issues.

One final criterion for effective historical fiction is that it reflect the value and spirit of the time period in which the story is set. This criterion is, in part, why some pieces of historical fiction come under attack by would-be censors. Take, for example, a book set in Colonial America that deals with the place of women in society. Elizabeth George Speare's *The Witch of Blackbird Pond* springs immediately to mind. Here is a young heroine who is uncomfortable with the rules of the society in which she finds herself after moving from her home in the Caribbean to Connecticut. Kit may have some rather contemporary ideas about being allowed more freedom; however, she is aware of the strictures of the society and how society deals with strong-minded women (in this case, branding them as witches and ostracizing them from the community). This view of women as property or subservient in society may be hard to swallow for kids growing up in today's culture.

Likewise, the treatment of people of color in the past is one that is sometimes tough to view through contemporary eyes. *The Adventures of Huckleberry Finn* is routinely challenged because it uses what we consider today to be a racial epithet. *The Moves Make the Man* by Bruce Brooks contains a scene in which Jerome comes face-to-face with Jim Crow laws and their impact. Donald Crews's picture book *Bigmama's* includes an illustration of a "Colored Only" train car. To change the values of those times to suit modern values negates the power of historical fiction, the importance of examining the past. Rather, it is essential for all of us to be sensitive to the potential problems that using pieces of historical fiction might cause in the classroom. (For more information about censorship, see Appendix Y.) We can use these potentially volatile topics as a jumping-off point for writing and for class discussion that crosses over into the social studies classroom as well.

Biographies and Autobiographies

Reading about the lives of the famous, the infamous, and ordinary people provides more than a satisfying reading experience. Reading about other people can broaden students' acquaintance with other cultures, races, and ethnicities. It can supplement the textbooks that still give rather short shrift to the contributions of underrepresented populations. With the recent boom in reality television programming, it is apparent that as a society we want to know more about people. We are, in essence, snoops, eager to see into others' lives. As Mary Long suggested at a recent ALAN workshop, "Reality TV has nothing on reality reading."

When the time has come to discuss biographies in my college classroom, I generally begin by asking students to brainstorm with me a list of contributions made to science and history and math by women, by African-Americans, and by Hispanics. While the students are able to list some notable names, there is still a relative paucity of knowledge about the lives of people other than Washington, Lincoln, Jefferson, and a handful of others who dominate the pages of YA biographies. It is then I introduce them to some powerful biographies and autobiographies for YA readers (see Appendix N). Two, in particular, present perfect examples for the wide range of subjects for biographies and autobiographies for adolescents. *Warriors Don't Cry* by Melba Pattillo Beals and *King of the Mild Frontier* by Chris Crutcher embody many of the criteria for effective and interesting books in this genre.

Good biography and autobiography should first and foremost use many of the techniques of fiction to draw the reader into the life story of the subject (Norton 2003, p. 533). It should, then, tell a good story. Of course, along the way, it should provide accurate information. To do this, the best biographies and autobiographies use primary sources. In the case of *Warriors Don't Cry* and *King of the Mild Frontier,* both autobiographies, the primary source material is the life of the author. *Warriors Don't Cry* tells of Beals's courageous action in being one of the first students to integrate Central High School in Little Rock, Arkansas. Subjected to innumerable torments and attacks, Beals and her fellow African-American students were told never to show any sort of reaction to the hate thrust upon them daily. In dispassionate yet animated voice, Beals tells of her day-to-day experiences and how she tapped into the immense strength of her family in order to survive the ordeal of being one of the Little Rock Nine. What amazes readers of all ages is that Beals can be so forgiving of those who wished her great harm, who called her unspeakable names, who made each day of her high school career nightmarish. She describes the time spent at Central High as in part responsible for making her into the woman she is today. This spirit of courage comes through clearly in Beals's compelling autobiography. Other related biographies and autobiographies that might be used in connection with her book include *Freedom's Children* by Ellen Levine, *Malcolm X: By Any Means Necessary* by Walter Dean Myers, and *I Know Why the Caged Bird Sings* by Maya Angelou.

King of the Mild Frontier is far removed from Beals's autobiography. Here is part of the story of the childhood and adolescence of one of YA literature's finest authors, Chris Crutcher. Crutcher relates, in his usual mixture of humor and pathos, some of the classic moments of his youth. Some chapters will have students holding their sides and trying to contain laughter. Other chapters tackle more serious subjects. What shines above all, and what makes this an excellent example of good autobiography, is that Crutcher pulls no punches. This is not a glitzy, breezy work. Readers will see Crutcher at his best and worst, witness the highs and lows of his adolescence. In short, we get to see Crutcher, warts and all. Good biographies and autobiographies for YA readers need to do just that: present the whole picture of an individual. This is not the time for self-glorification or for an author to sing the praises of a subject without also mentioning the not-so-nice aspects most of us demonstrate in our lifetimes. Biographies and autobiographies do not shy away from the truth even when the truth is less than flattering.

Make Way for Sam Houston by Jean Fritz illustrates just how to tell the whole truth about a historical figure. As a longtime member of the faculty of Sam Houston State University, I was curious to know more about the person whose name is splashed across campus. What I discovered was the man behind the myth. Here was a legendary figure in Texas and American history made real by meticulous research and detailed writing. Sam's youth and adult life were rich with the kind of tiny details kids love. Sam was a daydreamer; he was a bit of a chauvinist; he had small feet for someone of his stature. Each semester, when my students read this remarkable biography, Sam Houston becomes more than a statue out on the interstate that runs by campus. He becomes a living, breathing person. Fritz brings her ability to create interesting biographies to other legends of history, including James Madison and Teddy Roosevelt. Imagine conducting an interdisciplinary unit with your social studies teacher in which students study different historical periods partly through their reading of biographies and autobiographies. Think of all the inferential thinking, of how students must use the details from their books to hypothesize how life was during that period in history. Such an activity might just be the textbook to life for these students. Of course, the same can be conducted with science or any other content area as well as electives such as music, art, and physical education. Helping students make connections is one way to ensure reading as a lifelong habit.

Pairing works from this genre could also make for an interesting classroom experience. *Bad Boy: A Memoir* by Walter Dean Myers, for example, shows what life was like in Harlem in the 1950s as Myers was growing up. *Carver: A Life in Poems* by Marilyn Nelson tells of the life of this amazing scientist through wonderful narrative poems. These two life stories, set decades apart, both provide insight into the minds of gifted African-American men. Pairing the two books can demonstrate the power of education, especially being able to read and write, in the lives of men of great accomplishment. Of course, the fact that one book is written in verse as a biography and one written in narrative prose as an autobiography will also provide an opportunity for students to write compare/contrast pieces. Another interesting pairing could be made with *John and Abigail Adams: An American Love Story* by Judith St. George and *Louis XVI, Marie Antoinette and the French Revolution* by Nancy Plain, both on the 2002 list of Notable Social Studies Books for Young People. This pairing of books examines the role of relationships in the lives of historical figures. The young women in class might find this of particular interest because it ties into the interest many of them have in romance literature. What better way to tap into that love of romance than to look at how a relationship really works? Biographies and autobiographies can make history come alive for contemporary readers who are much more centered in the *now.*

Informational Literature

At a conference of the National Council of Teachers of English (NCTE) several years ago, Dr. Robert Small focused a session entirely on nonfiction. Nonfiction, he declared, was the only genre defined by what it was not. It is not fiction. Then, he asked, exactly what is it? This is a question I have pondered over and over as I prepare lists of good books to suggest to students and teachers. If something is not fiction, how can we define it? How can we evaluate it? How should we approach using it in the classroom? Let's begin by discussing some of the inherent problems suggested by these questions.

What is nonfiction? The answer depends on whom you ask. Ask a librarian, and you will get a Dewey decimal answer: nonfiction is all those areas of Dewey classification outside of fiction (novels). Therefore, from a Dewey perspective, nonfiction includes poetry, drama, and folklore. However, if you ask someone in the English profession, nonfiction tends to be defined as expository rather than narrative text. For the purposes of the discussion here, I define nonfiction as comprising those books that provide information on various topics of interest to YA readers—thus, informational literature.

How do we evaluate nonfiction? Because this is a genre with a wide range of possible topics, it is sometimes tough to come up with only a handful of criteria to use when selecting the best in nonfiction. Since nonfiction covers topics about which we may not have much knowledge, we must rely on other sources to evaluate book for us. The typical sources, such as review journals, to which we might turn for insight do not always pay as much attention to nonfiction as they do fiction. Therefore, it becomes even more important to utilize a set of criteria by which we can judge informational literature.

Qualifications of the Author

One of the first questions I ask when I pick up a piece of informational literature is, What makes this author qualified to write this particular book? (Carter and Abrahamson 1990). I want to know if I can trust the author to bring me accurate information on this topic. How do we determine the qualifications of the author? I begin by reading the blurb on the inside back cover of the book. Generally, it is there that one finds information about the author. We can also look online to see if the author maintains a Web site so that we can glean his or her qualifications for writing about this subject. Sometimes, though, that information does not help in assessing the qualifications of the author. There are more than a few authors in this genre who write about topics as far-ranging as chimney sweeps, the history of the chair, and the life of Adolf Hitler (James Cross Giblin) or potatoes, gold, Langston Hughes, and the civil rights movement (Milton Meltzer), or perhaps blizzards, traveling across America as an emigrant, and the Great Chicago Fire (Jim Murphy). What next? Another good place to look is in any acknowledgments section the book might feature. Sometimes acknowledgments may be located in a separate part of the front matter of the book. Occasionally the acknowledgments are on the copyright page. An appendix might contain that information as well. If I cannot see the personal qualifications of the author, I at the very least want to know with whom he or she consulted during the writing of the book.

Accurate and Current Information

It is important, of course, that the information contained in an informational book be accurate (Norton 2003, p. 549). However as an English major, there are many subjects about which I know little or nothing. How, then, am I to ascertain the accuracy of the information? One resource is to turn to professional reviews. Review journals such as *School Library Journal, Booklist,* and *Horn Book* ensure that those who review books in the area of the arts and sciences have some expertise to comment upon the accuracy of the information. There are, though, far fewer reviews of nonfiction than

Selected Orbis Pictus Award Winners and Honor Books

The Great Fire by Jim Murphy

Safari Beneath the Sea: The Wonder World of the North Pacific Coast by Diane Swanson

Kids at Work: Lewis Hine and the Crusade Against Child Labor by Russell Freedman

Christmas in the Big House, Christmas in the Quarters by Patricia McKissack and Frederick McKissack

Across America on an Emigrant Train by Jim Murphy

Making Sense: Animal Perception and Communication by Bruce Brooks

Children of the Dust Bowl: The True Story of the School at Weedpatch Camp by Jerry Stanley

Flight: The Journey of Charles Lindbergh by Robert Burleigh

Now Is Your Time! The African-America Struggle for Freedom by Walter Dean Myers

Prairie Vision: The Life and Times of Solomon Butcher by Pam Conrad

Franklin Delano Roosevelt by Russell Freedman

The Great Little Madison by Jean Fritz

The Life and Death of Crazy Horse by Russell Freedman

Charles A. Lindbergh: A Human Hero by James Cross Giblin

Shipwreck at the Bottom of the World: The Extraordinary True Story of Shackleton and the Endurance by Jennifer Armstrong

No Pretty Pictures: A Child of War by Anita Lobel

Hurry Freedom: African Americans in Gold Rush California by Jerry Stanley

The Amazing Life of Benjamin Franklin by James Cross Giblin

America's Champion Swimmer: Gertrude Ederle by David A. Adler

Michelangelo by Diane Stanley

Kennedy Assassinated! The World Mourns: A Reporter's Story by Wilborn Hampton

of fiction materials in these journals, which means that some books do not get reviewed.

Another possible source to determine accuracy is to locate books on awards lists (see Appendix X). Prior to the last decade or so, very few informational books won the major awards. Now there are some awards specific to the genre. In 1990 the National Council of Teachers of English put into place the Orbis Pictus Award. This award is given annually to an outstanding informational book for children. Other books may be named as honor medalists. Past winners include *Black Potatoes* by Susan Campbell Bartoletti, *Leonardo Da Vinci* by Diane Stanley, and *When Marian Sang* by Pam Munoz Ryan.

The Association for Library Services to Children (ALSC) of the American Library Association (ALA) in 2001 created the Robert Sibert award for distinguished contributions to nonfiction for children. These works are not only accurate but interesting to read. In 2003 award winners dealt with the lives of such diverse people as Hitler, the artist Jackson Pollack, the singer Marian

Anderson, and the YA novelist Jack Gantos. Additionally, an informational book about the stock market crash of 1929 was honored. Award-winning books tend to be those we can trust.

We can also look to those lists mentioned earlier that are developed by teachers in various content areas and available through the Children's Book Council.

I would like to suggest a further strategy for assessing accuracy, one that involves students in a wide range of reading and research skills. It is something I used in my classroom to teach library/research skills in lieu of the more traditional (and greatly despised) research paper. First, gather multiple children's books on a particular topic of interest to students. I have several books about sharks, for example. I break students into small groups (two to four work best for this assignment), and give each group two to three books on one topic. (An alternative that includes yet another skill of using an online catalog or OPAC is to have students locate books on their own.) Create a three-column chart and distribute it to students. Then, follow this procedure:

1. Students read each book.
2. In the first column, they note all the facts that all the books agree upon.
3. In the second column, they note the facts about which there is disagreement from book to book.
4. In the third column, they note another outside resource (Web-based or reference) that they have consulted about the facts where there was disagreement, and what answer they received.
5. Groups compile a written report identifying the most accurate book based upon this process.
6. One additional assignment might be to write to the publisher of any books that they found to contain errors.

Let's examine the skills and strategies students use in the preceding activity. Comprehension skills are certainly necessary to read the books assigned to the groups. Differentiating between fact and opinion is also utilized in this activity. Various research skills, such as identifying specific resources for locating information to verify the integrity and accuracy of an online site, are also at play. Finally, writing skills are brought to bear at the end of the assignment. More important, we have transferred the burden of acquiring information to the learner, made the assignment more about seeking information than regurgitating it. This activity has remained a favorite of my students over the years.

Finally, the most up-to-date information is essential in some informational books (Carter and Abrahamson 1990). Pull a book on computers from twenty-five years ago, ten years ago, even five years ago, and the importance of having current information is readily comprehensible. Since information currently doubles every five years, many books become outdated almost as soon as they are published. Certainly, we want to offer students books on space exploration, environmental issues, and health-related topics that contain all the latest scientific facts and figures. How, then, do we check for currency of subject? The most logical place to look is on the copyright page of the book. A book with a 1990 copyright date that tackles the subject of global warming will not be as current as one with a 2002 copyright date.

A caveat here, though. Go beyond the copyright page and examine the bibliographic citations for the book. A book with a 2003 copyright but whose references do not go past 1999 is, in effect, a 1999 book in terms of the currency of its information. Remember, also, that despite some dating, most trade books contain information far more current than our textbooks. Texas adopts texts on a ten-year cycle, which means it is possible for my students to be using a science text from 1993. Imagine how much information is missing from that book—about Mars, the space shuttle, and disease-resistant forms of tuberculosis, for instance. Social studies books may show George Bush the elder as President if their copyright dates are older. Supplementing the curricular texts with more recent informational books can bring material up to the minute for our classes.

No Stereotypes

It is of prime importance that informational books avoid stereotypes. This is especially important when it comes to the photos and illustrations used in the book. One of the reasons I use Gail Gibbons's book *New Road!* in my class is that it shows how roads are constructed. Highway construction is a fact of life for my students, who commute to campus daily. We chuckle that a picture book makes the task seem so simple that construction should be completed in half the time it truly does take. However, I use this book for an even more critical reason: it shows men and women of all races working on all phases of planning and construction of roadways. Stereotypes are avoided. As a matter of fact, the illustrations serve to reverse some of the stereotypes my students might already have. Sometimes it is fun to bring into class a group of books from past decades and have students identify stereotypes in the illustrations and in the text. Learning about the role of gender will come in handy later as we examine the social milieu of a piece of literature.

Balanced Treatment of the Subject

Finally, informational books need to present information on the entire range of a topic. Notice that in the discussion about biographies and auto-biographies, I noted the need to tell everything about a subject, not just what would be considered flattering. The same is true here. Books about reproduction and sexuality, therefore, have to be comprehensive. Unfortunately, that frequently makes these books the target of censors.

In the past year, two books about sexuality and reproduction were pulled from the shelves of the local public library. *It's Perfectly Normal* and *It's So Amazing*, both by Robie Harris, were challenged as inappropriate for the YA and children's collection. A citizen panel, fortunately, recommended that they be returned to the shelves. (See Appendix Y for more information on censorship.)

It is not only books about sexuality that come under scrutiny for includ-ing all the relevant information. Books critical of U.S. policies and leaders may cause consternation from time to time; books about other controver-sial issues (death penalty, birth control, alternative lifestyles, evolution, UFOs, tattooing, cloning, terrorism and security issues, medical ethics, piercings, skinheads) can also raise some eyebrows. But when students need to find information, we need to be certain they are presented with multiple viewpoints. Libraries possess materials from those different points of view. They may contain materials that present biased information. They must be as eclectic as possible, especially in terms of the informational material made available to their patrons.

Our classroom libraries should mirror that diversity of information as much as possible. The Gale Group (www.galegroup.com/) offers online, print, and video resources for presenting all points of view with its Opposing Viewpoints Resource Center, Opposing Viewpoints Series, and Opposing Viewpoints Video Series, which present experts' opinions, pro and con, on controversial contemporary issues such as abortion, the aging population, biological warfare, Custer's Last Stand, the death penalty, endangered oceans, gun control, hate groups, immigration, and the para-normal. Teacher guides for discussion are provided.

Other Gale Group series are Teen Decisions and At Issue. Teen Decisions offers books on areas that affect individual teens' lives, such as dieting, per-formance-enhancing drugs, gangs, body image, and alcohol. The At Issue series provides full articles with source notes by experts considering current issues like abortion rights.

Finally . . .

Studies have indicated that a love of nonfiction begins as early as elementary school. I think in the past we, as teachers, have not encouraged this interest as much as we might because we have focused on fiction trade books. I know that during all my time at the university, I had few classes in using informational books with students, and most of those were limited to content areas. So, we need to push ourselves, I think, to read more in this genre (see Appendix N).

I would have to say that I'm both an avid reader and an eclectic reader. I can read all day, but it doesn't really matter what I read, as long as the book offers me a chance to be whisked away to an interesting place. This week I might find myself immersed in Tolkien's *The Two Towers,* next week I might spend my bedtime hours thumbing through the pages of a Star Trek novel, a month from now I might decide to return to my earlier childhood years and revisit my favorite collection of fairy tales or a Judy Blume book. To me reading is as natural and as necessary as eating a plate of food. It has always been great nourishment for my mind *and* my soul. During my teen years I mostly read famous literature and poetry written for African-American adults. I buried myself in books by James Baldwin, Richard Wright, Claude Brown, Zora Neale Hurston, Nella Larsen, Gwendolyn Brooks, and many other great writers, desperately trying to find out about my culture and how I fit into the world. Out of all the books I read I enjoyed Wright's *Black Boy* and Brown's *Manchild in the Promised Land* the best, because they were primarily told from a young perspective that I could relate to.

Reading: Natural and Essential by Lori Aurelia Williams

As for my writing, I've always said that I have no idea how I started writing for young people. I just became a YA writer like I became a person who loves watching *Buffy the Vampire Slayer* and *Masterpiece Theatre,* enjoys hanging out at the local computer hardware store, adores glitter fingernail polish, and owns a collection of *Mad* magazines dating back to the 1970s. Like most writers I am what I am, a combination of all the people and things that have affected my life, and what seems to have affected me more than anything is how young people are viewed and treated in our society. I became interested in this when I was still a teen myself. Growing up in the 'hood, in an abusive household, I saw and met several children who were going through what I was going through, or something much more difficult. Like me, they suffered in silence, afraid to tell the things the adults around them didn't want them to say aloud.

Today when I write it is with those kids in mind. I write mostly edgy stories that deal with poverty, physical and mental abuse, drug and alcohol problems, teen pregnancies, and even death. My kids are good children, but they are also children that have been hardened by the environments they are growing up in, and the lives they are forced to lead. My girls' biggest fears don't center around whether or not they will be asked to the homecoming dance, and my boys' largest concerns aren't whether or not they can make the varsity wrestling team. My kids have deeper problems, problems that sometimes make people uncomfortable—and it's that uncomfortable feeling that I'm trying to achieve. I want that uneasiness to help people remember characters like twelve-year-old sexually abused Kambia and thirteen-year-old alcoholic Lemm. Hopefully recalling their tales will help people spot real-life Kambias and Lemms when they see them in the kids next door, the kids in their classrooms, and the kids that their children hang out with. Perhaps if this happens there won't be so many mistreated and frightened children in the world, and the only stories that young people will hide deep inside them will be the normal childhood memories of play and friendship that they will eventually pass on to their own children.

From the minute I figured out that C-A-T spelled cat, I was hooked. Even before that, when my big sister used to read Dr. Seuss books to me. I loved the sound of the words. I loved looking at the pictures. And I loved the feeling of closeness with her that I got from sitting in her lap.

When I was growing up, every summer all of my friends used to go off to camp or their beach houses, while I languished at home, feeling terribly deprived. So I turned to books for solace and for escape—from the heat, from loneliness, from boredom. I may not have been as well traveled as my friends, but all I had to do was walk around the corner to the library, and I could take far more exciting journeys than any of them.

Riding the Roller Coaster by Sonya Sones

All those Nancy Drew books I read must have influenced me, because I grew up to be a deeply snoopy person. In my later teen years, the diaries of Anaïs Nin were a big influence on me—they inspired me to continue keeping journals, and to try to write beautifully in them, and honestly. The poetry of Richard Brautigan was another major influence on me. The first time I read it, I sat down and wrote reams of my own poetry because Brautigan had made it look so easy.

I never really made a conscious decision to write for young adults. But when I began writing stories, the stories I felt like telling were always about teenagers. Being a teenager is a little like riding a roller coaster that you can't get off of, no matter how scared you are, or how sick to your stomach. You've got to ride that sucker till it's over. It's scary, but exhilarating. And so stories about teenagers are, too, which is what I like so much about reading them, and about writing them.

PART III

Making the Match

In third grade our class was divided into three reading groups: the Airplanes, the Jets, and the Rockets. I wanted to be a Rocket, but I was a Jet. Each afternoon when Mrs. Baylor called to the Rockets, I watched my smarter classmates pick up their books and form a circle in the back of the class. What was their secret? How did they earn a place in the best group?

Lift Off

by Kimberly

Willis Holt

Then one Monday after my reading group finished our session, Mrs. Baylor said, Kimberly, tomorrow you may read with the Rockets. All day long I felt giddy. Then a dreadful thought occurred to me—how did I become a Rocket? What did I do that day that I hadn't done before? What skill gave me passage into the elite group? Instead of basking in my grand achievement, anxiety about the next day nipped at my heels. I racked my brain trying to remember what method I'd used so that I could do it again the following day.

I practiced reading aloud in front of the mirror. I mastered great speed. Words flew from my tongue and I became impressed with how many sentences I could say without taking a breath. My confidence grew. Pictures formed in my mind of the other Rockets, jealous of my newfound talent. Wait until Mrs. Baylor hears me tomorrow, I thought. She'll wonder what to do with me. She'll wish for a group higher than the Rockets. Maybe she'll create one. And if she does, I'll fly straight there, becoming the first third-grader in the history of Larrymore Elementary School to ever spend only one day in the Rockets.

The next day, I couldn't wait to hear Mrs. Baylor announce, All Rockets, please get in your reading circle. When she did, I squeezed my chair between Brainy Alice and Science Whiz David. They wouldn't want to miss this.

My heart pounded so fast I thought it would eject from my chest. Anticipation built as Mrs. Baylor called on each student to read. When it was finally my turn, I took a deep breath, knowing it would have to last me at least an entire page. I began a little slower than I'd hoped, but by the end of the sentence I returned to my superfast pace. Periods and commas didn't stand a chance. Sentences slid together without one pause. I ended my session with a great big gasp for air.

I glanced across the circle at my teacher. Mrs. Baylor looked stunned. She sat in a daze that I interpreted as being highly impressed. After the Rockets ended and our circle broke, Mrs. Baylor motioned me aside and gave me the news. I was already thinking of names for the new reading group. If she asked, I planned to suggest the Light Years. Since light does indeed travel faster than sound, the name was quite fitting.

Unfortunately Mrs. Baylor had another plan in mind and it didn't include the creation of a superior reading group. However, part of my prediction was correct. In one day I had orbited my way back to the planet of the Jets.

CHAPTER 8

Reading Aloud: The Power of the Spoken Word

Snapshot of a Reader: Teri Lesesne, 50

My earliest memory of reading is still associated with the smell of Old Spice aftershave and the touch of cold metal. I could not have been very old, because the book we would share was Pat the Bunny. *Pop Pop, my maternal grandfather, would hold out his arms; someone would help me climb into the wheelchair and onto his lap, where he would read my favorite book over and over again to me. Pop Pop's reading aloud to me became part of the routine for our Sunday visits. Over time the titles must have changed. I am certain that I outgrew* Pat the Bunny *eventually. Still, when I pick up my dog-eared and disreputable looking copy of that book today, I am immediately transported back to those Sundays spent being read to by my grandfather. I see that same sort of magical transportation when I work with kids. Generally, when I am in a school these days, I am there to talk to kids about books (see Chapter 9) they might want to read in their spare time. You can imagine the dismayed reaction of students who are all herded into an auditorium or library when they are told what the presentation will entail. I know I have to capture their attention immediately, so I always begin my session with a read-aloud. Appendix A has a list of those never-fail read-alouds that work for me time and again.*

A Second Snapshot: Jennifer Webb, Librarian, Cary Memorial Library, Lexington, Massachusetts

I love hearing people's stories about how reading aloud has formed/helped/changed them. I just had to chime in. My dad read aloud to me from the very beginning, and we didn't stop until high school homework loads got in the way. I'm now twenty-five, and a few nights ago my sweetie and I went over to my parents' for dinner. After dinner, we started reading Pride and Prejudice *out loud for the zillionth time. I read Mr. Collins's proposal scene. We were laughing so hard we could barely continue. Even the Colombian exchange student living with my folks got the jokes, and his English skills wouldn't usually extend to nineteenth-century syntax. I still love to read aloud; we try to do it every night. (Used by permission)*

What was so magical about that time my grandfather and I spent together each week? Why does reading aloud still seem magical to Jennifer? Why do middle school and high school students respond so well when someone reads aloud to them? A few years ago, Kylene Beers and Barbara Samuels asked to me explore those questions for a book they were editing called *Into Focus: Understanding and Creating Middle School Readers* (1998). Their request that I write about a subject near and dear to my heart gave me a chance to explore my thoughts and feelings in some depth. When it came time to write this chapter, I was not certain that I could add anything to what I had already written. However, as I began to revisit reading aloud, I thought the context of the classroom had changed a bit. New questions, ones I had not considered, began to emerge.

Why is reading aloud so important for and to our students? Why should we read aloud even after our students become independent readers? What are some features of a good read-aloud selection? When is a good time to introduce read-aloud to our students? How should we prepare and present a read-aloud? What role do audiobooks play in this process?

In *Voices of Readers: How We Come to Love Books* (1988), Carlsen and Sherrill present the results of decades of investigation into the development of readers. They discuss those childhood and adolescent experiences that lead to a lifetime of reading. One experience seems to dominate: Students had teachers who read aloud to them in school. If you visit an elementary school, it is not unusual to see teachers reading aloud to classes. However, as students become more and more independent in reading, the amount of reading aloud seems to diminish. Teachers stop reading aloud; parents do as well. Suddenly, an enjoyable activity, one that develops readers, is absent from the lives of some kids who might just need it the most.

Jim Trelease knows the value of reading aloud to kids as well. His *The New Read-Aloud Handbook* (2002), now in its fourth edition, discusses the research behind why reading aloud is a good way to spend instructional time. *Reading Magic* (2001) by Mem Fox, also praises this simple activity: "The fire of literacy is created by the emotional sparks between a child, a book, and the person reading. . . . It's the relationship winding between all three, bringing them together in easy harmony" (p. 10).

And more than a decade ago, *Becoming a Nation of Readers* (1985) proclaimed that the single best activity for bringing kids into a lifetime of reading was reading aloud. It is also one of the least expensive and time-consuming activities we can implement in the classroom. A sustained program of reading aloud can increase test scores (always valuable in these test-conscious times) and motivate kids to want to read more.

The Three P's of Reading Aloud

What skills do we need to be proficient in reading aloud? It is important to remember that reading aloud is a performance of sorts. We should keep in mind what I call the three P's of reading aloud: *preview, practice,* and *personalize.*

Before reading anything aloud to the class, always *preview* the material. Is this read-aloud piece appropriate for our students (see the discussion in earlier chapters about the development of adolescents)? One year I decided to read aloud the opening chapter of *A Day No Pigs Would Die* by Robert Newton Peck. I had not previewed it. In this scene, young Rob comes across one of his farm's cows in labor. The calf is a breech birth, and Rob removes his overalls to tie around the legs of the calf and help in the birthing process. The cow takes off with Rob in tow. He suffers some injuries to his posterior—all in all, a humorous read. However, Rob refers to the cow in question as a bitch. I am certain that you can picture the faces of my eighth-graders as that word escaped my lips. It did not matter that I then instructed the kids about the nature of this word in the context of the story. Had I previewed the chapter, I could have addressed the use of the word in advance and saved myself some embarrassment.

Practicing the piece to be read aloud is also a good idea. I want to maintain eye contact as I read aloud. In order to accomplish this, I read the piece aloud several times beforehand so that I become familiar enough with the material to glance up at the students. Eventually, some of these pieces became memory pieces for me as well. Practice also means that I eliminate stumbling over unfamiliar words, names, and the like. By the way, names can be a tricky thing. Until I listened to the Harry Potter books on tape, I was mispronouncing a few of the odder names of the characters. However, none of my students objected. As a matter of fact, we talked afterward about how each of us had determined how to pronounce names. This led to a discussion of phonics and syllabication, two topics that seldom arise in class but were now beneficial to know.

I *personalize* the reading aloud with my own facial expressions, gestures, pauses, and emphases. I am, admittedly, a frustrated actor; I enjoy hamming it up from time to time, exaggerating accents into full-blown dialects. I try to make the book my own in whatever way I can. The read-aloud is a performance, after all. We need to demonstrate that we are moved by what we are reading. I have been known to cry when I read aloud certain books, for example, *The Velveteen Rabbit* (Margery Williams), *Where the Red Fern Grows* (Wilson Rawls), and *Pink and Say* (Patricia Polacco). I make no effort to hide the emotion because I think kids need to see adults moved by books and reading. Likewise, I giggle and laugh, wince and moan, in books that cause those reactions, too.

How to Begin

I like to begin reading aloud on the first day of each school year. This accomplishes two things right off: it lets kids know that books and reading are important to me, and it sets the stage for the process early. Generally, by the end of the first few weeks of class, kids know that I will begin reading as soon as the bell rings for class. A nice bonus of doing this is that kids tend not to be tardy to class, especially if they are enjoying the selections for read-aloud time.

At the outset, I use short read-alouds. Picture books for older readers, especially those with great humor, are often my first choices for those early weeks (see Appendix H). For example, I may begin with several variants of the Cinderella story, like *Bubba the Cowboy Prince* by Helen Ketteman, a Texas version of the story replete with a fairy godcow and Ms. Lurlene, the apple of Bubba's eye. Bubba loses a cowboy boot after Lurlene's fancy party, and Lurlene goes all over looking for her prince with one boot missing. This allows me to put on my biggest Texas drawl and really whoop it up. For the next several days, I read other variants. Finally, I take a little extra time and read the Grimm Brothers version of the story, in which the stepsisters cut off parts of their feet to fit into the shoes. Kids generally are familiar with the Disney versions of familiar fairy tales and will *adore* the more bloody and gruesome versions from Grimm.

After kids get accustomed to the read-aloud routine, I might elect to read a short novel or a collection of poetry for a change of pace. Or, I could tie those two elements together and read one of the dozens of novels in verse, such as *Out of the Dust* by Karen Hesse or *Who Killed Mr. Chippendale? A Mystery in Poems* by Mel Glenn. I also share poems from my students' childhoods that I suspect they still secretly love, such as Shel Silverstein's "Sick" or Jack Prelutsky's "Homework." Judith Viorst and Shel Silverstein also have poems about Cinderella that would tie into the earlier theme. Making connections among books is something that good readers do, and it is something we can make happen for kids through careful planning of the read-aloud.

Anything, even reading aloud, can become stale, so I always look for ways to vary once kids are aware of the routine. I invite guests to come in and read aloud. My students particularly enjoyed listening to the building principal and other administrative staff. Occasionally, I invite other teachers to come in. A colleague of mine even managed to get some of the local sports figures to come and read aloud as part of their service to the community. Any such guests can impress the kids and provide a welcome change. I also vary read-aloud time by using audiobooks. From time to time, I will play a chapter from a book or sometimes even the entire book for the class.

For instance, if I were forced as part of the curriculum to teach a Dickens novel, I might resort to an audiobook version. I hate to admit it as a former English major and English teacher, but I just do not care for the works of Dickens. I think part of my aversion goes all the way back to fifth grade, when I was forced to read *Great Expectations*. I made it through several chapters and then opted for Cliff Notes. Since then, Dickens and I have not been on the best of terms. I would also use an audiobook version of a story that used dialects or that was set in a foreign country. I do not do many dialects convincingly and would prefer to let professional readers do that job for me. Jim Dale is an outstanding reader of the Harry Potter books. While I can hear a British accent as I read silently, I cannot imitate one. Dale's easy style of reading is a perfect way to enjoy Harry Potter with the kids.

Here is a recent posting from a listserv about audiobooks, by Sarah Denton, a librarian in Berkeley, California (used with permission):

I take audiobooks into sixth-, seventh-, and eighth-grade classrooms. In these classes, about two thirds of the kids are ESL students (wildly varying levels), and the rest have cognitive or behavioral difficulties or some combination of all three special needs.

With audiobooks, these kids are able to experience literature they never would have had access to by reading. The teachers are amazed and pleased at the students' response. The students are thrilled to be finishing books—a first for many of them. And I have to tell you one story: one boy was drawn immediately to Joey Pigza, who like himself has to take medication to calm down. He loved the fact that there were books about characters who got into trouble! Just a few weeks later, he chose The Incredible Journey [Sheila Burnford] to listen to. I was surprised and asked how he liked it. He told me that it was a little slow but that it was a wonderful way to see the whole country. So here's a kid who thought books were for other people, who now understands that they make the entire world available to him. And it wouldn't have happened without the experience of hearing books being read.

This is powerful stuff we do, folks.

Keeping It Fresh

Reading aloud is not just one particular type of reading. Over the years, I have defined several distinctly different ways in which we can read aloud to our students. Sometimes I use a model I call "read and tease," in which I read just a sentence or two or maybe an opening chapter from several books. The idea is to give my students a sense of what is in store for them should they choose to read one of these books. "Read and tease" works well within the confines of booktalking (see Chapter 9). Opening lines and paragraphs from books such as *Whispers from the Dead* by Joan Lowery Nixon, *Ash: A Novel* by Linda Faustino, Robert Cormier's *The Chocolate War,* and Laurie Halse Anderson's *Speak* are all wonderful for this method of reading aloud.

In addition to "Read and tease," I often use read-aloud to introduce a topic, genre, or subject in class. How better to whet the students' interest and bring focus to something new than to include a read-aloud that ties in to the class? So, if I am about to begin a unit on poetry, I begin by reading aloud some of my favorite poems. I read "Lasagna" by X. J. Kennedy, "Factoids" by Kristine O'Connell George, or "Sarah Cynthia Sylvia Stout" by Shel Silverstein. All three are humorous and serve to make students' reaction to poetry more positive. I use a nonfiction book as a read-aloud when

---

Good Books for "Read and Tease"

The Adventures of Super Diaper Baby (Captain Underpants series) by Dav Pilkey (INT/MS)
Alan and the Animal Kingdom by Isabelle Holland (MS)
Angus, Thongs and Full Frontal Snogging by Louise Rennison (MS/HS)
Ash: A Novel by Linda Faustino (HS)
Caleb's Story by Patricia MacLachlan (INT/MS)
The Chocolate War by Robert Cormier (HS)
Cirque Du Freak series by Darren Shan (INT/MS)
Dead Girls Don't Write Letters by Gail Giles (HS)
Fat Camp Commandos by Daniel Pinkwater (INT/MS)
Forged by Fire by Sharon Draper (MS/HS)
Give a Boy a Gun by Todd Strasser (MS/HS)
Jinx by Margaret Wild (HS)
Loch by Paul Zindel (MS)
Locomotion by Jacqueline Woodson (MS)
Monster by Walter Dean Myers (HS)
No More Dead Dogs by Gordon Korman (INT/MS)
The Rag and Bone Shop by Robert Cormier (MS/HS)
Rats by Paul Zindel (MS)
Shattering Glass by Gail Giles (HS)
The Silent Boy by Lois Lowry (MS)
The Sisterhood of the Traveling Pants by Ann Brashares (HS)
Son of the Mob by Gordon Korman (HS)
Speak by Laurie Halse Anderson (HS)
Stand Tall by Joan Bauer (MS)
The Steps by Rachel Cohn (MS)
Stuck in Neutral by Terry Trueman (HS)
Tears of a Tiger by Sharon Draper (HS)
The True Confessions of Charlotte Doyle by Avi (MS/HS)
We All Fall Down by Robert Cormier (HS)
Whale Talk by Chris Crutcher (HS)
Whispers from the Dead by Joan Lowery Nixon (MS)
You Don't Know Me by David Klass (MS/HS)

INT = intermediate grades, 4–6   MS = middle school grades 5–9   HS = high school grades 8–12

---

my students are preparing a new unit in social studies or science. *Phineas Gage* by John Fleischman is a great introduction to the science of the brain. *Chimney Sweeps* by James Giblin gives teachers an interesting way to introduce another time and place. Even math has some good books to read aloud. My all-time favorite for math is *Math Curse* by Jon Scieszka. Reading can also serve as a model for English class, especially when it comes to tight writing. Picture books use few words and yet pack a punch. I might read Eve

Bunting's haunting *The Wall* and talk about the impact of the final five words of the book and how an author can accomplish much with just a handful of exactly the right words.

Of course, I also use read-aloud in more conventional ways. About one third of the way into the school year, I select an entire novel that we will read as a class over a period of weeks. I try to have different books for the different classes (mostly for my benefit because I cannot bear to read the same book aloud five or six times a day). Word spreads from class to class, and sometimes kids from one class will check out books that I am reading to another group. Sometimes a teacher will ask me what happens if a student checks out the book and finishes it before the read-aloud in class is complete. One teacher even forbade kids from doing this. I don't forbid them to read, but if kids are going to read ahead of the class, I ask that they keep what happens a secret. Generally, they do. Those same kids still tend to enjoy the read-aloud. I know I have listened to books on tape after I have already read the book. The duplication does little to diminish either experience. As a matter of fact, sometimes I pick up more of the nuances of plot or character as I listen to a book with which I am already familiar.

Finally, I sometimes read aloud pieces in what I call a "read and think" activity. Occasionally, when I am reading a book, I run across a sentence or paragraph that makes me stop and catch my breath, ask a question, go back and reread. That is how I identify the think pieces from books. Paula Fox's award-winning *One-Eyed Cat* has a scene in which the main character is talking about the difference between lies and truth. He makes an analogy that truth is messy, rather like an untidy attic, whereas lies can be neat and well made. Needless to say, that took my breath away. It made me think of times when, indeed, a lie was tidy and neat and the truth would have been much more messy. Likewise, Brooks's *The Moves Make the Man* deals with similar issues and has many wonderful think pieces, including the last line of the book: "There are no moves you truly make alone." These think pieces lead nicely into journal writing and class discussion, too.

Finally . . .

When I used to see five or six classes a day, I had students keep a chart in their binder listing the books I had read aloud for their class as well as their reactions to each one. I had them devise a rating scale of some kind and make brief comments. In that way, I tried to make sure they were paying some attention. Even now, in my university classes, I ask students to keep a list of the books I read aloud. They rate them using a scale from 1 to 10, with

10 being a book they love. This charting helps them assemble the beginnings of what will become their classroom libraries. I encourage them to use the lists to distribute to family members who want to buy them something for a birthday or holiday.

A word or two about student behavior during read-aloud: I let kids close their eyes and even lean their heads on the desk. I listen best with eyes closed sometimes, too. I also never follow up a read-aloud with any sort of assessment tool, like a quiz. I might ask someone in class to summarize what we read the day before for the sake of a student who was absent from class. But now is *not* the time to make an enjoyable activity miserable by adding a test or a worksheet. Keep the read-aloud a time of intimacy between you and your students. Keep it enjoyable.

The research on read-aloud is definitive. Reading aloud works. It takes little time (you can read aloud for five or ten minutes a day and still have an impact on the kids) and very little investment. The paybacks are terrific.

Wondering What's Around the Bend

by Sharon Creech

I am always rather envious of writers who can recall a long list of titles of books they read when they were young. Although I can remember enjoying reading—the feel of the books in my hands, the feeling of being in the book and in the world of the stories—I remember the title of only one of these books: *The Timbertoes,* by Edna Aldredge and Jessie McKee, with color illustrations by John Gee.

I read it in school, with my class, our first chapter book. It's about a family of wooden people who live in the forest. I have such a vivid memory of that reading experience, of being completely in the world of the book, eager to know what would happen to the family in each new chapter. I also remember the day we finished the book. At the end of the story, the family has built a raft, and they set off down the river on their raft: "Around the turn it went, and out of sight." I stared at the final page a long time, reluctant to leave the world of the book, and also deeply curious about what was going to happen to this wooden family on their trip down the river.

A few years ago, I rediscovered this book and was surprised how many of the images I often use in my own books are also present in *The Timbertoes:* the family, the woods, rafts, and rivers. I don't know whether those images were already in me, and that is why I responded so strongly to the book, or whether it was because of those images that I responded as I did. In any case, I find it astonishing that that story and its central images have stayed with me all these years.

In a quiet tribute to this book, my own book *The Wanderer* closes with the characters building a raft and contemplating setting off down the river. One of the characters asks, "Don't you wonder what's around that bend?" I always wonder what is around that next bend, and maybe that is one reason why I write and why I enjoy reading so much.

CHAPTER 9

Booktalking: Making Personal Introductions Between Books and Readers

Snapshot of a Reader: Wes, 15

> *Wes is an unmotivated reader. Even from my perch in the back of the room, that is obvious to me. I watch as his class files into the library. I know this is something the class does on a regular basis. However, each time I have seen this particular class, I have noticed that Wes generally wanders around the shelves for a while before taking up residence on a sofa near the circulation desk. There he waits for the rest of his classmates to finish checking out books before joining them in a line and returning to his classroom. What is different this day is that his librarian, Ms. Buckman, has called the class to come and sit in one of the library's alcoves. She pulls a cart laden with books into the narrow space. As the librarian picks up a book and begins her talk, Wes settles down, attentive. At the end of her presentation, Wes approaches the cart and removes a book. He heads to the circulation desk, checks the book out, and sits on the sofa reading while his classmates locate their books.*

What I observed was the power of the booktalk. Lois Buckman had been watching Wes and other students for weeks wandering the library without much success in locating a good book to read. Wes and his companions are what I call "nomads of the library." They wander aimlessly along the shelves, hoping, I suspect, that a good book will announce itself and fly off the shelf magically. These are kids who will tell you straight-faced that there are no good books in the library. So, the librarian had decided to give students a personal introduction to some good books.

While one-on-one discussion about possible books to read is wonderful, most of us see hundreds of students during the week. How can we reach those hundreds and let them know about the good books that are stubbornly hiding on the shelves? How can we persuade the nomads of the library to settle down and find a book to read? One way to provide students with information about books is through booktalking. Booktalking provides us the chance to talk about dozens of books in a relatively short period of time. Five minutes at the start of class, ten minutes at the beginning of a library visit: even these brief opportunities can increase the chances of making the match between reader and book.

What Is a Booktalk?

Although the word might suggest that we are simply talking about a book, a booktalk is a bit more involved than that. A booktalk is not a review of the book. It is not simply a plot summary or an alternative to a traditional book report. It is a presentation planned by the teacher or librarian in which students are provided a personal introduction to one book or to several books. Think of a booktalk as an ad for a book, a book you wish to sell to a reader. The goal of the booktalk, then, is to whet the appetite of the audience, make them want to pick up some good books. Booktalking allows readers the chance to hear a little something about some books, to make a more educated decision about what to read. Few of us would purchase a car without a test drive and some information about the performance of the vehicle. Think of a booktalk, then, as a test drive for a book.

Components of a Good Booktalk

Know the Audience

Begin planning a booktalk with a specific audience in mind. What is the age range of the audience? Do you have only eighth-graders or will this be a cross-grade presentation? Are there different levels of reading ability within the group? What do you know about their current reading interests? (Don't forget to take into account what you know about the culture of this group outside of school as well.) Are there goals other than motivating them to read a book, some curricular objectives you hope to meet through the books?

Connect the Books

Once you have determined the audience for the booktalk, decide on a theme or agenda for the talk. If you are planning to talk about more than one book, it is essential to pull together books that relate to each other in some way. This helps readers make connections between and among books. Most of us make connections between and among books without giving it much thought. We read a book and think, "Gee, this reminds me of book X or author Y." Good readers make those connections. However, students do not always make those connections naturally. Booktalking along a theme or topic can help make those connections clear to potential readers.

The themes you select can be broad. One of my favorite broad themes, which permits me to include just about any title, I call "What would happen if?" Basically, this theme takes the premise that members of the audience are placed in the shoes of the main character of each book. What would they do if they were Jerry in Robert Cormier's *The Chocolate War* or Izzy in Cynthia Voigt's *Izzy, Willy-Nilly* or Harold in Gary Paulsen's *The Schernoff Discoveries*?

Of course, the themes and topics can be much narrower in focus. In April, I do quite a few themed talks on books of poetry. For a talk like this, I include some oldies but goodies (kids of any age still love hearing Shel Silverstein's and Jack Prelutsky's poems) as well as newer collections. I might plan a booktalk on mysteries or another genre. Sometimes I use what I call "variation on a story," where I include different versions of the same story. For example, there are several YA versions of the classic *Romeo and Juliet*. I might decide to do a quick talk about books such as *If You Come Softly* by Jacqueline Woodson and *Romiette and Julio* by Sharon Draper and perhaps add Bruce Coville's picture book version of the play as well.

Read (or Reread) the Books

One of the cardinal rules of a booktalk is that you must read the books first. I know there may be some who disagree about the necessity of reading the books in advance of the presentation. However, I think it is imperative for two reasons. First, when I present a book in a booktalk, I am endorsing this book. That means I want to be certain that I know and will vouch for its contents. Many years ago, I had a colleague who talked about a book she had not read in its entirety. When a student complained about content he found objectionable, the teacher was startled to discover that, had she read the book fully, she would not have presented it to the class. It was developmentally inappropriate for her students. I also encourage reading the entire book because I think that the more knowledge we have of the content, the better prepared we are to develop the booktalk.

Plan How the Books Will Connect

Generally, when I read a book I plan to booktalk (and that is *any* book these days), I keep a notepad or some Post-it notes nearby. I jot down names of characters, an occasional incident I find interesting, and perhaps a passage or two I might wish to read aloud either as part of the booktalk or in a separate read-aloud session. If I have notes for each book, it is easier for me to see how I might make connections for the audience.

Then I gather the books I plan to include in my presentation. The number of books is dictated by the length of time I have for the booktalk. If it is a short time such as five or ten minutes, I might only talk about two or three books. If I have thirty minutes or more, I can easily handle five or ten books. What is essential at this point is to find the idea or event or character to help me hook one book to another. The *segue* is an important component of the booktalk if I am to make connections for my audience. So, when I have all the books gathered, I arrange them in the order I will talk about them, working to find one common trait for that segue from one book to the next.

Plan the Presentation

Now that I know my audience, have read the books, and know how I will make connections among the books, it is time to prepare the presentation as a whole. I generally like to open and close the booktalk with what I consider to be my two strongest talks. In many cases, that means using the two books I know best or liked the best as I was reading them.

The middle of the booktalk presentation, especially in longer booktalks, is just as crucial as a good opening and closing. The pace has to be brisk so that the attention of the students will not wander. So, more often than not, I open with a lengthy booktalk and then move into a series of briefer, faster-paced booktalks in the middle before closing with a final booktalk of some detail.

I make certain that I know the names of the main characters of the books, although when you are first getting started, you might find it more comfortable to use Post-it notes attached to the back cover of the book with names and other pertinent information you might forget in front of the audience. I rehearse what I want to say for each book. If there is a section I plan to read aloud, I mark it carefully so that I can find it at the appropriate time and place in the presentation. Now is the time to do a run-through and time check. My first practice is generally done in front of a mirror or in front of my cats (they are a picky pair of cats, so I know if I can keep their attention, I can keep the attention of a human audience). I do not worry as much about time as about content at this stage. I can always cut, add, and edit once I am comfortable with what I want to say about the books.

Finally, I am ready to do my presentation in a dress rehearsal format. For this, I like to present to colleagues or my own children. I run through the presentation for this smaller audience and make any necessary adjustments. All the rules of normal presentation apply. You have to be able to project your voice. Speak in an interesting, modulated tone. Develop some characterization, either by using different voices (volume change will do nicely) or facing in different directions for various characters. Speak clearly and distinctly. I always have to remember to s-l-o-w down because I have a tendency to speak too quickly when nervous or excited. Finally, I try to remember to smile; this is supposed to be fun. Of course, the more times you do the presentation, the more familiar and easy it becomes. So, volunteer to go to the library and present to other classes. Travel throughout the building over the course of several weeks and make presentations in the classrooms. The more at ease you are, the better your performance.

A Sample Booktalking Agenda

Audience: Grades 8 and 9
Theme or Topic: How Authors Come Up with Stories

I move from one story to the next by using one of the questions authors have in their arsenal as they are thinking up ideas for their books. Authors note events from the real world around them and ask, "What would happen if . . ." to begin to formulate the story. In the case of *Whispers from the Dead,* Nixon lived in a neighborhood where an awful murder had been committed. She wondered what would happen if a teen who had experienced a near-death episode picked up on the fact that something awful had transpired in the house when she moved in from another state. Presto, there is a premise for the book. On the other hand, Gary Paulsen did not have to ask, "What would happen if . . ." because *Harris and Me* is autobiographical.

Sometimes, an author asks, "What would happen if . . ." and the result is a mystery. Sometimes that same question yields a realistic story. It can also cause an author to ponder something other than realistic, as evidenced by books such as Paul Zindel's *Rats, Among the Hidden* by Margaret Peterson Haddix, and *Others See Us* by William Sleator. Moreover, the question is not a new one. Storytellers and authors have used it for centuries. Even *Cinderella* began with a similar question. Roald Dahl's question was more along the lines of, "What would happen if I decided to tell a funny version of *Cinderella* or another older story?" Priscilla Galloway speculated about taking the darker versions of the stories and changing them to suit her idea. (Note: this is a gloriously broad theme or topic that can be used to tie together all sorts of books.)

Opening Book

Whispers from the Dead by Joan Lowery Nixon. Read aloud the first three or four paragraphs of the opening chapter and then tell a little about Sarah's near-death experience with her friends at a lake near her home. Sarah and her family move to Texas and into a home in which, unbeknownst to them, an unsolved double homicide has taken place. Sarah's near-death experience puts her in touch with the "vibes" of the events that have transpired in the house. She is compelled to find out more information about the murder. In doing so, she draws the attention and anger of the murderer. He begins to plan her death. If she does not solve the crime, she will become another victim in this house.

Closing Book

Harris and Me by Gary Paulsen. Tell the students about the misery Harris has inflicted on his cousin over the course of the summer. Gary must get revenge because of the incidents with the pigs, the skiing of the haystack, and the disruption of Gary's conversation with a pretty girl. His revenge: to get Harris to urinate (I use the word *pee*) on an electric fence with predictably hilarious results.

Other Books

In the Middle of the Night or *Tunes for Bears to Dance to* by Robert Cormier. These are realistic stories that are nicely suspenseful. They tie to *Whispers from the Dead* but do not have the supernatural overtones. I use *In the Middle of the Night* in the fall around Halloween. At other times, I use *Tunes for Bears to Dance to* instead. Other Cormier books will work, such as *The Rag and Bone Shop* or *Tenderness* or *We All Fall Down*. Cormier's works are intense. Again, know the development of your audience, and take care about which titles you include.

Rats by Paul Zindel or *Among the Hidden* by Margaret Peterson Haddix or *Others See Us* by William Sleator. These three books are science fiction. In *Rats* a group of rats escapes from the city dump and begins to terrorize a suburban neighborhood. This is a gruesome, bloody book that will make toes curl. Sometimes I use it to show kids that books can be scary. *Among the Hidden* is futuristic and can make a nice tie in to *The Giver* or *1984* or another classic dystopian novel. *Others See Us* is about a young man who acquires the ability to hear what folks are thinking. He discovers, much to his chagrin, that his grandmother also has this capability when she tells him telepathically that if he squeals on her she will kill him. This book presents a nice surprising twist on the sweet old grandma character.

Revolting Rhymes by Roald Dahl and *Truly Grim Tales* by Priscilla Galloway. Here are two variations on *Cinderella* (although you could just as easily do any other familiar tale). Most students have a mental image of Cinderella formed by Walt Disney. The variations I like to include are Dahl's hilarious poetic version (please preview the poem because it refers to Cinderella as Cinderslut) and the Brothers Grimm version, which has the stepsisters cutting off parts of their feet to fit into the shoes (ties nicely to *Rats*). Then I move on to a different story in the Galloway book, which features Little Red Riding Hood and some mutated wolves.

Dos and Don'ts of Booktalking

Here are some suggestions for making booktalks successful.

Some Dos of Booktalking

- Take notes as you are reading the book. These notes will help you decide the focus of the booktalk. Since books tend to swim together after I have read several in a row, I find notes are a handy way of keeping the stories separate. If you use Post-it notes, you can keep them inside the book and refer to them for a quick refresher before any booktalk.

- Try for a variety of genres in each presentation. Not every member of the audience will share your love of poetry or mystery or science fiction. I always try to have at least three different genres within a longer talk unless the talk is themed around one particular genre.

- Hook one book to the next to the next, and so on. See how the broad theme can help you connect books one to the other for the booktalk. Sometimes the connection can be a similarity in plot or story line. However, connections can also be made by linking characters, setting, tone, and so on.

- Use openings to focus your audience's attention. I generally try for a shocking opening or a humorous one. You have to get their attention quickly if a booktalk is to be effective. More often than not, I begin with a read-aloud. It settles me down as the presenter and tends to get kids involved as well.

- Vary the length and content of the individual booktalks. I once heard someone talk about four or five books and always end with the phrase "and if you want to know what happens next, read the book." By the third book, I had lost interest because I knew where the talk was heading. Sure, use that line occasionally. But if you want to keep the attention of the audience, vary the content of the talk. I also plan to use a few short talks (what Joni Bodart calls flash talks) along with more detailed ones. It keeps the pace fresh for me and for the audience.

Some Don'ts of Booktalking

- Don't talk about a book you have not read from cover to cover. It is imperative that you know the content of the book. When you include any book in a presentation, it is an endorsement. Make certain that the book is appropriate for the audience. You do not want any surprises.
- Don't talk about a book you did not enjoy. How can you possibly convey the pleasure of reading if you did not like a book? With adults, I occasionally refer to a book I just could not get into. I generally find that someone else loves the book. Let another person talk about that book to the group. So, if I am not a real aficionado of fantasy, I will try to locate another teacher who is. We can then take turns presenting books to one another's classes.
- Don't oversell the book. Remember, if you say this is the best book in the world, it has to live up to that for all readers. There are few, if any, one-size-fits-all books, so do not hype. Let the book sell itself.
- Don't tell too much of the book's plot or give away the ending. Why would I want to read a book if I knew the ending? Remember how differently you viewed *The Sixth Sense* once you knew the secret. Don't give away too much. Leave some delicious surprises for the reader.
- Don't use someone else's booktalk or read a written booktalk. It's okay to borrow ideas from other booktalkers. However, the best booktalks are not scripted and memorized. They are individual and idiosyncratic. Stick with what works for you.

Resources for Booktalking

Appendixes B and C list some terrific resources to help you as you add booktalking to your repertoire. Resources to provide more information about booktalking include books, articles, videos, and online pages.

Reading when we're young is a very different experience from adult encounters with books. When you're a kid, reading is more powerfully immediate, more emotionally engaging, more attention-consuming (hence the phrase "lost in a book") and more, well, *transporting*. When you're young, books truly do have the power to take you out of yourself and out of the place you call "the real world." I think that's why I loved to read so much when I was a little kid suffering through a miserably unhappy childhood. Frankly, the farther away from the real world that books could take me, the better I liked them. So it's no wonder I loved fantasy—the Oz books, E. Nesbit, *Winnie the Pooh, The Wind in the Willows,* and most of all, the Freddy the Pig books

Books Make

Life Easier

by Michael Cart

by Walter R. Brooks. The Freddy books were a different kind of fantasy, set in a recognizably real world but with an important difference: animals could talk! And Freddy, the chief actor in the animals' dramatic adventures, was more real to me than the people I encountered in the daily business of my life. And in my book-fueled fantasies, I became a character in the Freddy series; I lived with Freddy on the Bean Farm, the one place where I felt that I belonged and where the friendship I felt for Freddy and his friends never failed to fill the empty spot in me that was my loneliness.

It's because of Freddy that I fell head-over-heels in love with books and reading as a boy, and it's because of Freddy that I developed an academic interest in children's literature when I grew up.

That said, I'm a little surprised that young adult literature should have become my personal and professional passion, since I was a teenager in the 1950s long before the "invention" of young adult literature by S. E. Hinton, Robert Lipsyte, and Paul Zindel. There simply were no young adult books to engage my imagination and emotions when I was a teen. But maybe that aching absence is the very reason I'm so hooked on books for teens. Maybe it's because I so vividly remember my adolescent longings for books about kids like me who were experiencing the same trials and traumas, tribulations and terrors, that I was encountering as a teen. I desperately wanted to see my face reflected from the pages of a good book. And I couldn't.

Or maybe it's simply because somewhere inside I'm still a teenager myself. And while the details of my everyday life then have faded, the sharp edges of the emotions I felt are still as honed as razors.

Life is hard. Life is especially hard for teens. Books can make it easier. They can make it easier by showing kids that they are not alone, something I didn't know when I was a kid. They can make it easier by showing kids coping. They can make it easier by showing capable kids the reality of a world that can and does destroy other kids who are less fortunate. And in showing that kind of grim reality they can help the luckier, more privileged kids grow their consciences and a corollary conviction to make a better world when they grow up. And I guess that's the real reason why I'm such a loud-mouthed advocate for young adult literature and why I create books for teens. Books about things that matter: love, sex, tomorrow, personal crisis, alienation, family, and friendship.

Bottom line? I write for and about teens because I believe that books can save lives.

It's as simple as that.

CHAPTER 10

Motivating Readers

Snapshots in a Photo Album

Because I am fortunate enough to visit a host of schools over the course of a year in a variety of capacities, I hear a symphony of voices. Students speak candidly to me about books and reading. After all, I am someone who seems to know about books they might like to read, someone who is not one of their teachers, someone in whom they can confide. Seldom, though, do I have the chance these days to spend more than one day in any particular school. That sometimes makes it difficult for me to assess whether the read-alouds and booktalks have had an impact. I rely on reports from teachers and librarians about kids' continued reactions to my visit. So, how do I assess the success? From time to time, I hear from the students after my visit. Occasionally, a teacher has the class write thank-you notes. I cherish these. I also hear from kids via my e-mail account because I share my e-mail address with them during the presentations.

I also have been working in one particular school as a mentor and booktalker for more than ten years now. The school is a grades 7–12 campus and has permitted me the wonderful opportunity to track kids over the course of several years to see how various strategies and activities motivate them to continue reading. So, here are several voices of readers. Though the voices are distinct, there are some commonalities that, in my opinion, are helpful in directing what we do in our classes.

Sean was one of my eighth-grade students the final year that I taught middle school. He is now a doctoral student at my alma mater. Recently, he was asked to write his reading autobiography and wrote that his eighth-grade experiences were responsible for helping him to become a lifetime reader. Sean credits especially Free Reading Fridays and Directed Individualized Reading.

Wes was a ninth-grader who had been in one of my mentoring classes as a seventh-grader. As a seventh-grader, Wes was more than a reluctant reader. He was one of those challenges we love: he just feigned lack of interest no matter what teachers did. His librarian, Lois Buckman, finally enlisted his aid in selecting some new books for his classmates. She handed him a book she told him she thought might be too mature for his peers and asked Wes's opinion. Before long, Wes was reading all the new books we could feed him. He was even getting into trouble for not doing other assignments because he was acting as a "special consultant" for the mentoring program. He still dropped by the library as a ninth-grader to check out the new books the seventh-graders were reading. He always volunteered his opinion of the newest offerings.

Jack pasted all the e-mails he received from his university mentor on his wall at home to remind himself that now he was a reader. Sara still e-mails her university partner. The two go to a movie from time to time. They still select books to read together and write about them electronically. This semester we have a class of thirty seventh-graders who have already read more than fifty books. All the students who have participated over the years have received passing scores on the state proficiency exam in reading. Not one has dropped out of school prior to graduation (in a state where the dropout rate ranges from 10 to 20 percent).

Several schools in Texas have been participating in the International Reading Association's Children's Choices program. I am one of the coordinators of this project, which means I am able to pass along to schools hundreds of new

books for Pre-K to eighth grade. Kids select books on their own to read. They

complete a simple ballot indicating their opinion of the book. Ballots are tallied

nationwide, and a list of favorite books is published in The Reading Teacher

each fall. The list is also available online at www.reading.org/. Here is what

some of the participants had to say about the project and the books.

"Thanks for letting our school read all those good books. We would be very

happy if you would donate even more books but we're not saying you have to.

Books rule!"

"Thank you for the Children's Choice books. We take really good care of

them. I want to read them all."

Growing Lifetime Readers

In Chapter 2, I indicated the stages in the development of lifetime readers. Now let's examine these stages in terms of what we can do in the classroom to facilitate each stage.

Unconscious Delight

Unconscious delight is that initial stage in the development of a lifetime reader when, as you read, the real world slips away, and you become lost in a book. I suspect many of you can recall reading and being sucked into the world of the novel, losing track of time. Many of us still find that pleasurable sense of losing ourselves in a book today. I can fall so deeply into a book that I do not hear fire trucks pass my street, do not hear the phone ringing right away, or do not see someone trying to get my attention. I have seen students in this same trance. How do we encourage this stage of unconscious delight?

One of the first things we can do as teachers is to provide time and space to read. For the last ten years that I taught middle school I instituted Free Reading Fridays. I practiced curriculum compacting, fitting instruction and practice into the Monday through Thursday routine so that we could take thirty minutes from each class on Friday to read for pleasure. There were just a few rules: no textbooks could be used or homework done during this time; reading material had to be appropriate for the school guidelines (no mature magazines); and students could sprawl anywhere as long as they read quietly. I allowed some group reading but asked those students to find a place away from the rest of the class so as not to disturb others reading silently. I bought beanbag chairs and pillows at garage sales and allowed kids to bring in blankets and pillows from home. After all, no one I know reads sitting at a desk while reading for pleasure. The idea was to make the environment comfortable for reading.

By the end of the first six weeks of school, students were able to sit for extended periods of time and read silently. I made certain, of course, to have plenty of reading materials in the classroom library, including magazines and newspapers, series books, nonfiction, and fiction. There never was an excuse about not having remembered to bring something to read from home. There was always material in the classroom.

In addition to providing time at school for reading, I sent regular letters home to parents asking that they set up a time and place for their children to read at home. I encouraged family reading time as well. Students kept a log of the reading they did at home; parents signed it every day, and I collected the logs weekly. As the mother of a student in band for five years, I had to sign forms similar to this log. I told parents that the only homework I would give routinely was for students to read materials of their own choosing. Periodically, I would send suggestions of books the family could all enjoy together and books that parents might want to buy for special occasions.

Finally, to promote unconscious delight, I made sure to have lots of serial reading material on the shelves. I also read these books so that I could talk to kids about them (see Chapter 9). Many of us read for pleasure serially. Serial reading includes reading series books. When I was in the middle school classroom, I could not keep copies of the Goosebumps series on the shelves despite having multiple copies. The same with Francine Pascal's Sweet Valley High series and Christopher Pike's Chain Letter series. When I was growing up, it was Cherry Ames, Nancy Drew, and the Hardy Boys. Today, kids are reading Series of Unfortunate Events, Animorphs, Magic Treehouse, Dear America, and countless other series books. Right now, on the *New York Times* bestseller list for children, seven Series of Unfortunate Events books are among the top ten. Other slots are filled with entries from the Princess Diaries series by Meg Cabot and the Georgia Nicolson series by Louise Rennison.

Serial reading is not confined to series books, though. I still read serially because there are certain genres in which I read extensively. I am a mystery buff; my sister reads mostly biography. There are those who eschew all but fantasy or science fiction or nonfiction. When we read in one genre almost to the exclusion of others, we are still engaging in serial reading. Likewise, I read serially because I read books by a handful of authors. I love being frightened by Stephen King and Dean Koontz. A new YA book by Joan Bauer or Chris Crutcher gets my immediate attention; a new professional book article or book by Kylene Beers or Janet Allen is always at the top of my "to read" stack. One has only to glance at the bestseller lists to see that is true for many others. On the *New York Times* list for adults are books by John Grisham, James Patterson, and Danielle Steel, all perennial favorites of adult readers. We read serially as adults as well as children.

By the way, for anyone concerned about kids who read series books, Catherine Ross interviewed readers several years ago about their reading habits as children and then as adults. She published her findings in a study titled, "If They Read Nancy Drew, So What? Series Book Readers Talk Back" (1995). Dr. Ross's research indicated that reading series books does not prevent kids from becoming widely read as adult readers. Indeed, after reading the autobiographies of my students for the past twenty-five years, I can testify that series books are generally one of the phases of students' lives as readers.

Reading Autobiographically

Reading about yourself in a book is an important stage in the development of lifetime readers. As a child and teen, I searched for characters like me in books. I grew up in a single-parent family in the 1950s; there were no books about kids like me, unfortunately. There were few books about kids of other cultures until very recently as well. Multicultural literature is a key ingredient for this stage of reading development.

Too often we define multicultural literature as books about different races and ethnicities. I think the time has come to broaden that definition. Begin by examining what is meant by the term *culture*. I share in many cultures. I am female; thus, gender defines part of my culture. My level of education, my chosen profession, my place of residence, my family situation, my religion, my political leanings, my marital status: all define part of "culture" as it applies to me. The same is true for the kids we teach. Culture includes (but is not limited to) religion, socioeconomic status, music preferences, education, race, ethnicity, physical characteristics (height, weight, hair color and texture, acuity of vision and hearing), learning styles and preferences, family structures, and so much more. I find it an interesting exercise to ask students to brainstorm all the different cultures with which they feel kinship.

This means, of course, that our classroom library needs to reflect a great deal of diversity. My first class was 99 percent African-American, but my collection of books could not be limited to that culture. It needed to reflect not only the kids in my class but others with whom they might some day come into contact. We live in a global community, and the books we feed to kids need to reflect that same global nature (see Appendix S).

There is one final strategy I want to mention here as it relates to this phase of reading development. Often when I am faced with reluctant readers, I ask them this question: If an author could write the perfect book just for you, what would it be like? I find that as students describe the book that would perfectly meet their needs and interests, I can scan the lists of books I have read and find a book that comes closest to their description. Often students are amazed. As Peter put it one time after reading *The Outsiders* by S. E. Hinton, "I cannot believe that a woman could understand a man like me so well." Indeed, there are many books already on the shelves that can reflect the lives of our students.

Reading for Vicarious Experiences

While it is essential to see ourselves in books, we also read for the vicarious experience of being in another place and, perhaps, in another time. I grew up in a house full of women. As the oldest of four daughters, I longed to be an only child. One of my dearest friends in childhood was an only child who longed to be part of a larger family. So, we read different books. I loved Nancy Drew: she was an only child; her mother was dead and her father often absent; she had a neat car (a roadster back in those days) and went on exciting adventures at the drop of a hat. I also developed an early affection for fantasy and science fiction. *A Wrinkle in Time* by Madeleine L'Engle offered me the chance to travel through time with Meg and Charles Wallace as they raced to rescue their father. I loved, too, the sad books about horses and dogs. As an inner-city dweller, I had no pets and desperately wanted a house and yard full of them.

I do not think I was much different from today's readers. After all, look at how many millions of copies J. K. Rowling's stories about Harry Potter have sold to date, and you have some idea of the appeal of reading for vicarious experiences. Harry and his adventures with Ron and Hermione at Hogwarts School fulfill that need for escape to a different place and time for contemporary readers. Likewise, the Lemony Snicket series offers a chance to read vicariously. Here are three children who suffer so much loss and pain. Better to read about them than to have to experience that loss and pain ourselves. Add to that the fact that they are deliciously droll, and you have another example of reading for vicarious experience.

What does that mean in terms of the books we offer readers? If we work in an urban school, we need to be sure that some of our books are about suburbs and rural communities (and other countries as well). Stories set in other times and places—historical fiction—are also something that will meet the needs of kids in this stage of reading development. Fantasy and science fiction meet the need, too. Offering kids biographies and autobiographies of a diverse group of people is a good idea. And do not forget nonfiction about places outside of the hometowns of our kids. Reading for vicarious experiences can mean different books for different readers.

Reading for Philosophical Speculation

At some time during our development as readers, we read to "figure out stuff," as Cali told me one day. Kids search out books on topics of interest to them, especially subjects about which they need to come to some sort of judgment. For example, many of my students are reading *The Lovely Bones*, an adult book by Alice Sebold. It is the story of a young girl killed by a serial murderer. She narrates her story from heaven following her death. Sebold's concept of life in heaven is one of the factors readers find compelling about this novel. What sort of life is there after death? Do those whose death is horrific find peace? Can they communicate with those left behind? Cali's mother died of complications from breast cancer last summer. Cali found, in her grief, that *The Lovely Bones* offered some solace. It suggested that her mother was finding peace and happiness in heaven.

More often that not, however, it is nonfiction that meets the needs of readers during this stage of development. *It's Our World, Too!* by Phillip Hoose offers a collection of stories about young people who have made a difference with their activism. In this book we meet kids who interceded on behalf of the environment and got a tuna-canning company to begin using dolphin-safe nets. A group of students pressured McDonald's to stop using styrofoam containers for their burgers. Yet another young woman organized a soup kitchen out of her own house. For kids looking for ways in which they can help make the world a better place, Hoose offers some concrete examples. Kids may choose to read books about birth control, sexuality, capital punishment (a topic of huge interest in my community, which is surrounded by a few prisons, including the infamous death chamber), poverty, world hunger, and a host of other subjects. (See Appendix N for nonfiction books on a wide range of topics.)

Since many of the books kids explore during this phase are nonfiction, we would do well to engage the cooperation of the other content area teachers in our school. I had the great good fortune of working in a team teaching situation for ten years. Four teachers formed the core of the team: English, math, social studies, and science. We shared the same set of students and tried to cross discipline boundaries as often as possible. Students read *The Witch of Blackbird Pond* by Elizabeth George Speare for credit and discussion in both English and history classes. Dan Wilson, my history teammate, talked about the historical aspects of the novel while I handled the literary end of things. Since the kids were learning about the time in which the story was set, they had some knowledge of the social milieu of the time and place. That made entering the story world easier for most readers. It also provided a purpose to read for both classes: they read for the history and for the story. Of course, we tied the issue of religious freedom to current events (and strangely enough that discussion is once again relevant). Reading for philosophical speculation helped students make connections among the disciplines.

Reading for Aesthetic Experiences

Reading for the sheer beauty and enjoyment of reading is the final stage in the development of a lifetime reader. Certainly, this is one that many of us never outgrow. I know I am still knocked out by words and sentences and phrases and paragraphs. One of my students asked me recently why every book she has borrowed from me has pages turned down (one of the perks of owning books is being able to turn down pages and write in them). Those, I told her are my favorite parts of the book. I might flag several poems in the new collections by Naomi Shihab Nye, Mel Glenn, and Paul Janeczko. Perhaps it is one of the short stories in the latest offering by Don Gallo or Michael Cart. Of course, there are the splendid passages in new books from Joan Bauer and John H. Ritter and Kimberly Willis Holt and Gail Giles to consider. When I read some passage or part that makes me pause to reread or exhale sharply or just stop in awe, I mark that point so that I can revisit it.

I received an e-mail just today from a middle school student raving about a passage in Paul Zindel's *Rats*. He talked about it being the "most perfectly scary and nauseating" passage he had ever read, and of course he loved it because it scared him and made him sick at the same time. Generally speaking, aesthetic experiences with books do not entail stomachaches, but it is as valid a response as any. In Chapter 8, I called such passages "think pieces." These are those parts of the book that can generate some interesting discussion or writing. One activity that works with this phase of reading development is the reading log.

Reading logs can take various forms and structures. At the beginning of the school year, I tend to provide more structure and form in order to help kids get comfortable with keeping reading logs. As the year progresses, it is

Directions for Reading Logs

Use a spiral-bound notebook with at least 100 pages. For each book you read for class this ___ week, create an entry in the Reading Log Notebook. [Note: If kids want to do an electronic entry, that is fine. They can create the entries in Word and e-mail them or post them to the class Web site for grading.] I will collect this notebook on _____ for one of your test grades. Follow all directions carefully. A sample entry is included below.

• In the upper right-hand corner of the page, note the date on which you prepared the entry. [This allows me to determine if kids are "keeping up" with the work.]

• In the upper left-hand corner of the page, note the number of pages in the book you read. [In this manner I can keep an easy tally of how many pages kids read in any given time frame. I do not do this for competition; I simply note it so that kids get a sense of accomplishment as they see the pages mount up in total.]

• Note the title and author of the book and the year in which it was published. [You could make a bibliographic citation a part of this assignment and teach those skills.]

• Write a good summary of the book. An adequate summary addresses the following questions. [These questions make it less likely that kids will copy the book flap because they ask for more detailed information.]

    Who are the main characters?

    What is the conflict or problem central to the story?

    How do the characters go about solving this problem?

    How is the situation resolved at the end?

• Tell me about your response to the book. You may use some of the following questions to guide your response if you feel you do not have much to say. [Kids need the questions at the outset, but eventually they come to trust that I want their honest appraisals and opinions and begin to move away from them after a few entries.]

    Who is your favorite character? Why?

    What part of the story was the most or least believable? Why?

    To whom might you recommend this book? Why?

    Would you read another book by this author? Why or why not?

    What do you think was the strength of this book? Why?

    Were there any weaknesses, in your opinion? What were they?

    What were your reactions (feelings) to this book? Why?

    Did the characters seem real to you? Why or why not?

    Who do you think the intended audience is for this book? Why?

    Did you like or dislike the book? Why?

• Rate the book on a scale of your own devising. The rating should follow logically from your response to the book. In other words, do not give it a high rating if you found flaws or did not like the book. [The rating system allows them to represent their thoughts visually.]

simple enough to allow students to develop some of their own guidelines for reading logs. Of course, you might also want to vary using logs with some of the other activities that are mentioned later in this chapter.

Sample Reading Log Entry

142 pp. April 8, 2003
CUBA 15 by Nancy Osa

Violet has just turned fifteen. Her abuelita tells Violet that it is time for a quince celebration, a traditional celebration for a young woman coming of age. Violet's father and his parents are Cuban, and this tradition means a great deal to the family. Violet, however, does not see herself dressed in a pink dress the color of Pepto Bismol. She informs her family that, if the quince is to take place, she, Violet, needs to be placed in charge of making the important decisions for the ceremony. Violet selects her court and dress and the theme of the celebration. "All the World's a Stage" allows Violet to pull in her newfound interest in speech competitions. Of course, all the best laid plans cannot keep last-minutes problems from threatening the success of Violet's quince party. She triumphs at the party, managing to make amends for the errors and hurt her actions have caused.

   Even though I am not Hispanic and have never planned a quince, I know how overwhelmed Violet felt about trying to take care of all the details and still handle school and friends and family. Like Violet, I performed in high school in the speech competitions and enjoyed getting over my fear of speaking in public. I think the way Violet managed to get her way about the dress was so clever. She used her brain instead of just whining until she got her way. This book had a lot of funny scenes and I would recommend it to other people who like humorous books.

RATING: The time FLEW by as I read this book.

Directed Individualized Reading

In the 1970s, Terry Ley wrote two landmark articles on a program for getting kids involved in books and reading called Directed Individualized Reading (DIR) (1979). Over the years, I have made modifications to Ley's concepts; however, the underlying principles remain the same. The basic principles behind DIR are that teachers provide time in class to read during DIR; teachers read books selected by their students; after the book is read, teacher and student meet to confer about the book; the conference is student-led.

The following is a schedule for a typical DIR session.

Day One

Students select books from the classroom or school library, or they may bring in a book from home. Students provide the teacher with the title of the books they have selected. When I was first starting out, I limited the books kids could select to a list of about fifty books I had already read. Gradually, this list became longer and was not as restrictive.

Days Two–Five

Students are given class time to read. The teacher also spends class time reading the books students have selected. Typically, I can read one YA book a day, which means I can complete about five books in class per week. The rest of the books become at-home reading. I can skim some books; others will already be familiar to me.

Days Six–Ten

As students complete the books, they sign up for a conference. I have gathered some questions that students can use as a basis for planning their discussion with me (see Peck's Questions later in this chapter; you can also use generic discussion questions) and have placed them in folders, or students may elect to plan the conference without any assistance from the teacher. As I confer with students, the other class members continue to read books.

Even though the discussion is student-initiated and student-led, I can always ask questions and make sure that students understood the book they read. There is accountability here as well as higher-level thinking. What I love best about DIR is that it affords me the chance to discover the books that are speaking to my students. It also gives me the chance to do some reading, to keep more abreast of YA books.

Books on Tape

For some students, there is little time during the school day to read. They are involved in all sorts of extracurricular activities or have responsibilities at home that prevent them from finding time to read. Others find the act of reading painful because of reading disabilities. Still others prefer to hear a book than to read it. For those students, audiobooks may be the answer. For many years, Lois Buckman and I have been working with at-risk readers. We have done booktalks and have assisted teachers in coming up with alternatives to the traditional book report (see Appendix V). However, we still had a few students who were not reading. Some of these kids spent nearly ninety minutes a day on the bus getting to and from school. We wondered what would happen if we purchased audiobooks and cassette players and headphones and allowed kids to check them out as they would a book. I wrote a grant proposal, and with the $1,000 we purchased cassette players, headphones, and books on tape. When Lois booktalked, she also included the titles she had in audio format. Before long, the audiobooks were circulating as well as the hard copies of the books.

Audiobooks for Middle School Students

The Amber Spyglass by Philip Pullman
Cut by Patricia McCormack
Eva by Peter Dickinson
The Golden Compass by Philip Pullman
Harry Potter I–IV by J. K. Rowling
Hatchet by Gary Paulsen
Holes by Louis Sachar
Joey Pigza Loses Control by Jack Gantos
Jocy Pigza Swallowed the Key by Jack Gantos
The Lord of the Rings by J. R. R. Tolkien
Many Stones by Carolyn Coman
Monster by Walter Dean Myers
My Louisiana Sky by Kimberly Willis Holt
The Princess Diaries by Meg Cabot
The Sisterhood of the Traveling Pants by Ann Brashares
Speak by Laurie Halse Anderson
Stargirl by Jerry Spinelli
The Subtle Knife by Philip Pullman
Wolf Rider by Avi

Audiobooks were appealing to the kids who did not have time to read traditionally. They could plug into a book on the ride to and from school or in the evening before bed. Some of the audiobooks became part of the family commute as well. Students reported that they listened to the tapes with parents and siblings on trips over the weekend and holidays. Some kids found they preferred listening to a book and following along with the hard copy (we always purchase unabridged audiobooks). I take books on tape in the car during vacation and listen to audiobooks when I walk every day. It is about the only way I can keep up with adult books, given all the wonderful YA books stacking up and awaiting me.

Lois and I have secured several small grants thanks to ALAN, the Texas Library Association, DEMCO, VOYA, and YALSA. We continue to add to the audiobook collection and now are adding books on CD. In preparation for an author visit by Jack Gantos, the eighth-grade teacher played *Joey Pigza Loses Control* for her classes. Seventh-graders got to listen to another Gantos book on tape. Sometimes Lois plays part of an audiobook during her routine booktalks to the classes in the library. The English as a Second Language teacher is planning with us for a pilot program involving audiobooks for the next school year. Since listening comprehension is often higher than reading comprehension, we predict that her students will be able to enjoy books more on their interest level without the frustrations that crop up because of language differences. Finally, some teachers permit listening to audiobooks during DIR and silent reading time.

USSR, DEAR, and Other Silent Reading Programs

Finding time to read is sometimes one of the biggest challenges I face. Imagine how tough it is for our students to find time during their hectic days. Corrie has band practice and homework every night. Cali is involved in speech and drama after school. Even fourth-grader Natalie has activities that take time after the school day is over. As a classroom teacher, I found it imperative to provide time for reading at school. I had read about USSR, Uninterrupted Sustained Silent Reading, which is also called DEAR, for Drop Everything and Read, and I decided to give it a try in my classes.

The week prior to initiating this activity, I placed signs around the team area to whet students' curiosity. On Monday, as kids trooped in for afternoon classes, I greeted them with bean bags, pillows, and blankets. "Grab a book and find a comfortable place to read," I announced. Kids dove for the floor and corners and settled in to read. There were few objections. I also had a huge bag of popcorn spread into various containers around the room so that kids could snack as they read. At the beginning, I set a timer for five minutes. Gradually, we moved to ten and then to fifteen minutes. Fifteen minutes a day for reading may not sound like much, but it does add up over the course of a week.

Because I taught in an open concept school, it was not long before word spread that my class got to come in an lie down on the floor. My teammates had little choice but to agree to schedule those fifteen-minute sessions in their classes as well. Before much longer, the principal decided it might be a good idea for the entire school to have SRA (Silent Reading Activity). Then *everyone* in the school read for those fifteen minutes, including the administrators, the secretarial staff, and the custodial crew joined in. It set the school climate for reading wonderfully. This time was for free reading—no textbooks, no testing. Kids were encouraged to bring in pillows and sleeping bags, whatever they needed to make reading comfortable.

Finally, I moved into Free Reading Fridays. By compacting the curriculum, pretesting kids to determine baseline knowledge, and other methods I was able to find time to take one day and devote it to reading. I chose Fridays for this free reading. After a small-group instruction or the traditional spelling test (ten minutes), we spent the remainder of the fifty-minute class reading. We could read aloud, listen to audiobooks, do buddy reading, conduct DIR conferences, or engage in silent reading. I tried to vary the activities for the sake of motivation. Fridays, instead of being a day of dread, became a relaxing way of entering the weekend refreshed.

Peck's Questions

After all that time spent reading, it became apparent that I needed to provide options for kids to report on what they were reading. DIR and book logs were fine, but I wanted some more alternatives. It was then that I ran across an article by author Richard Peck (1978) in an issue of the *ALAN Review*. Peck talked about the importance of asking kids good questions about the books they were reading. He suggested the following ten questions as one place to begin purposeful discussion. After each question, I note the sorts of examples and explanations I gave my students as I introduced them to the questions.

1. *What would this story be like if the main character were of the opposite sex?* This question gets at the role gender plays. For example, in a romance, how would the story change if the guy told the story instead of the gal? What would happen if Brian Robeson in Paulsen's *Hatchet* were really Brianna? How would the story change?

2. *Why is the story set where it is? (not What is the setting?)* Does this story have to take place where it does? *Slake's Limbo* by Felice Holman has the main character fleeing bullies and ducking into a subway tunnel, where he survives on his own for months. Obviously, this story needs to be set where there is an underground system of some kind. Sometimes setting is essential (imagine Harry Potter without Hogwarts School and Privet Drive).

3. *If you were to film this story, what characters would you eliminate if you couldn't use them all?* This question asks students to consider the important role even a minor character might play in the story. For instance, Shakespeare often uses a minor character to break tension in his tragedies or uses someone like Falstaff to deliver some important news. Before you eliminate a character, you need to be certain that person does not play a critical role. How could you eliminate John or Lorraine or Mr. Pignati from *The Pigman* by Paul Zindel and retain the integrity of the story?

4. *Would you film this story in black-and-white or color? Why?* Most kids will answer "color" because they do not really know black-and-white.

There are some good black-and-white movies, though, with which they may be familiar. I use *Psycho,* the original version, and tell kids that Hitchcock used Hershey's chocolate syrup for the blood in the shower scene. However, when I watch that movie, I see red; it takes me a few days to not feel spooked in a shower afterward. *Pleasantville* is another good example because it switches from color to black-and-white and back to color. *The Wizard of Oz* does the same. This helps kids think of mood and tone in writing.

5. *How is the main character different from you?* Generally, this is not a tough question to answer. What readers tell you here, though, can provide insight into their lives and into how they relate to the story. See question 7 as the follow-up to this. I am different from the characters in most books because of my age. However, there are other ways in which I am different. I am not a slave like Sarny in *Nightjohn.* I have not been on MTV's "The Real World" like Judd Winnick in *Pedro and Me.*

6. *Why, or why not, would this story make a good TV series?* Some stories end with all the problems neatly wrapped up. There are books, however, where there is no clear-cut resolution, where the ending is open to further exploration. Obviously, series books lend themselves to a series format on TV.

7. *What is one thing in this story that has happened to you?* Here is where kids can make personal connections to the text. I once had a student tell me he was like a main character whose friend had drowned in *On My Honor* by Marion Dane Bauer. Richard had watched helplessly as his own father suffered a heart attack and died in a lake. I had not known this about Richard, but his answer allowed me to reach out to him about this great sadness in his life.

8. *Reread the first paragraph of Chapter 1. What's in it that made you read on?* This question makes kids aware of narrative hooks. This is nothing new. The Nancy Drew series of the early twentieth century generally began with a car hurtling toward a cliff or something equally exciting. Contemporary books have come a long way but many draw you in immediately. I always read the first page of Joan Lowery Nixon's *Whispers from the Dead,* which ends with the main character talking about writing down what has happened in her life beginning with the day she died. *That* is a hook. I also want kids to know that if a book is not making them want to read on, it is permissible to take the book back and select another one to read.

9. *If you had to design a new cover for this book, what would it look like?* Please include a copy of the cover you are discussing. There are so

many skills that can be taught using this question alone. It does give readers a chance to represent characters, moods, and plot in more abstract styles. I generally do not permit kids to use clip art and magazine photos. I prefer they use colors and shapes to approximate what the book is about. Molly Bang's *Picture This: Perception and Composition* is a good book to guide you in an assignment like this one.

10. *What does the title tell you about the book? Does it tell the truth?* Sometimes this question alone can bring out the essence of the book. The title of *Speak* by Laurie Halse Anderson has both a literal and a figurative meaning. *Monster* by Walter Dean Myers is what the prosecutor calls the defendant, Steve, who is telling the story from his point of view. Do "The Moves Make the Man"? How does a title like Crutcher's *Whale Talk* bring readers information about the book?

A few final words about these questions. Teachers might assign all ten for a book report alternative. But my favorite way to use these questions is to ask readers to select the two questions they think are most important to answer about the book. They must not only answer those two questions, they must also make their case as to why each was selected. Of course, you could also ask kids to answer the odd-numbered or even-numbered questions or the first five or any other variation that suits your needs for assessment.

Pass It On

Janet Allen (2001) calls this activity the Book Pass. I ran into it about fifteen years ago in Julie Hydell's classroom. She told me that too often her kids got to the library and did not have a clue about how to find a good book to read. So, she checked out thirty books (for the thirty kids in her class) and placed one on each desk. Every two minutes, kids would pass along their book to the person behind them. In a class period, kids would have the chance to preview all thirty books. "Chances are," she told me, "kids will find one or two that interest them. Then, when we go to the library, they are on a cart so that kids can find them easily. If someone has not found a book this way, I can spend some time with them or ask the librarian to make some suggestions." Of course, I immediately stole the idea and use it today in my classes at the university. Any book is bearable for two minutes.

I give kids the option now to pull out of the rotation once they find a book they want to read for longer than two minutes. Of course, if after ten minutes, they change their minds, they can opt back into the rotation of books.

As a classroom teacher, I took my kids to the library every other week to check out books. My motivated readers would conduct their business quickly and settle in to read on the couch or at a table. However, I always had one or two "nomads of the library." They wandered along the shelves and never settled on a book at all. These kids were overwhelmed by the sheer quantity of books from which to choose. Kylene Beers (2002) talks about this same phenomenon. These kids want to select from a more narrow choice. That is why I would ask the librarian to place books on a cart or a table so that kids could make a selection more easily. The librarian, Rosemary Smith, and I would booktalk from this smaller grouping of books, giving kids a personal introduction to them. This seemed to help those less-than-eager readers find books they might actually like to read.

Annotations

An annotation is a short piece of writing that combines a summary of the book with a critical comment from the reader. That comment could be a reader response of some kind or a reference to another book on a similar theme or an indication of strengths and weaknesses of the book. Kids tend to perceive this assignment as a relatively simple one to do. What they discover, though, is that writing succinctly is a bit tougher than anticipated. Generally, I read aloud a storybook in class (*Where the Wild Things Are* by Maurice Sendak works well) and then we write the annotation together in class. Once we have written about the book, we go back through and tighten the writing. I limit the word count in an annotation to somewhere between one hundred and two hundred words. That means we have to lose anything extraneous. I require a bibliographic format of some kind for this assignment so that I can help kids feel comfortable with compiling the information for a citation. This will come in handy as we do research projects later in the semester.

Reading Autobiography

When I took a YA literature course with Dick Abrahamson, the first assignment he had us complete was our reading autobiography. In this writing, we were to tell him about our lives as readers. It was a pleasant assignment for me because I had many wonderful feelings about reading as a child, teen, and adult. However, that is not always the case. As the autobiographies were shared, I began to see that not all kids loved reading early on as I did. Some had come to a love of reading as teens; some had lost the read-

---

Sample Annotation

Cheripko, Jan. *Rat.* Boyds Mills Press, 2002. 201pp., $15.95. ISBN 1-59078-034-5

Jeremy Chandler is known as a gym rat. He spends hours hanging out in the gym, shooting baskets. Born with a birth defect that left him with a deformed right arm, Jeremy has had to overcome tremendous obstacles. None of those, though, is as devastating as what faces him after he testifies against the basketball coach accused of molesting a cheerleader. He is no longer a gym rat but a rat fink in the eyes of the players on the team. He is targeted by one player in particular, a young man who seems determined to get revenge. Jeremy is unexpectedly befriended by the new coach and his family. However, even this newfound friendship carries with it problems of its own. Cheripko explores interesting moral territory in his latest novel. Jeremy is forced to make difficult choices throughout the novel. While he knows what is the right thing to do, following his conscience is not always easy or rewarding. Sometimes, Jeremy learns, telling the truth can hurt. An interesting pairing for *Rat* might be *The Moves Make the Man* by Bruce Brooks. It, too, explores, the nature of truth.

---

ing spark as young adults. Some found little time to read as adults. I decided to use this same assignment in my classes. I still do. I feel I get to know my students well in terms of their literacy development after reading their autobiographies.

The basic assignment asks students to think back to their childhoods and talk about the positive and negative experiences they have had with books and reading. The experiences can be in or outside of the school. I ask them to consider their reading lives as they grew older and to talk about important books, times, people. I do not set a limit in terms of length, but I do encourage them to be thorough without rambling. I share my reading autobiography with the class before asking them to write to give them some idea of what I am looking for in this writing.

Here are two sample reading autobiographies. One is mine, the one I share with my students as I give them the same assignment. The second example is from one of my students who grew up in the Rio Grande Valley of Texas. They serve both to show the commonalities many readers share and to point out some of the differences that exist because of age, ethnicity, culture, and other variables.

Dr. Lesesne's Reading Autobiography
I can still smell the Old Spice aftershave my grandfather wore whenever I pick up my battered copy of Pat the Bunny. *My earliest memory of reading is my "Pop Pop" turning the pages of this book and helping me see,*

smell, and touch the pages. I know I was fortunate to grow up in a family where books and reading and learning were important. My mother read at night after she thought we were asleep. As soon as I was able to walk what seemed to be miles to the local library, my mother made sure I got a library card. Once a month we would visit the Carnegie Library (and wasn't I disappointed when I discovered that not all libraries have dinosaur exhibits and floor after floor of books?) and check out the maximum number of books allowed. It was never enough as I would read all of my books in a flash and then have to be content to reread them until the next trip to the library. Christmas meant a pile of books, too.

Once school started, I was startled to learn that not all books were created equal. I remember the horrible basal readers with their Dick and Jane and Spot nonsense. I sped through them as quickly as I could and then begged to move on to something more interesting. Unfortunately, at school there was not a real library, so I had to wait to get home to read the real *books. I was a good reader in the classroom and learned how to get through what the teachers wanted me to read somehow. I do recall that I was in the top reading group, so whatever method the teacher had devised to keep us unaware did not work.*

Serial reading was next for me. I fell in love with The Five Little Peppers and Trixie Belden and Nancy Drew and Cherry Ames. One Christmas, my mom gave me the complete Cherry Ames and Nancy Drew collections. I spent the holidays blissfully saving lives and solving mysteries. Soon, though, I was ready for more racy stuff. I found my mother's stash of True Confessions *magazines and began to read them even though she would punish me every time she caught me reading them. If they were forbidden, I wanted to read them!*

School reading continued to be a chore for me. I still recall with displeasure having to read Great Expectations *in fifth grade. To this day, I cannot abide Dickens novels thanks to what Sister Fabian did to the novel in class. Pure torture was reading a chapter at a time and then being quizzed to death over characters and setting and details. Outside of school, though, I continued to read. One night, while I was babysitting, I came across a collection of plays by William Shakespeare, and a whole new world opened up for me. I think if I had not met the Bard on my own, I would not have enjoyed him in school. Since I already knew the plays we did in school, I think I appreciated learning about them more. My senior English teacher also recited and acted out plays and poems. He is largely responsible for my continued love of poetry. In college I read what I was assigned to read and not much more. I went into a sort of hiberna-*

tion, waiting for summers so I could read the latest romance or mystery for grownups.

As a teacher, I finally found the books I love reading to this day— young adult novels. Most of the good YA books were written after I left my teens. However, I wanted to read what my students found interesting, and I got hooked! I still prefer reading children's and YA books. I keep up as best I can with adult books on tape. I seem to spend more and more time in my car and have discovered that books on tape are a wonderful way to make the commuting less painful. Lately, I have listened to Stephen King, and I have some other audiobooks waiting. Now, though, it is more likely that I will be listening to YA and children's books on tape because the kids insist on listening, too. I reread via audio the Tolkien series and am listening to Pullman's His Dark Materials books on tape with the kids now.

I still find time most days to do some reading. Even if all I get to is the bathroom book, I like to spend some of my day lost in a book. Then, there are those lovely rainy days spent reading and time on long flights reading. I actually look forward to having to wait somewhere with a book.

I cannot understand people who do not like to read. To me, books are life!

Velma Vela's Reading Autobiography
One Book Is Never Enough

I am standing next to a canal where the gushing water screams past my father and me. It is late at night, and I listen to the deafening tossing and tumbling of the water when suddenly everything goes silent. My father stretches out his arms and holds out his hands; slowly he turns them over for me to see and, in that moment, I brand the unforgettable image of the calloused hardworking hands into the very essence of my existence. With tears in his eyes, he struggles to say, "Por eso, quiero que vallas a la escuela mi'ja. Por eso quiero que estudies. Yo no quiero ver estsos callos en sus manitas." [For this, I want you to go to school, my child. For this, I want you to study. I do not want to see calluses on your hands.] These words are all I hear—no roaring irrigation pump, no gushing water—just my father's love and his vision of my future.

My family has always been gung-ho on education. My father's greatest desire was for his children to finish high school and go to college. Somehow, though, the concept of raising a reader escaped my father and mother. Reading was never stressed in our house. My parents placed their confidence in the educational system, believing we would be exposed to *reading, believing that the school would provide us with the print-rich environment foreign to them. I was a student yearning, waiting for a teacher to enrapture me with the wonder of a book. But somehow I fell through the educational colander. My passion for reading, my need for reading, lay dormant throughout school because of the lack of stimulation, the lack of nurturing, the lack of enthusiasm.*

I read a book or two, but my true love of reading did not blossom until I was pregnant. I wanted my child to love to read, so I purchased a book called How to Raise a Reader *and read about* The Very Hungry Caterpillar, The Velveteen Rabbit, *and* Pat the Bunny. *I joined the Children's Book of the Month Club and found the wonders of children's literature as a twenty-eight-year-old. I ripped open every book package as if it were a Christmas present. The most vibrant and vivid colors and images amazed me, as did the format of these books. I was hooked.*

I discovered my love for literature, especially children's literature, as a child trapped in an adult's body. I am old, but when it comes to the reading world, I am but a child, constantly seeking new challenges, new dreams, new ways to tell a story. As a child I stood beside the canal, and my father inspired me to excel, to succeed, to be happy. Today, as a parent, I too hold out my hands. In them I have a book, and with it I can impart a magic beyond the dreams of my father. A book is an explosion, a rainbow illuminating and morphing the imagination. And one book is never enough.

I read Velma's reading autobiography on the screen of my computer several months ago as her class turned in their assignments electronically. Something made me hit the print key. Here was a incredible testament to the power of books and reading. Though Velma and I had grown up miles and years apart, we still had an important connection, one forged by our mutual love of reading.

Finally . . .

This chapter barely scratches the surface of the variety of strategies and activities we can use to bring kids and books together. For the past twelve years, I have been asking my YA literature university students to be mentors and e-pals for reluctant readers in the middle school. The Student-Teacher Online Mentoring Project (STOMP) has worked well. Past research suggests that mentors are important for kids. Mentors add an additional literacy role model for students.

Alternatives to traditional book reports might also be a key factor. See Appendix V for a listing of some other ideas for holding kids accountable for their reading. However, I do want to issue a caveat here: Sometimes it is best to read for the sheer pleasure of reading. I know when I finish a book that sometimes I want to talk to someone else who has read the book (DIR), sometimes I want to write about my response to the book (annotations, reading log, Peck's questions), and sometimes I just want to savor the feeling with which the book left me. I certainly do not wish to take a test over each book. I do not normally care to write a new ending (unless I disliked the way the book ended). I might send a letter or e-mail to the author. However, most of the time, I simply want to move on to another book, to get lost once more in the story the author has created for me. I think that we need to offer this same opportunity to our students, too. It's enough for me to know that I have once again successfully made the match and found the right book at the right time for the right reader.

Afterword

Of all the letters I've received from readers, the two-and-a-half-page single-spaced epic from a fifteen-year-old girl named Holly stands out among my favorites. Holly began by informing me that she was *not* a reader. She had tried repeatedly to make her teacher understand this, but her teacher continued to "force-feed" her literature and had the gall to insist she write about it. Holly did not like to write; she felt it was a colossal waste of time, but she was writing to me as part of a class assignment. Her teacher had suggested that she read my second novel, *Thwonk*, and Holly had fought this at every turn. Then, Holly confided, the funniest thing happened.

She liked my book.

Now, being Holly, she backed into the compliment. She thought the cupid was funny, and she would have done exactly what A. J. had done. She thought being popular wasn't all it was cracked up to be, and like A. J., she had a father who didn't understand her. She was considering reading another one of my books, but she wasn't promising anything. She closed with this: "You should feel pretty good about what you do for a living, Mrs. Bauer, because it isn't every day that Holly Goldsmith picks up a book."

I sat there with that letter feeling very good indeed. I wrote Holly back, not sure how to break it to her. She was both an insightful reader *and* a good writer.

I've often wondered about Holly's teacher. It's easy to give up when faced with resoundingly reluctant readers, easy to just say, fine, don't read. But teachers are made of this remarkable stuff—part resilience, part hope—which allows them to press in. It's the pressing in that brings those precious breakthroughs.

Dr. Teri Lesesne is one such warrior. I have been privileged to know her as a colleague and a friend. Armed with books and her indomitable love of literature, she marches into libraries, schools, classrooms, and hearts and makes books come alive for people of all ages. She is a matchmaker of the highest order, determined to connect readers with the right books. What a blessing that can be. Think of the rewards.

The right books can travel the years with us and mean different things at different times. The right books from the past speak to us now. The right books teach us how to use our lives—to think through where we are versus where we want to be. The right books show us the steps to take out of big problems, the truth of the human condition; they expose us to radical thinking; encourage us to grow beyond ourselves. The right books always enlarge us because reading is not solitary. It is a merging of at least two people—the reader and the author.

As I'm writing this, I look at my bookshelf—I have two shelves devoted to the well-worn novels that have spoken to me deeply at different times in my life. The first is *Grandpa Bunny Bunny,* a little-known Golden Book that was ahead of its time, way beyond Bambi and the other big headliners—a book about art, life, death, and leaving the best of your self behind. Next to that are *The Wind in the Willows* [Kenneth Grahame], *Charlotte's Web* [E. B. White], *The Good Earth* [Pearl Buck], *The Call of the Wild* [Jack London], *A Separate Peace* [John Knowles], *To Kill a Mockingbird* [Harper Lee], *The Catcher in the Rye* and *Nine Stories* [J. D. Salinger], *The Great Gatsby* [Scott Fitzgerald], *A Moveable Feast* [Ernest Hemingway], *Catch 22* and *Good as Gold* [Joseph Heller], *Lake Wobegon Days* [Garrison Keillor], *The Remains of the Day* [Kazuo Ishiguro], *The Shipping News* [E. Annie Proulx], and *A Prayer for Owen Meany* [John Irving]. Just looking at those books floods me with memories and emotions of the times I was ever so fortunate as to have them intersect with my life and my heart and my needs. Some were presented, some I discovered, some we had on our bookshelves at home, just waiting to be picked. None of those books were ever read just once. They got me through the weirdness of the '50s, the complexity of the '60s, when for a long time I wasn't sure who I was or what I wanted. They were there when my dad died suddenly, when I changed careers, when I tried to make sense of a world that wasn't equal, safe, or fair. They followed me through my life in sales, my life as a wife and mother. They are part of me, these ripples of memory, pressing in at every turn. Perhaps this is where cellulite comes from. I certainly hope so.

As a writer, these books have greatly influenced how I approach my work. I'm always delighted when someone comes up who just "discovered" one of my early novels. The story is fresh to them, like I just wrote it. And as I hear them talk about it in the now of their lives, it begins to feel new to me as well.

"Dear Mrs. Bauer," a freshman girl wrote. "I just finished *Hope Was Here.* I read it in one morning. I started it in study hall, I read it during math class and all the way through World History."

I laughed, of course; and then I thought about that year in which I sweated, wept, opened veins, and rearranged major organs to finish that book.

It took me a year to get it right.

It took her a morning to read it.

Interesting math, this writing business.

Years ago, in a supreme moment of dating despair, I contracted with a singles dating service to be matched with an interesting man. They sent Roger, who was agonizingly unfunny; crass to our waitress (if you've read my *Hope Was Here,* you know how I feel about food service). The only thing we had in common was that we both needed oxygen to live.

It was the longest lunch of my life.

"So," I said to him, trying to be polite. "What are you reading these days?"

Nothing. He was reading nothing.

And it showed.

I have always been a reader. Even in my darkest moments, I have read. Even when I was a kid at risk in high school, determined to be a supreme rebel and wear black leather and look tough, I read.

I was born into a family of readers who taught me that a book is a living thing; an ecosystem that invites us inside to live with the characters and breathe their air.

To fully enter in, then, is the point of reading. To understand the doors that must be opened so that students can do that is the point and the power of this book.

Let Teri Lesesne help you make the match, light the match, and pass the fire to your students.

Teaching Kids to Love to Read

by Lee Bennett Hopkins

As a young teenager, book were not an important part of my life. Growing up with a single, hardworking mother who had to raise three of us, survival loomed above reading. I came to books and reading via my eighth-grade teacher, Mrs. Ethel K. MacLaughlin. Since I was a nonreader of books (I did devour magazines), she led me to begin reading via play scripts. I soon read every one I could get my hands on. This led me into the world of true books.

When I found *Little Women* by Louisa May Alcott, I devoured it. Perhaps this was because of the family I did not have. I still adore the novel. Lines from it have been part of my lifelong memory. There is no specific reason I write or collect poems for young adult readers. I enjoy creating books for all ages. Can you put an age on a poem? Some poems can be read and *felt* at age 5 or 50 or 80. I have always professed that we spend too much time teaching children to read and not enough time teaching them to *love* to read.

Book Lists and Resources

I am constantly asked to recommend a book for a sixth-grade boy or for a ninth-grade science class. Someone will ask for a book on a certain topic or theme at a workshop. To be honest, I do not generally keep lists that are categorized by grade level or content area. Each year for the past decade or so I have kept lists of the books I read that I thought would prove useful in some way in the classroom. Some books made excellent read-aloud selections; others seemed perfect for reluctant readers or gifted readers. However, asking teachers to wade through hundreds (if not thousands) of books for one that might meet their needs would not be terribly helpful. So, in these appendixes are lists of books that might just meet the needs of your classroom. Some are new. Others are classics in the field. While some may have gone out of print, I suspect that they can be found on library shelves in your school or public library (or even from used book sellers). Some of the lists are annotated; some are not. However, you can always look up annotations, summaries, or reviews of books on the Internet or sites such as your school's OPAC (online catalog).

Once again, let me stress the importance of your role in selecting materials for your classroom. It is up to you to preview a book and decide if it meets your individual needs. I have indicated a general age range as follows:

INT = intermediate grades, 4–6
MS = middle school grades 5–9
HS = high school grades 8–12

There is a deliberate overlap in these designations. Grade ranges have been provided to indicate the age appropriateness of the materials.

The best lists, however, are the ones you develop. As a new teacher, I would post the books I had read on a bulletin board in the classroom. At the beginning of the year, students were required to read from my list. That meant I could talk about a book with any student at any time. As the year progressed, I encouraged students to bring in books that they thought I should add to the list. I pledged to read one book recommended by each student over the course of the year. Some of the books students recommended became part of my list. Gradually, the list grew longer, as will yours.

I have categorized books in a variety of ways here; some are on multiple lists. It is as tough to pigeonhole a book as it is to label a child. Select a few books you do not know and make a concerted effort to read and add them to your own lists. Ask students to select one or two they think they might like and to review them for you. Give the lists to your school librarians, and ask them to tell you which are already in the collection (and perhaps order some that are not).

Read-Aloud Selections

C hapter 8 discusses all the ins and outs of reading aloud to students of all ages. Remember the cardinal rules of reading aloud: preview the materials; practice reading with plenty of expression; read only those pieces you yourself enjoy. I have included several short works here. Begin reading aloud with these shorter pieces until students get accustomed to the activity. Gradually begin using longer works, but intersperse picture books, poems, and short stories from time to time for variety. Be sure to ask others to be involved in the read-aloud time. The speech and drama teachers are perfect for read-aloud guests. My students always loved having the school principal come in and do a guest read-aloud. Sometimes I would swap out with a colleague to give the kids a chance to hear someone new. Invite people from the business community, especially ones familiar to the students.

Appelt, Kathi. "Just a Kiss, Annie P." from *Kissing Tennessee and Other Stories from the Stardust Dance.* Here is a story with another twist, perfect for teaching kids about making assumptions. (MS)

Bauer, Joan. *Stand Tall.* The opening chapter in which Tree discovers the bureaucracy of the school system is sure to strike a chord with your students. (MS)

Brashares, Ann. *Sisterhood of the Traveling Pants.* Read the introduction, the story of how the pants came into the lives of the main characters. (HS)

Cart, Michael, ed. *911: The Book of Help.* Any story or poem from this collection would make excellent material for reading aloud. I particularly favor the poem by Sonya Sones and the short story by Joan Bauer. (MS/HS)

Cisneros, Sandra. "Eleven," from *Woman Hollering Creek and Other Stories.* This story perfectly encapsulates what adolescents are all about. The narrator talks about how growing another year older does not necessarily mean we lose the child inside us. (MS)

Creech, Sharon. *Love That Dog.* This slim novel tells the story of Jack and his beloved dog, Sky, in a series of poems. The entire book can be read in one class period. (INT/MS)

Crutcher, Chris. *King of the Mild Frontier: An Ill-Advised Autobiography.* Any chapter would make an interesting read-aloud. Be sure to have other books by Crutcher on hand, too. (HS)

Dahl, Roald. "Little Red Riding Hood" from *Revolting Rhymes.* This comic poetic rendition of the fairy tale with a surprise twist at the end proves poetry can be fun. (INT/MS/HS)

Fleischman, John. *Phineas Gage.* This gruesome story of how one man survived a severe brain injury is just bloody enough to satisfy reluctant readers. Read the chapter in which Gage is struck in the head by his tamping rod. (MS)

Giles, Gail. *Shattering Glass.* The first sentence will be enough to send kids scurrying for this book. (HS)

Hesse, Karen. *Witness.* A brilliantly conceived and written novel which uses nine points of view to tell about the Klan's arrival in a New England town in the 1900s. This is perfect for reading aloud or for Readers Theater. Select one poem from each of the nine characters to introduce point of view to students. (MS)

Klass, David. *You Don't Know Me.* The opening chapter works well as a read-aloud, as do Chapters 2 and 3, where John describes his futile attempts to produce music from his tuba. (MS/HS)

Korman, Gordon. *No More Dead Dogs.* Wallace hates books in which the dogs die. Imagine his frustration when he discovers that his new English teacher's favorite book features another hapless canine. (INT/MS)

Korman, Gordon. *Son of the Mob.* This also works wonderfully in read-aloud. (HS)

Lynch, Chris. *Slot Machine.* Read aloud some of the letters Elvin writes home to his mother from summer sports camp. (MS/HS)

Nixon, Joan Lowery. *Whispers from the Dead.* Mystery lovers will be enchanted by this story about a house haunted by the ghosts of two women found murdered in the entry hall. Read the riveting opening pages and you will be sure to grab the attention of your students. (MS)

Paulsen, Gary. *Harris and Me.* Read aloud any of the chapters of this rollicking, funny book. My favorite read-aloud is the scene in which Gary dares Harris to pee on an electric fence. (INT/MS)

Paulsen, Gary. *Guts.* Here are all the true stories behind Paulsen's action-adventure novels. What is it like to eat a raw turtle's egg? How does one survive a moose attack? Those and other answers make for perfect reading aloud. (MS)

Peck, Richard. "Priscilla and the Wimps" in *Sixteen,* edited by Don Gallo. A school bully gets his comeuppance from an unlikely challenger: Priscilla Roseberry. Perfect for a unit on irony. (MS)

Rice, David. "California Cousins" from *Crazy Loco.* What happens when some stuck-up cousins come to visit the family and sneer at having to use an outdoor bathroom? It can only be hysterically funny. (INT/MS)

Ritter, John H. *The Boy Who Saved Baseball.* Read aloud the first four paragraphs of Chapter 7 as a way of introducing style to students. In addition to making an excellent introduction to the novel, these chapters might also serve as a starting point for a discussion of drawing inferences. Can students surmise what the story is about from these paragraphs? (MS)

Schwartz, Alvin. *Scary Stories to Tell in the Dark.* 3 vols. Any of the urban legends and ghost stories from these books are excellent read-aloud selections. Be sure to save some for Halloween to read with lights out and a flashlight under your chin for effect. (INT)

Shan, Darren. *Cirque Du Freak.* Darren is lured to an abandoned house one evening to see what is billed as a one-of-a-kind freak show. What he sees that night alters the course of his life and of those he loves most. Read the prologue to the book as one way to entice readers. There are five books in the series, each with a riveting opening to read aloud. (INT/MS)

Trueman, Terry. *Stuck in Neutral.* The opening chapter is a perfect lure into this book about a young man stricken with cerebral palsy. (HS)

Books to Booktalk

Here are my no-fail, sure-to-hook books to use when trying to bring kids and books together. Remember, the best booktalks are not canned presentations from someone else. Rather, your own take on what will interest kids in the book is the direction to go when planning booktalks. I try to limit talks to one to two minutes per book so that I can discuss as many books as possible in a short time. Chapter 9 provides tips and suggestions for successful booktalks.

Avi. *Wolf Rider*. Andy picks up the phone in his house. A voice on the other end of the line announces that someone has just been murdered. When Andy reports this call to the police, they do not believe him. Suddenly, Andy is caught between a killer and his victim. (MS)

Bauer, Joan. *Thwonk*. What would it be like to have your own personal Cupid, one who could grant you one wish that could change your life? Remember the old saying, though, be careful what you wish for as it might come true. A. J. McCreary learns her lesson when she asks for help in the romance department. (MS)

Brashares, Ann. *Sisterhood of the Traveling Pants*. A pair of magical jeans unites the lives of four friends. (MS/HS)

Cooney, Caroline. *The Terrorist*. Laura's younger brother Billy is killed when a terrorist hands him a package bomb in a crowded London train station. Laura needs to know who is responsible for her brother's death. (MS)

Cormier, Robert. *The Rag and Bone Shop*. Jason is the last person to have seen his young friend alive and is the prime suspect in her murder. He protests his innocence, so a police lieutenant skilled in the art of interrogation has to work his magic and extract a confession at any cost. (MS)

Crutcher, Chris. *Ironman*. Bo Brewster competes in the triathlon despite the obstacles placed in his path by his domineering father. (HS)

Duncan, Lois. *Who Killed My Daughter?* This horribly true story relates the story of Duncan's search for the person or persons responsible for murdering her teenage daughter. (HS)

Fleischman, John. *Phineas Gage*. This true story of a workman whose injury led doctors to know more about the brain and how it works is sufficiently gruesome to lure even reluctant readers. (INT/MS)

Galloway, Priscilla. *Truly Grim Tales*. This collection contains twisted and darker retellings of classic fairy tales. Imagine being Little Red Riding Hood and having to traverse the forest where genetically mutated wolves carry semiautomatic weapons. (MS)

Gantos, Jack. *Hole in My Life.* True account of the years Gantos spent in federal prison for running drugs. (HS)

Glenn, Mel. *Who Killed Mr. Chippendale?* Glenn crafts a mystery told in verse about the murder of an English teacher. (MS/HS)

Gutman, Dan. *The Kid Who Ran for President.* What happens when a twelve-year-old runs for President of the United States makes for fun reading. Judson Moon sues the federal government for age discrimination and begins his campaign for the Office of President. (INT/MS)

Hoose, Phillip. *It's Our World, Too.* This nonfiction collection examines how ordinary teens changed the life of their communities through social activism. (MS/HS)

Korman, Gordon. *No More Dead Dogs.* Wallace has vowed never to read another book in which the dog ends up dying. Unfortunately, his new English teachers has other plans. When Wallace writes a book report expressing his disgust for *Old Shep, My Pal,* he is faced with consequences he could never have expected. There are too few funny books for this age group. Kids miss having a good laugh. (MS/HS)

Levine, Gail Carson. *Ella Enchanted.* Ella, brought to the castle to prepare for her marriage to the prince, finds that she does not really want to marry him after all. (INT/MS)

McDonald, Janet. *Spellbound.* Miserable because she feels trapped at home with her baby, a teen mother is given a chance at completing school and attending college. All she has to do is win a spelling contest. (HS)

Nixon, Joan Lowery. *Whispers from the Dead.* Sarah Darnell and her family move into a house where an unsolved double murder has taken place. Sarah, following a recent near-death experience, begins to be haunted by scenes and sounds from the murder. Once she begins to investigate, she is targeted as the next victim. (MS)

Paulsen, Gary. *Harris and Me.* What happens when a naive city boy spends a summer on the farm with his cousin Harris? (MS)

Paulsen, Gary. *The Schernoff Discoveries.* Schernoff is always interested in experiments. As the school year begins, the experiments become more risky. They include how to attract girls. (INT/MS)

Pfeffer, Susan Beth. *Twice Taken.* A young teen sees a photo of herself and her father on a late night feature on missing and abducted children. She discovers that she has been taken by her father away from the rest of her family. What would it feel like to be removed from the only person you know as family? (MS/HS)

Shan, Darren. *Cirque Du Freak.* Darren must become a servant to Crepsley after he steals something valuable from the vampire. (MS)

Zindel, Paul. *Raptor.* Zach takes an egg from an underground cavern despite the fact that he knows this is wrong. An adorable little oviraptor hatches. However, when the raptor's mother comes looking for her lost youngster, Zach's life is imperiled. (MS)

Zindel, Paul. *Rats.* Imagine what would happen if some rather upset rats made their way into the city water supply. (MS)

Resources for Booktalking

Books

Bodart, Joni Richards. 2002. *Radical Reads: 101 Young Adult Novels on the Edge.* Lanham, MD: Scarecrow Press.

Bromann, Jennifer. 2001. *Booktalking That Works.* New York: Neal-Schuman.

Jones, Patrick. 1998. *Connecting Young Adults and Libraries: A How-to-Do-It Manual.* 2d ed. New York: Neal-Schuman.

Littlejohn, Carol, and Cathlyn Thomas. 2001. *Keep Talking That Book! Booktalks to Promote Reading.* Westport, CT: Libraries Unlimited.

Rochman, Hazel. 1987. *Tales of Love and Terror: Booktalking the Classics, Old and New.* Chicago: ALA. Also an instructional video.

Schall, Lucy. 2001. *Booktalks Plus: Motivating Teens to Read.* Westport, CT: Libraries Unlimited.

Articles

Anderson, Sheila, and Kristin Mahood. 2001. "The Inner Game of Booktalking." *Voice of Youth Advocates* 24 (2): 107–110.

Bromann, Jennifer. 1999. "The Toughest Audience on Earth." *School Library Journal* 45 (10): 60–63.

Guevara, Anne, and John Sexton. 2000. "Extreme Booktalking: YA Booktalkers Reach 6,000 Students Each Semester!" *Voice of Youth Advocates* 23 (2): 98–101.

Herald, Diana. 1995. "Booktalking to a Captive Audience." *School Library Journal* 41 (May): 35–36.

Osborne, Marcia. 2001. "Booktalking: Just Do It!" *Book Report* 19 (5): 23–24.

Online

The ABCs of Booktalking. www.uelma.org/conven00/booktalk.htm

Booktalking discussion group. groups.yahoo.com/group/booktalking

Booktalking ideas. www.albany.edu/~dj2930/yabooktalking.html. Basic concepts and sample booktalks on many YA books.

Booktalking Web site of the Professional Development Task Force of Young Adult Library Services Association (YALSA). www.ala.org/, "Professional Tools," search for "Booktalking."

Books on Tape

Available from the Listening Library, www.listeninglib.com/kids/catalog/index.html.

Anderson, Laurie Halse. *Speak*. (HS)

Avi. *Wolf Rider*. (MS)

Brashares, Ann. *Sisterhood of the Traveling Pants* and sequel. (HS)

Cabot, Meg. *The Princess Diaries* and sequels. (MS/HS)

Coman, Carolyn. *Many Stones*. (HS)

Cormier, Robert. *The Chocolate War*. (HS)

Curtis, Christopher Paul. *Bud, Not Buddy*. (INT/MS)

Curtis, Christopher Paul. *The Watsons Go to Birmingham—1963*. (INT/MS)

Dickinson, Peter. *Eva*. (MS/HS)

Gantos, Jack. *Joey Pigza Loses Control*. (INT/MS)

Gantos, Jack. *Joey Pigza Swallowed the Key*. (INT/MS)

Gantos, Jack. *What Would Joey Do?* (INT/MS)

Hiaasen, Carl. *Hoot*. (MS)

Paulsen, Gary. *Harris and Me*. (INT/MS)

Paulsen, Gary. *Nightjohn*. (MS/HS)

Pullman, Philip. His Dark Materials series: *The Amber Spyglass; The Golden Compass; The Subtle Knife*. (MS/HS)

Sachar, Louis. *Holes*. (INT/MS)

Shusterman, Neal. *The Dark Side of Nowhere*. (MS)

Silverstein, Shel. *Where the Sidewalk Ends*. (INT/MS)

Snicket, Lemony. Series of Unfortunate Events: *Bad Beginning* and sequels. (INT/MS)

Spinelli, Jerry. *Stargirl*. (HS)

Tolkien, J. R. R. *The Hobbit;* The Lord of the Rings trilogy. (MS/HS)

Popular Authors of Young Adult Books

Several hundred teachers, librarians, and experts in the YA field responded to a survey I posted on several listservs about which authors should be considered important. The following list represents the top twenty-five authors identified in this survey, listed in order of importance. I include links either to the author's personal home page or to sites where information about the author and his or her works can be located.

Gary Paulsen.
 www.randomhouse.com/features/garypaulsen/.
Robert Cormier.
 www.randomhouse.com/teachers/authors/corm.html.
Walter Dean Myers.
 www.randomhouse.com/teachers/authors/myer.html.
 greenwood.scbbs.com/servlet/A4TStart?authorid=wmyers&source=introduction.
Jerry Spinelli.
 www.randomhouse.com/teachers/rc/rc_ab_jsp.html.
 greenwood.scbbs.com/servlet/A4TStart?authorid=jspinelli&source=introduction.
Chris Crutcher.
 www.aboutcrutcher.com/.
 greenwood.scbbs.com/servlet/A4TStart?authorid=ccrutcher&source=introduction.
Katherine Paterson.
 www.terabithia.com/.
S. E. Hinton.
 www.sehinton.com/.

Madeleine L'Engle.
 www.randomhouse.com/teachers/authors/leng.html.
Philip Pullman.
 www.randomhouse.com/features/pullman/.
Mildred Taylor.
 www.randomhouse.com/teachers/authors/tayl.html.
Paul Zindel.
 www.randomhouse.com/teachers/authors/zind.html.
 greenwood.scbbs.com/servlet/A4TStart?authorid=pzindel&source=introduction.
Sharon Creech.
 www.sharoncreech.com/.
 www.harperchildrens.com/hch/author/author/creech/.
J. K. Rowling.
 www.scholastic.com/harrypotter/author/.
Cynthia Voigt.
 www.scils.rutgers.edu/~kvander/voigt.html.
Lois Lowry.
 www.loislowry.com/.
 www.randomhouse.com/teachers/authors/lowr.html.

Christopher Paul Curtis.
  www.randomhouse.com/teachers/authors/
  curt.html.
Karen Hesse.
  www.kidsreads.com/authors/au-hesse-
  karen.asp.
  teacher.scholastic.com/authorsandbooks/
  events/hesse/.
Virginia Hamilton.
  www.virginiahamilton.com/.
Louis Sachar.
  www.randomhouse.com/teachers/rc/rc_ab_
  lsa.html.
Lois Duncan.
  loisduncan.arquettes.com/.
  www.randomhouse.com/teachers/authors/
  dunc.html.

Virginia Euwer Wolff.
  greenwood.scbbs.com/servlet/A4TStart?
  authorid=vwolff&source=introduction.
Jane Yolen.
  www.janeyolen.com/.
Judy Blume.
  www.judyblume.com/.
Richard Peck.
  www.richardpeck.smartwriters.com/.
  www.randomhouse.com/teachers/authors/
  peck.html.
Brian Jacques.
  www.redwall.org/.
  www.mystworld.com/youngwriter/authors/
  brian_jacques.html.
  www.randomhouse.co.uk/redwall/
  conversation.html.

Popular Young Adult Books for Teens

W hat ten works, present or past, should anyone working with teens need to know?" This query was posted originally to the YALSA-BK, the NCTE-MIDDLE, and CHILD_LIT listservs, and sent to dozens of YA literature experts. Lists were compiled from the more than one hundred responses received. After the lists were compiled, books that had appeared on multiple lists (at least five lists) were included here. The top books, appearing on more than forty lists, were *The Chocolate War* and *The Giver*. The books on the list range from the earliest publications in YA literature (*The Outsiders* and *The Pigman*) to more recent works (*Monster* and *Speak*). They include works by several of the Margaret Edwards winners (Cormier, Crutcher, Paulsen, Garden, Hinton) and Printz honorees (Anderson, Wolff, Myers).

Among the Hidden by Margaret Peterson Haddix. Luke is the third child in a futuristic society that permits each family to have only two children. Thus, he is forced to stay hidden from all save his own family. (INT/MS)

Annie on My Mind by Nancy Garden. This classic is one of the first books to tackle the relationship between two girls who fall in love. Annie and Liza face overwhelming odds but decide their love is one they need to share. (HS)

Beauty by Robin McKinley. Retelling of the tale of Beauty and the Beast, perfect for YA readers, especially girls. (MS/HS)

Blood and Chocolate by Annette Curtis Klause. Vivian is part human, part wolf. She has fallen in love with a boy and wants to reveal her true nature to him so that their relationship can develop. (HS)

Bridge to Terabithia by Katherine Paterson. Jess wants to be the fastest runner in his class. When he is beaten by a girl, no one could have suspected that Leslie would become his best friend. (INT)

The Chocolate War by Robert Cormier. Jerry Renault takes a moral stand against the Vigils, the group who leads his school. When he dares to "disturb the universe," the consequences are severe. (HS)

Ender's Game by Orson Scott Card. Science fiction tale of a grim future where Ender Wiggin is being trained to be part of an elite militia to protect the human race from further alien invasions. (MS/HS)

Eva by Peter Dickinson. When Eva is seriously injured in an accident, her parents give permission for doctors to save her life by any means necessary. This futuristic novel examines several questions about medicine and ethics and the environment. (MS/HS)

Fallen Angels by Walter Dean Myers. Richie's tour of duty in Vietnam changes his life and the lives of his family forever. This novel follows an all-African-American platoon into the jungles of Southeast Asia. (HS)

Forever by Judy Blume. Katherine thinks that the time has come for her and her boyfriend Michael to take the next step in their relationship. (HS)

Freak the Mighty by Rodman Philbrick. An unlikely friendship develops between Max, a giant of a boy, and Freak, a genius afflicted with physical limitations. (INT/MS)

Gathering Blue by Lois Lowry. In this companion novel to *The Giver,* Kira is taken in by the Grand Council and given an important task: she is to embroider the robe of The Singer. Again, evil things are occurring just beneath the surface of Kira's society. (MS)

The Giver by Lois Lowry. Jonas's society appears perfect on the surface. However, there is more going on than Jonas ever expected until he becomes the Receiver of Memory for his people. (MS)

Go Ask Alice edited by Beatrice Sparks. When Alice is slipped a drug at a party, her descent into the world of drug use and abuse begins. This classic novel was written by a psychologist as a warning to teen readers. (HS)

Harry Potter and the Sorcerer's Stone and sequels by J. K. Rowling. Harry and his adventures at Hogwarts School for Wizardry have won the hearts of millions of fans all around the world. (INT/MS/HS)

Hatchet by Gary Paulsen. Brian Robeson is on the way to see his father when the pilot of the small plane in which he is riding suffers a heart attack and the plane crashes in the wilderness. Several sequels. (MS)

Holes by Louis Sachar. Stanley Yelnats, he of the palindrome name, is sent to Camp Green Lake when he is wrongfully convicted of stealing the sneakers of a famous ballplayer. There he "unearths" a mystery about buried treasure. (INT/MS)

I Am the Cheese by Robert Cormier. Adam Farmer finds himself under interrogation and house arrest. Can he escape? (HS)

Ironman by Chris Crutcher. Bo Brewster wants to compete as an adult in the Ironman Triathlon. There are many obstacles, not the least of which is his own father. (HS)

Jacob Have I Loved by Katherine Paterson. Two sisters, Louise and Caroline, have a turbulent relationship. Louise looks back on her childhood memories in an attempt to discover the cause of her intense jealousy. (MS/HS)

Make Lemonade by Virginia Euwer Wolff. LaVaughn begins to babysit the two small children of Jolly, a teen mother who has a host of troubles. (MS)

Maniac Magee by Jerry Spinelli. Jeffrey "Maniac" Magee unites the two ends of a small town with his antics. (INT/MS)

Maus: A Survivor's Tale by Art Spiegelman. 2 vols. This graphic novel tells of Spiegelman's father's experiences in a concentration camp during World War II. (HS)

Monster by Walter Dean Myers. Sixteen-year-old Steve is accused of being the lookout for a robbery turned homicide. He avows he is innocent. His trial is told as if it were a movie script being written by Steve. (HS)

The Moves Make the Man by Bruce Brooks. Jerome and Bix make for unlikely friends in this story of friendship, family, and faking. (MS)

Nightjohn by Gary Paulsen. Sarny is a young slave girl taught to read by the newest slave on the plantation, John. She must keep her education secret to protect them both. (MS)

Nothing but the Truth by Avi. Philip is suspended from school. He will tell you that the reason he is suspended is that he was being patriotic. Is he telling the whole truth? (MS)

Out of the Dust by Karen Hesse. Billie Jo's life could not be dustier. A fire causes her to lose her mother as well as the use of her hands. Somehow she must rise from the ashes of her life. (MS)

The Outsiders by S. E. Hinton. The Socs and the Greasers battle against one another. (MS/HS)

The Pigman by Paul Zindel. John and Lorraine adopt Mr. Pignati, an elderly gentleman they meet while making prank phone calls. He becomes a friend and mentor. (HS)

Roll of Thunder, Hear My Cry by Mildred Taylor. The Logan family is the focus of this story set in Mississippi in the 1930s. (INT/MS)

Rules of the Road by Joan Bauer. Jenna Boller is hired to drive Mrs. Gladstone across country for the summer. Along the way, she will learn a lot about shoes and about life. (MS/HS)

Running Loose by Chris Crutcher. Louie Banks is thrown off the football team for refusing to make a cheap hit. Now his perfect life is falling apart a little piece at a time. (HS)

Shiloh by Phyllis Reynolds Naylor. When one of Judd Travers's dogs escapes and finds his way into Marty Preston's life, he would do anything to keep "Shiloh." (INT/MS)

Sixteen, edited by Donald R. Gallo. This collection features sixteen stories written by YA authors such as Richard Peck and Ouida Sebestyen. (MS)

Speak by Laurie Halse Anderson. Shunned by her peers, Melinda must find her voice and warn her best friend about the dangerous young man she is dating. (HS)

Stargirl by Jerry Spinelli. Leo is smitten when Stargirl, a new student, enters the drab world of Mica High School. (HS)

Staying Fat for Sarah Byrnes by Chris Crutcher. Moby, an overweight young man, cares what happens to Sarah Byrnes, a young girl horribly disfigured in what people assume was a kitchen accident. (HS)

Swallowing Stones by Joyce McDonald. Seventeen-year-old Michael fires a shot into the air from a rifle given to him for his birthday. Later he learns that his bullet killed a man working on his roof. What does he do now? (HS)

Tangerine by Edward Bloor. Paul is haunted by the memory of how his eyesight became so damaged. His older brother has played some sort of role, he is certain. (MS)

The Watsons Go to Birmingham—1963 by Christopher Paul Curtis. The weird Watsons travel from Michigan to Alabama during one fateful winter. (INT/MS)

Weetzie Bat by Francesca Lia Block. Weetzie, Dirk, and Grandma Fifi redefine what it means to be a family. (HS)

Where the Red Fern Grows by Wilson Rawls. Billy loves his two coon dogs, Old Dan and Little Ann. Their loss is almost more than he can bear. (INT/MS)

Z for Zachariah by Robert O'Brien. This story centers on life after a nuclear holocaust. (MS)

Books to Motivate Reluctant Readers

This is the list of books Lois Buckman and I collected for our Student Teacher Online Mentoring Project (STOMP) over the past ten years.

Anderson, Laurie Halse. *Speak*. Melinda is thrilled to be at a party for high school students since she has not even begun her freshman year. Then, the unspeakable happens, and Melinda does not know how to get help, how to tell others what has happened to her. (MS/HS)

Avi. *Nothing but the Truth*. Phillip tells his parents that he has been suspended from school for simply being too patriotic. Will the full truth ever surface? (INT/MS)

Bloor, Edward. *Tangerine*. Paul's older brother is a gifted athlete. The family has made many sacrifices for Eric in hopes he will obtain an athletic scholarship and play college ball. Paul may have made the greatest sacrifice of them all. (MS/HS)

Bode, Janet. *Hard Time*. This book provides a real life look at the victims and perpetrators of juvenile crime. (MS/HS)

Bode, Janet. *Heartbreak and Roses*. Teens in love is the focus of this nonfiction book. Bode allows teens to talk about abusive relationships, mixed-race relationships, and all the other trials and traumas of love during adolescence. (HS)

Brashares, Ann. *Sisterhood of the Traveling Pants*. A pair of magical jeans unite a group of friends separated for an entire summer. (MS/HS)

Carter, Alden. *Between a Rock and a Hard Place*. Mark and his cousin Randy are thrown together for a weekend adventure in canoeing. Randy is diabetic and, at first, uses this as an excuse to get out of work. When Randy's supplies are lost overboard, though, the situation becomes more grave. This survival and adventure story pushes the boundaries of the genre. (MS/HS)

Coman, Carolyn. *Many Stones*. As Berry travels with her father to South Africa to the memorial service of her sister who was murdered, her relationship with her father strengthens. (HS)

Cooney, Caroline. *Driver's Ed*. Remy, Morgan, and Nickie steal a stop sign as a lark. They didn't realize what could happen until that night a woman, new to the neighborhood, drives through the intersection, is hit by a cement truck, and killed. Wracked with guilt, they are torn whether to tell or not. (MS/HS)

Cooney, Caroline. *Flash Fire*. If you had only moments to decide what could be salvaged before your house was consumed by fire, what would you save? That is the situation facing a group of kids home from school alone when a wildfire enters their normally quiet community. (MS)

Cormier, Robert. *We All Fall Down*. When Jane and her family come home, they find the house trashed and her sister in a coma. Later, Jane takes comfort from Buddy and falls in love with him, unaware that he is one of the vandals. (HS)

Couloumbis, Audrey. *Getting Close to Baby*. Willi Jo and Little Sister are staying with their aunt after the death of their baby sister. One day Willi Jo goes up on the roof and stays there. If she comes down, she will have to explain what she was doing there, and she really doesn't know what her feelings are. (INT/MS)

Couloumbis, Audrey. *Say Yes*. When Casey wakes up one morning to find her stepmother missing, she will do whatever she has to so she can survive on her own. (MS)

Curtis, Christopher Paul. *The Watsons Go to Birmingham—1963*. Kenny watches his older brother making one wrong decision after another until his parents say that is it and they pile into the car and go from Flint, Michigan, to Birmingham so his grandmother can straighten him out. Life is much different and dangerous in Birmingham for this African-American family. (INT/MS)

De Vries, Anke. *Bruises*. This is an intense novel that examines the life of an abused teen. Judith's mother often beats her. Judith has learned how to hide her bruises from authorities. When Michael enters her life, he offers her a means of escape. Can she reach out to someone in trust? (MS/HS)

Ewing, Lynne. *Drive-By*. When Tito's brother is killed in a drive-by, he realizes that the brother he idolized was involved in a gang. (MS)

Gallo, Donald R., ed. *Ultimate Sports*. This story collection, featuring works by prominent YA authors, looks at a variety of themes and issues related to sports. (MS/HS)

Glenn, Mel. *Who Killed Mr. Chippendale?* A mystery in poetry follows the murder of a high school English teacher. Who killed the teacher, and why? (MS/HS)

Hautman, Pete. *Stone Cold*. Denn plays one hand of poker and he is hooked. He is a natural and can tell what his opponents are thinking, so he never loses. He becomes so enthralled that he quits school, doesn't see his family, loses his friends. Ultimately, his life becomes one card game after another. (HS)

Holt, Kimberly Willis. *Dancing in Cadillac Light*. Sometimes you can get lost in a family. Eleven-year-old Jaynell finds solace in sitting in one of the abandoned cars in the junkyard as she pretends to drive away from her troubles. She is overjoyed when her grandfather buys a car and allows her to drive in the empty fields near her home. (MS)

Holt, Kimberly Willis. *When Zachary Beaver Came to Town*. Toby expects the summer to be the same as all the rest until the fattest boy in the world comes to his small Texas town. (MS)

Klass, David. *Danger Zone*. When Jimmy Doyle joined the teen "dream team" that was predominantly African-American, he wasn't prepared for the lessons he would learn. Racism and prejudice had to be dealt with before they could be a real team. (HS)

Klass, David. *You Don't Know Me*. When John's mother is home, her boyfriend treats John with kindness. In her absence, though, John is subjected to physical and verbal abuse. (MS/HS)

Korman, Gordon. *No More Dead Dogs*. Wallace has vowed never to read another dead dog book again. His new English teacher has other plans. (MS)

Korman, Gordon. *Son of the Mob*. Vince's dad is a mobster. For Vince, that means all sorts of complications in life including a trussed-up body in the trunk of Vince's car on his first date. (MS/HS)

Korman, Gordon, and Bernice Korman. *The D-Poems of Jeremy Bloom*. When the hapless Jeremy oversleeps the first day of school, he is forced to sign up for an elective he did not want. Jeremy realizes his mistake when he shows up for pottery class and discovers it is, in reality, a poetry class. (MS)

Levy, Elizabeth. *The Drowned.* Lily is spending the summer with her aunt and needs to earn some money. She decides to take groups of people on a tour of the haunted houses in Atlantic City. The last house on the tour proves to be almost the death of Lily. (MS)

Lowry, Lois. *The Giver.* In this haunting tale of a future society, Jonas learns that beneath the surface there is true evil in his world. He must find a way out before he is "released." (MS)

Lynch, Chris. *Slot Machine.* Elvin Bishop is not having any fun at summer sports camp. He is a fat kid who is decidedly unathletic. (MS)

Martinez, Victor. *Parrot in the Oven.* Manny's life is one full of turmoil at home and at school. (HS)

Myers, Walter Dean. *Monster.* Steve is in a battle for his life as he stands accused of participating in a robbery turned homicide. Will anyone believe he is innocent? (MS/HS)

Nixon, Joan Lowery. *Shadowmaker.* When Katie's mother, an investigative reporter, decides to go to a small town in order to find quiet to write her book, Katie had to go along. Instead of quiet, they are terrorized one night by some townspeople who are willing to murder to keep their secret about the chemical waste being put into the river. (MS)

Nixon, Joan Lowery. *Spirit Seeker.* Holly will do all that she can to help her friend Cody, who is accused of killing his parent, even though it may mean going against her father, who is a police detective on the case. (MS)

Nixon, Joan Lowery. *The Weekend Was Murder.* A weekend murder game becomes frighteningly real for Liz when she discovers an actual body. (MS)

Nixon, Joan Lowery. *Whispers from the Dead.* After Sarah nearly drowns, she seems haunted by the incident. Her father accepts a transfer, thinking new surroundings

would be good for her, but when Sarah enters the house, she is the only one who knows that a horrible murder has taken place there. (MS)

Nixon, Joan Lowery. *Don't Scream.* When two new good-looking boys enter her school, Jess is immediately attracted to them, but something isn't quite right. Who are they, and why are they suddenly at her school? Jess is determine to find the answer regardless of her own safety. (MS)

Nixon, Joan Lowery. *Kidnapping of Christina Lattimore.* When Christina is kidnapped and being held for ransom, her family thinks that she is an accomplice because she desperately wants to go on a trip to Florida and her father said no. (MS)

Nixon, Joan Lowery. *The Other Side of Dark.* Stacy awakens after being in a coma for four years. Will she be able to identify the person who attacked her and killed her mother? (MS)

Nixon, Joan Lowery. *The Séance.* When a group of girls are holding a séance, they hear a scream. They turn on the lights to discover that one of the girls, Sara, is missing. The next morning police find her body. What will happen to the others involved in this séance? (MS)

Nixon, Joan Lowery. *Search for the Shadowman.* While doing a school assignment, Andy discovers the name Coley Joe in the family Bible, an outcast that no one wants to talk about. Andy is determined to clear his ancestor's name. (INT/MS)

Paulsen, Gary. *The Glass Café.* When a young man enters the drawing of a woman in an art contest, he sets off a chain of events that lead to all sorts of confrontation. The subtitle of the book says it all: *Or the Stripper and the State: How My Mother Started a War with the System and Made Us Kind of Rich and a Little Bit Famous.* (MS)

Paulsen, Gary. *Harris and Me.* Harris takes advantage of his cousin, who has never been on a farm. (INT/MS)

Paulsen, Gary. *How Angel Peterson Got His Name, and Other Outrageous Tales About Extreme Sports*. Basically, all these stories could start with the same phrase: it seemed like a good idea at the time. These short and wildly humorous stories make for excellent read-alouds. (INT/MS)

Paulsen, Gary. *The Schernoff Discoveries*. Schernoff is, well, he's a science geek. His experiments place Harold and Gary in situations fraught with danger but always resulting in hilarious consequences. (INT/MS)

Paulsen, Gary. *Woodsong*. This slice-of-life autobiography tells of Paulsen's life in the woods. (MS)

Rowling, J. K. *Harry Potter and the Sorcerer's Stone*. Harry is whisked away by Hagrid for five glorious years of adventure at the Hogwarts School of Wizardry. (INT/MS/HS)

Sleator, William. *Interstellar Pig*. Barney's summer becomes much more interesting when he starts to play the board game with his unusual neighbors who turn out to be aliens. (HS)

Sleator, William. *Others See Us*. Jared discovers that he and his grandmother are both able to read the minds of others. This power carries with it some terrible responsibilities. (MS)

Spinelli, Jerry. *Stargirl*. When Stargirl shows up at Mica High School and stands on the table in the cafeteria during lunch, playing her ukulele and singing, Leo knows things will never be the same. (HS)

Tashjian, Janet. *Multiple Choice*. Monica has a hard time making decisions because she is a perfectionist, and to help control her obsessive behavior she invents a multiple-choice game that will help her make a quick decision. She rolls the dice and has to accept what it says even if it means such things as wearing her pajamas to school. (MS/HS)

Thomas, Rob. *Green Thumb*. Grady wins the national science fair for the second year in a row, and his notoriety brings him an offer to work on a rain-forest project in the Amazon region. The rain-forest has been genetically engineered and has grown to full size in just a few years. Grady notices that there is not a sound in the forest. Where are the birds, insects, and animals? (MS)

Thomas, Rob. *Rats Saw God*. Steve is a National Merit semifinalist and is failing senior English. His counselor offers him one chance to avoid summer school. Steve is willing to grab on to anything at this point. (HS)

Wolff, Virginia Euwer. *Make Lemonade*. LaVaughn is babysitting to make some money for her college fund. However, she soon learns that Jolly needs much more help than she can provide. (MS)

Yolen, Jane. *The Devil's Arithmetic*. Hannah didn't want to go to her grandparents for Passover because she was tired of hearing about how bad it was during the Holocaust. When she opens the door for Elijah during the seder ceremony, she finds herself in Poland during 1942. When she is returned to the seder table, she knows now why it is important to remember the past. (MS)

Zindel, Paul. *The Doom Stone*. Jackson goes to visit his aunt who is on an anthropological dig at Stonehenge. He is fascinated by the large stones. One day he sees someone being attacked by what can only be described as a beast, and concerned for his aunt's safety, he sets out to try to destroy the creature. (MS)

Zindel, Paul. *Loch*. Luke discovers an ancient species of pleiosaur living in the waters his father is exploring for a relative to the Loch Ness Monster. (MS)

Zindel, Paul. *Rats*. What would happen if a group of rats infiltrated the city sewer system looking for revenge? (MS)

Picture Books for Older Readers

Although I suggest ways in which to use each book in the curriculum, sometimes the simple act of reading the book is sufficient. Do not make each book the target of a lesson plan, or you will diminish the effectiveness of using picture books with older readers. Note that levels are omitted here as most of these books work well from fourth to twelfth grade.

Ada, Alma Flor. *Dear Peter Rabbit.* This book combines several fairy tales into one hilarious story told through letters between the main characters. Also by this author: *Yours Truly, Goldilocks* and *With Love, Little Red Hen.* Perfect for teaching kids about writing letters and about how one story can be told through multiple perspectives.

Appelt, Kathi. *Bubba and Beau.* Bubba is a redneck baby and Beau is a red tic hound. Together, the two grow to love one another and their precious blankie. The sequel is *Bubba and Beau Go Night-Night.* Use this book to teach kids about voice and dialect.

Appelt, Kathi. *Elephants Aloft.* A nearly wordless or textless picture book uses prepositions to show the travels of an Asian and an African elephant. Look for the hidden peanut in each illustration. Great for having kids write sentences using prepositions and prepositional phrases.

Appelt, Kathi. *Bayou Lullaby.* Gentle poetic rhythms describe the bayou at the close of day. Terrific to teach about word choice, rhythm, and rhyme.

Baylor, Byrd. *Everybody Needs a Rock.* This prose poem talks about the rules for finding a special rock. Use this book to teach kids that poems do not have to rhyme. Other books by this author: *I'm in Charge of Celebrations, The Best Place in the World,* and *When Clay Sings.*

Bridges, Ruby. *Through My Eyes.* Bridges's first-person narrative recounts her days as the sole student in her kindergarten classroom when other parents refused to allow their children to attend class with a black student. Photographs and sidebars illuminate this troubled time in our history.

Brown, Ruth. *The World That Jack Built.* A futuristic version of the cumulative rhyme shows what happens when the environment in Jack's town begins to pollute the community.

Bunting, Eve. *Terrible Things.* An allegory for the Holocaust, this story is set in a forest and talks about what happens when one species fails to protect another from the "terrible things." History teachers will appreciate the references to the Holocaust, but the strength of the book lies in making clear what an allegory is.

Childs, Lauren. *That Pesky Rat.* A rat wants to be adopted and live as a pet. Though he advertises, most folks prefer more normal pets. Language use is rich. Also good for teaching about different levels of humor and about empathy.

Coerr, Eleanor. *Sadako and the Thousand Paper Cranes.* Based on a true story, this picture book version is illustrated by Ed Young. The dropping of the bomb on Hiroshima has consequences for its residents many years later.

Cronin, Doreen. *Click, Clack, Moo, Cows That Type.* The cows demand electric blankets to keep warm at night in a letter to Farmer Brown. Keeping writing pointed is a great lesson with this book. A sequel is *Giggle, Giggle, Quack.*

Crummel, Susan Stevens. *Jackalope.* Ever heard of the jackalope and how it came into being? Here is the tall tale behind this legendary creature. Use this to teach tall tale writing or hyperbole as a figurative device. Also by this author: *And the Dish Ran Away with the Spoon.*

Denim, Sue. *The Dumb Bunnies.* Some familiar folktales in the antics of Poppa, Momma, and Baby Bunny. Sequels include *Make Way for Dumb Bunnies* and *The Dumb Bunnies' Easter.*

Fanelli, Sara. *My Map Book.* Maps can be of locations and other more unusual places. Fanelli's book includes maps of her heart and stomach.

Feelings, Tom. *The Middle Passage.* The kidnapping and transport of slaves from Africa to America is the topic for this incredibly powerful picture book.

Frasier, Debra. *Miss Alaineus: A Vocabulary Disaster.* When Sage misses class, a friend gives her the spelling list. Sage mistakes *miscellaneous* for *Miss Alaineus* with hilarious results. Good for teaching homonymns, homophones, and homographs as well as vocabulary.

Garland, Sherry. *The Lotus Seed.* A family flees Vietnam, taking only the barest of necessities. When a lotus seed blooms in the new country, it holds out hope for a new beginning. This simple story can teach kids about word choice and spareness in writing. Also by this author: *My Father's Boat* and *I Never Knew Your Name.*

Howitt, Mary. *The Spider and the Fly.* This Caldecott honor book brings an old poem to life with an interesting twist at the end. Use to teach kids about limited point of view in a story.

Janeczko, Paul. *A Poke in the I.* Chris Raschka illustrates this collection of concrete poems.

Keller, Laurie. *Arnie the Doughnut.* Arnie the doughnut is thrilled to be purchased and to leave the confines of the display case. However, when he learns he is to be eaten, he is appalled. How could someone even consider ending his too short life? Point of view is an easy lesson with this funny picture book.

Keller, Laurie. *The Scrambled States of America.* The states have a meeting and decide to swap places. Things do not work out smoothly. Tell geography teachers about this one.

Ketteman, Helen. *Bubba, the Cowboy Prince.* This is a Texas version of *Cinderella.*

Leedy, Loreen. *Mapping Penny's World.* A good companion to *My Map Book,* this nonfiction selection is a great book for math class, too.

Lester, Julius. *From Slave Ship to Freedom Road.* Lester chronicles the history of African-Americans in the United States. Report writing could be the focus of using this book.

Lester, Julius. *What a Truly Cool World.* Here is a version of the creation story with humor and attitude. Meet God and his wife, Irene, as they set out to make a truly cool world. Pair this with other creation stories such as those found in Virginia Hamilton's *In the Beginning.*

Lester, Julius. *Sam and the Tigers.* This update of *Little Black Sambo* shows how to outwit forces seemingly beyond your control.

Could be used for a lesson in how to use repetitive language for emphasis.

Lewis, J. Patrick. *Arithmetickle*. Here are poems to use in math class. A good way to show kids how to write word problems that are not boring, too.

Lewis, J. Patrick. *Doodle Dandies*. Concrete poems are the focus of this picture book.

Locker, Thomas. *Sky Tree*. A science lesson along with magnificent oil paintings of the various phases in the life of a tree make this book perfect for integration into a science classroom. The text contains both informational paragraphs as well as lyrical poems about the tree. Also by the author: *Cloud Dance*.

Martin, Bill. *I Pledge Allegiance*. Martin takes each word in the pledge and defines it with concrete examples. Illustrations by Chris Raschka elaborate the simple text.

Medina, Tony. *Love to Langston*. Poems written about the life of Langston Hughes in the styles of Hughes are an excellent way to demonstrate style to kids.

Miller, William. *Tituba*. Before sharing *The Crucible* with your students, use this simple picture book to give them a back story of the slave woman accused of conjuring the devil.

Munro, Roxie. *The Inside-Outside Book of Texas*. Part of a series, this book highlights the flora, fauna, climate, geography, and major cities of Texas. It can readily be used as a model for writing expository text.

Muth, Jon. *The Three Questions*. Based on a story by Tolstoy, this book can be used to show students how to retell a story in simple language.

Myers, Christopher. *Wings*. This is a retelling of the Daedalus and Icarus story.

Myers, Walter Dean. *Patrol*. A young soldier begins to see his enemy as a real person. This could be used as a prereading activity for "The War Prayer" by Mark Twain or Hemingway's *A Farewell to Arms*.

Perdomo, Willie. *Visiting Langston*. A trip to the residence of Langston Hughes in Harlem is the beginning of a young girl's adventure to the heart and soul of one of her favorite writers. Use in connection with a study of Hughes and his writing.

Pilkey, Dav. *Dog Breath*. Lots of tongue-in-cheek word play as the Tosis family seeks a cure for the bad breath of their dog, Hally.

Polacco, Patricia. *Pink and Say*. Polacco tells of two young men brought together by the Civil War. Both end up in Andersonville Prison, where many prisoners perished. Beginning a unit on the Civil War or just war in general with this book will help students enter the historical period more easily.

Polacco, Patricia. *The Bee Tree*. Reading can be tasty, a young girl discovers thanks to the help of her grandfather. Teaches about using illusion and allegory.

Radunsky, Vladimir. *Manneken Pis: A Simple Story of a Boy Who Peed on a War*. Based on the story behind a statue in Brussels, this book carries on the tradition of the folk hero, a little, seemingly powerless individual, who can change things greatly by simple acts.

Rappaport, Doreen. *Martin's Big Words*. This account of the life of Martin Luther King Jr., told in two levels of text, his own words and those of the author, demonstrates good expository writing techniques.

Raschka, Chris. *Mysterious Thelonious*. Rhythmic text bounces across the page in the be-bop rhythm of Thelonius Monk. Word choice could be the focus of this lesson.

Rohmann, Eric. *Time Flies*. This textless book traces some of the important events in history. Great for social studies integration as well as to show the power of illustration for a visual literacy lesson.

Scieszka, Jon. *Squids Will Be Squids*. Modern-day retellings of fables à la Aesop. You could also pair this with Anno's *Aesop and Fables Aesop Never Wrote but Robert Kraus Did* and *Fables* by Arnold Lobel. Also by this author: *The True Story of the Three Little Pigs, The Book That Jack Wrote*, and *Math Curse*.

Sierra, Judy. *Monster Goose.* Rhymes in the tradition of Mother Goose but with much more humor. Be certain to share stories behind the Mother Goose rhymes with *The Annotated Mother Goose.*

St. George, Judith. *So You Want to Be President?* Delightful caricatures of each of the presidents along with interesting facts and tidbits show that report writing need not be boring. Also by this author: *So You Want to Be an Inventor?*

Stanley, Diane. *Rumpelstiltskin's Daughter.* This feminist version of the classic fairy tale has a nice surprise ending as well.

Teague, Mark. *Dear Mrs. Larue: Letters from Obedience School.* A dog writes letters from obedience school indicating that things do not always turn out as expected. Use to teach irony.

Thomas, Velma Maia. *Lest We Forget: The Passage from Africa to Slavery and Emancipation.* Here is a movable book that provides information about the freeing of the slaves. Not a simple pop-up, its appearance belies the gravity of the writing.

Van Allsburg, Chris. *The Mysteries of Harris Burdick.* A single illustration, title, and caption are all that remain of the mysterious work of (fictitious) Harris Burdick. These make ideal story starters and the book is available in Big Book format as well.

Wiesner, David. *The Three Pigs.* There are many ways of telling the same story, as this version of a familiar classic proves. Pair this with Scieszka's *The True Story of the Three Little Pigs* for an interesting piece of classificatory writing.

Wild, Margaret. *Let The Celebrations Begin.* Set in a concentration camp at the end of World War II, this book tells of ladies who begin to make stuffed toys for the children who have never known a life outside of their hut. Bring history to life and make it real with this moving picture book.

Easy Reading

Anderson, Laurie Halse. *Speak*. Melinda is thrilled to be at a party for high school students since she has not even begun her freshman year. Then the unspeakable happens, and Melinda does not know how to get help, how to tell others what has happened to her. (MS/HS)

Appelt, Kathi. *Kissing Tennessee and Other Stories from the Stardust Dance*. During a dance eighth-graders at a junior high are filled with hope. This story collection tells of the fate of a handful of the people at the dance. (MS/HS)

Atkins, Catherine. *When Jeff Comes Home*. Jeff, kidnapped while at a rest stop by a pedophile when he was thirteen, now is sixteen and back but won't talk about anything that happened to him. (MS)

Atwater-Rhodes, Amelia. *Demon in My View*. Jessica is writing a book about vampires, and to her astonishment, one of her characters shows up in her class. (MS)

Atwater-Rhodes, Amelia. *In the Forests of the Night*. Risika has been a vampire for three hundred years and is tired of her life. Things change when she finds a black rose on her pillow. (MS)

Avi. *Wolf Rider*. When Andy gets the wrong number, the caller admits to killing someone. Andy wants to find out what really happened and possibly prevent a murder. (MS)

Bechard, Margaret. *Hanging on to Max*. When his girlfriend had a baby, Sam fights for

custody because he is sure that he can raise his son while still in high school. He soon learns that babies require a great deal of care. (HS)

Blume, Judy. *Tiger Eyes*. Davey is devastated when her father is killed during a robbery. She goes with her mother and younger brother to New Mexico, where she meets Wolf, who helps her with her grief. (HS)

Cabot, Meg. *All American Girl*. Samantha, in love with her sister's boyfriend, saves the President's life and becomes famous. That should be good news, but the worst thing is that the President's son has a crush on her. (HS)

Cart, Michael, ed. *Love and Sex*. Ten original stories about teenage love and romance form this frank collection. (HS)

Cohn, Rachel. *Gingerbread*. After being kicked out of boarding school, Cyd stays with her mother for six months and then is shipped to her biological father. She just can't find a place she thinks she belongs. (HS)

Cohn, Rachel. *The Steps*. Since both of her parents have remarried, Annabel has too many stepbrothers and stepsisters. When she goes to visit her father, she hopes to get him to come back home even though he is remarried and his wife is expecting a baby. (MS)

Cole, Brock. *Goats*. Howie and Laura are the goats at camp. As the ultimate joke, they are stripped naked and put on an island.

They decide to fight back, and when the counselors come to get them the next morning, they are gone. (MS)

Cormier, Robert. *The Rag and Bone Shop*. Jason was the last one to see the little girl alive. The police are sure that he beat her to death, so they bring in an expert to get a confession out of him. (HS)

Cormier, Robert. *In the Middle of the Night*. Twenty-five years ago, there was a fire in the movie theater where Danny's father worked. Twenty-two children were killed, a tragedy that his father can't recover from. Suddenly there are mysterious phone calls and Danny decides to meet the caller. (MS/HS)

Curtis, Christopher Paul. *The Watsons Go to Birmimgham—1963*. Kenny watches his older brother making one wrong decision after another until his parents say that is it and they pile into the car and go from Flint, Michigan, to Birmingham so his grandmother can straighten him out. Life is much different and dangerous in Birmingham for this African-American family. (INT/MS)

Danziger, Paula, and Ann M. Martin. *P. S. Longer Letter Later*. Now that they are separated, Elizabeth and Tara*Star keep in touch via letters. Sequel is *Snail Mail No More*. (INT/MS)

Eberhardt, Thom. *Rat Boys*. Two girls find a magic ring and turn two rats into boys so they will have dates for the dance (MS/HS)

Ewing, Lynne. *Drive-By*. When Tito's brother is killed in a drive-by, he realizes that the brother he idolized was involved in a gang. (MS)

Flinn, Alex. *Breathing Underwater*. When Nick's girlfriend tries out for the school's talent show after he said she couldn't, he slaps her in a moment of uncontrolled anger. He is sentenced to attend violence management classes, but he thinks he doesn't belong there. (HS)

Flinn, Alex. *Breaking Point*. Paul is a scholarship student at a snobby school and the victim of many cruel jokes until Charlie befriends him. Charlie asks Paul to hack into the school computers and change his grade. This act is just the beginning of the price Paul must pay for Charlie's friendship. (HS)

Frank, E. R. *America*. After America tries to commit suicide, he is sent to a resident facility to get the help he so desperately needs and to find out who he is. (HS)

Gantos, Jack. *Joey Pigza Loses Control*. Joey goes to visit his father, who says if Joey really wanted to, he would do without his medication. He throws it down the toilet, and Joey soon feels himself beginning to lose control. Before it is too late, he calls his mother to come and get him. (MS)

Gantos, Jack. *Joey Pigza Swallowed the Key*. Joey is out of control in school and often at home because his medication doesn't work to control his attention deficit/hyperactivity disorder. (MS)

Giles, Gail. *Dead Girls Don't Write Letters*. Since Jazz died a year before in a terrible fire, Sunny has had to take care of her mother, who is still completely grief-stricken. One day a letter arrives from someone claiming to be Jazz, saying she is coming home to explain things. (HS)

Giles, Gail. *Shattering Glass*. Simon Glass is picked on all the time until a campaign is started to make him the Class Favorite. As he gains popularity, a darker side of him is shown. (HS)

Glenn, Mel. *Foreign Exchange*. An exchange program where inner-city high school students visit country students seems like a good idea until a pretty girl with long beautiful blond hair is found murdered. She was last seen in a rowboat with an African-American exchange student, and the police automatically think he is the killer. (MS/HS)

Haddix, Margaret Peterson. *Among the Betrayed*. This is the third in the series that began with *Among the Hidden*. When Nina is arrested by the Population Police, she is told that she will be executed unless she can find three other "third" children and turn in who has been hiding them. (INT/MS)

Haddix, Margaret Peterson. *Among the Impostors.* This is the second installment, following *Among the Hidden,* and Luke, a third child, has been sent to a special school where he can finally act like everyone else. Even here he lives in fear of being caught by the Population Police. (INT/MS)

Horowitz, Anthony. *Point Blank.* Alex is called into service by the government to find out why suddenly these terrible students have become perfect in all ways. He will be entering the school as a student to see if he can find out what is being done to these boys. (MS)

Horowitz, Anthony. *Stormbreaker.* Alex is once again called on to help his government, this time searching for his uncle's killer. (MS)

Korman, Gordon. *No More Dead Dogs.* For a book report Wallace writes a paragraph about how much he hates the book. The book turns out to be the teacher's favorite, and Wallace is given detention until he writes a "real" report. (MS)

Korman, Gordon. *Son of the Mob.* Vince's dad is a mobster. For Vince, that means all sorts of complications in life, including a trussed-up body in the trunk of Vince's car on his first date. (MS/HS)

Lester, Julius. *When Dad Killed Mom.* Jeremy and his younger sister Jenna try to understand why their father killed their mother. (MS/HS)

Lowry, Lois. *Number the Stars.* When the Danish resistance learned that the Nazis were taking Jews to their death, they managed to take seven thousand Jews to Sweden and safety. (INT/MS)

Mazer, Harry. *When the Phone Rang.* When Billy answers the phone call, it is the airline informing him that his parents were killed in a crash. Kevin, his older brother, drops out of college to take care of Billy and his sister, Lori, so they can stay together. (MS)

McCormack, Patricia. *Cut.* Callie can't stop mutilating herself. Whenever something upsets her, she feels an uncontrollable need to cut herself. (HS)

Myers, Walter Dean. *Fallen Angels.* Here is a gripping story about the violence and death in Vietnam. (HS)

Myers, Walter Dean. *Monster.* Steve is on trial for murder, but he says he just happened to be standing outside the store where the crime took place. Steve shares his thoughts and feelings though his journal and excerpts from the trial. (MS/HS)

Naylor, Phyllis Reynolds. *Jade Green.* After her mother dies, Jade goes to live with her uncle with the provision that she cannot bring anything green into the house. She thinks the small green frame with her mother's picture wouldn't matter, but she is dead wrong. (MS)

Neufeld, John. *Boys Lie.* Gina hates her body because she is so well developed. One day she is swimming in a local pool when a group of boys molest her. The humiliation overwhelms her. (HS)

Nixon, Joan Lowery. *The Séance.* When a group of girls are holding a séance they hear a scream. When they put on the lights, Sara is missing. The next morning the police find her body. (MS)

Paulsen, Gary. *Brian's Return.* Brian isn't happy with high school life, so he plans to return to the woods. (MS)

Paulsen, Gary. *Tracker.* John thinks that if the deer he is tracking lives so will his grandfather. (MS)

Peters, Julie Anne. *Define "Normal."* Antonia is assigned to do peer counseling to Jazz, who looks like a "druggie," but it is really Antonia who needs the help. (HS)

Pilkey, Dav. *The Adventures of Captain Underpants.* George and Harold always get in trouble. They reach their pinnacle when they hypnotize the principal and turn him into Captain Underpants. There are several books in the Captain Underpants series including *The Adventures of Super Diaper Baby.* (INT/MS)

Pinkwater, Daniel. *Fat Camp Commandos*. When sent to a fat camp, four "inmates" flee and hide out rather than face the lectures they would have to attend. They are determined to expose the owner of the camp as a fraud. (INT/MS)

Qualey, Marsha. *Close to a Killer*. Barrie works in her mother's hair salon, Killer Looks, a good name because the employees are all convicted murderers. When clients' homes are robbed while their hair is being done, business falls off. Two murders place the shop and its employees in real trouble. (MS/HS)

Rennison, Louise. *Knocked Out by My Nunga-Nungas*. In this sequel to *Angus, Thongs and Full Frontal Snogging*, Georgia is now the "Sex God's" girlfriend. Everything is great until she learns that her parents want to go to Scotland and ruin everything. (HS)

Schwartz, Alvin. Scary Stories series. From the escaped criminal with a hook for a hand to the poisoned wedding dress, these stories are chilling. (INT/MS/HS)

Sleator, William. *Rewind*. When Peter is upset, he runs into the road and is hit by a car and killed, but he wasn't supposed to die. He is given twenty-four hours to repeat the day and avoid being killed. Can he rewind his life? (MS)

Sparks, Beatrice, ed. *Go Ask Alice*. Alice feels life is difficult with her perfect parents and finds the solution in drugs. Once someone spikes her drink with LSD, her addiction starts. (HS)

Spinelli, Jerry. *Crash*. "Crash" is a bully and literally goes crashing through life. No matter what he does, he doesn't get the attention that he desperately wants and needs. (MS)

Strasser, Todd. *Give a Boy a Gun*. After two troubled boys use guns at school, other classmates, family, and police try to find out where they got the guns and why they felt they had to use violence. (MS/HS)

Tarbox, Katherine. *Katie.com*. Katie is planning to sneak away when she is on a high school trip so that she can meet the man she has been writing to on the Internet. She thought that he was twenty-seven, but he turns out to be a pedophile in his forties. (HS)

Tomey, Ingrid. *Nobody Else Has to Know*. Webber's grandfather takes the blame for a car accident which has seriously injured a little girl. (HS)

Trueman, Terry. *Stuck in Neutral*. Shawn has suffered from cerebral palsy, and he can no longer move or talk, but he can think, even though no one suspects that his mind is sharp. Shawn realizes that his father is planning to kill him. (MS/HS)

Walter, Virginia. *Making Up Megaboy*. One day, Robbie, age thirteen, gets a gun and shoots a convenience store clerk. Different people give their opinions as to why he did this horrible thing. (MS)

Werlin, Nancy. *The Killer's Cousin*. When David is acquitted for the death of his girlfriend, he goes to live with a cousin to finish his senior year. Some strange things begin to happen, and David becomes very apprehensive about the behavior of his eleven-year-old cousin. (HS)

Winick, Judd. *Pedro and Me*. This novel in graphics tells about Pedro Zamora, who was on MTV's Real World, and his struggle with AIDS and wanting to educate others about the disease. (HS)

Zindel, Paul. *Rats*. What would happen if a group of rats infiltrated the city sewer system looking for revenge? (MS)

Humor

Bauer, Joan. *Backwater.* Ivy Breedlove does not want to become a lawyer and join in the family tradition. She is, instead, interested in history, especially in the mysterious history of her own family. (HS)

Bauer, Joan. *Hope Was Here.* Hope's career as a waitress had led her in many interesting directions. However, none has been as different as her latest stint in the Land of the Lactose. (HS)

Bauer, Joan. *Rules of the Road.* Jenna Boller is hired to escort Mrs. Gladstone, owner of the shoe store chain that employs her. The job will make great changes in the lives of both women. (HS)

Bauer, Joan. *Stand Tall.* Tree, a seventh-grader, is torn between his divorced parents and their expectations of him. Tree has his own ideas about the path he should take in life. (MS)

Bauer, Joan. *Sticks.* Mickey wants to win the pool tournament held in his grandmother's pool hall. Several folks step in to help and perhaps the greatest help will be a lesson in geometry. (INT/MS)

Bauer, Joan. *Thwonk.* A. J. McCreary's life is turned inside out when her own personal Cupid offers to help her. Be careful what you wish for as it might come true. (MS/HS)

Cabot, Meg. *The Princess Diaries.* Mia discovers she is the heir to the throne. Now, her long-absent father returns and demands that Mia learn how to be a proper member of the royal family. Sequels include *Princess in the Spotlight* and *Princess in Love.* (MS)

Cabot, Meg. *All American Girl.* When Samantha Madison saves the life of the President of the United States, she is not prepared for how much her life will change, and not all of it for the better. (MS/HS)

Coville, Bruce. *Odder Than Ever.* This collection of short stories includes tales of the Stinky Princess and some killer biscuits. Also by this author: *Oddly Enough.* (MS)

Creech, Sharon. *Absolutely Normal Chaos.* Thirteen-year-old Mary Lou's diary entries tell of her chaotic life as one of five children. She rants about school reading, a visiting cousin, and all the other trials of her adolescent existence. (INT/MS)

Crutcher, Chris. *King of the Mild Frontier: An Ill-Advised Autobiography.* Crutcher talks frankly about his childhood and adolescence. (HS)

Curtis, Christopher Paul. *Bud, Not Buddy.* Bud is an orphan in search of the father he never knew. When he finds family, it is not quite what he expected. (MS)

Curtis, Christopher Paul. *The Watsons Go to Birmingham—1963.* The weird Watson family travels from Michigan to Alabama. Along the way they have several humorous escapades. (INT/MS)

Danziger, Paula. *This Place Has No Atmosphere.* Forced by her parents to go to a new lunar habitat, a teenager is at first more than resistant. Are there any cute boys in outer space? (MS)

Dunn, Mark. *Ella Minnow Pea.* This story, told entirely in letters, tells of the land of Nollop, a place where the letters of the alphabet are held sacred. (HS)

Fleischman, Paul. *A Fate Totally Worse Than Death.* This send-up of the generic teen horror novel is spot on. A gang of high school girls get their comeuppance from a group of women in a nursing home. (MS/HS)

Gantos, Jack. *Jack on the Tracks.* In this fourth book about Jack Henry, the hilarious escapades continue after Jack's family moved to a place alongside the railroad tracks. He makes new friends, keeps losing pets, and deals with his older sister and little brother. (INT/MS)

Gantos, Jack. *Jack's New Power.* When Jack is thirteen, his family moves to the Caribbean. This provides plenty of material for him to continue his uproarious tales. In one he is forced to face his deepest fear, in a second he cuts off his own wart, and in the third he falls in love and his mother is arrested for murder. (MS)

Gantos, Jack. *Jack's Black Book.* Jack Henry is in seventh grade, and he starts a journal. This is the beginning of his hilarious misadventures in school and at home. In *Heads or Tails* the stories continue, as his family begins moving around. (MS)

Gantos, Jack. *Joey Pigza Swallowed the Key.* Joey has trouble paying attention or controlling himself when his medication wears off. Consequently, he is always in trouble in school. From trying to sharpen his nails in a pencil sharpener to literally swallowing the house key that he wears on a string, Joey does it all and keeps acting weirder and weirder. (INT/MS)

Gantos, Jack. *Joey Pigza Loses Control.* In a sequel to *Joey Pigza Swallowed the Key,* Joey is under control when he goes to visit his father and smoking, oxygen-sniffing

grandmother. Joey is okay until his father says only wimps need medication and flushes Joey's ritalin patches down the toilet. (MS)

Gantos, Jack. *What Would Joey Do?* In the last of the Joey Pigza trilogy, Joey is sent to be home-schooled by a very religious neighbor. This could be a good thing, but the only other student in the school is a blind girl intent on making Joey's life miserable. (MS)

Gutman, Dan. *The Kid Who Ran for President.* Sixth-grader Judd Moon, egged on by his best friends, decides that a kid would make a great President of the United States. After he chooses a beautiful blond "First Babe" and an African-American as his running mate, the campaign begins. (INT/MS)

Hiaasen, Carl. *Hoot.* Roy, with Mullet Fingers and his sister Beatrice, tries to keep Mother Paula's All-American Pancake House from building on the site of nesting grounds of the burrowing owl. They will stop at nothing, including putting alligators in the port-a-potties. (MS)

Horvath, Polly. *Everything on a Waffle.* Primrose loves the local restaurant where everything including lasagna is served on a waffle. While waiting for her parents to be found after a boating mishap, she has some hilarious misadventures. (MS)

Howe, Norma. *The Adventures of the Blue Avenger.* After his father's death, David decides to change his name to Blue Avenger. Normally a quiet boy, when he puts on his costume, he becomes a super hero. He gains national prominence when he saves his principal from killer bees. He sets high goals and in the end reaches them. (HS)

Howe, Norma. *Blue Avenger Cracks the Code.* In this sequel to *The Adventures of the Blue Avenger,* he searches to find out who really wrote Shakespeare's plays, and along the way he has some hilarious adventures. (HS)

Korman, Gordon. *No More Dead Dogs.* Wallace cannot tell a lie. So when he is assigned a book report, he reports his true reactions to the book. Unfortunately, the book is the teacher's favorite, and Wallace is assigned detention. The detention is held at the play rehearsals of that same book. Wallace wreaks havoc until the entire story is changed. (MS)

Korman, Gordon. *Son of the Mob.* What can be worse than being the son of the mob leader? Vince finds out when he falls for the daughter of the FBI agent in charge of finding enough information to arrest his father. Also by this author: *Losing Joe's Place, No Coins, Please, Son of Interflux,* and *A Semester in the Life of a Garbage Bag.* (HS)

Levine, Gail Carson. *Cinderellis and the Glass Hill.* In this fractured fairy tale, Ellis wants approval of his older brothers, but they laugh at his inane inventions. He finally meets Marigold, who has been placed on a glass hill, and they live happily ever after. (INT/MS)

Lynch, Chris. *Extreme Elvin.* In the second book Elvin is now in ninth grade and still going through the angst of teenage years. One of his problems is that he has hemorrhoids. How can he get rid of them without anyone knowing? Of course, there is still the small matter of trying to find a girlfriend. (HS)

Lynch, Chris. *Slot Machine.* Elvin is sent to a sports camp the summer before high school, and since he is a big fat kid, he is automatically put on the football team. He has absolutely no athletic ability and so is hurt on the first play. They try him on every team until he discovers a secret society in the basement of the deserted library. (MS)

Nodelman, Perry. *Behaving Bradley.* Brad, a picked-on outcast, thinks that if the code of conduct in his school is changed, life will be different for him. (HS)

Paulsen, Gary. *Harris and Me.* When a city boy goes to spend the summer with his cousin in the country, he quickly learns about farm life through his mischievous tormentor, Harris. He learns such things as not to go in the pen when you are feeding pigs, not to jump from the hayloft, and to watch out for kicking cows. Revenge can be sweet. (INT/MS)

Paulsen, Gary. *The Schernoff Discoveries.* Harold Schernoff is a geek who has a theory about everything from how to date a girl to buying a car. Things don't always work out the way he plans, and there are hilarious results. (INT/MS)

Paulsen, Gary. *The Glass Café.* Tony often goes with his mother to the club where she works as a stripper and hangs out around the dressing room. He decides to paint some of the women for an art project. Some people think the art is pornographic, and others think it is amazingly good. Social Services gets involved, but they don't know what they are dealing with until they meet his very protective mother. (HS)

Paulsen, Gary. *How Angel Peterson Got His Name, and Other Outrageous Tales About Extreme Sports.* These are Paulsen's stories of growing up with boys who liked to outdo each other in sports. They would fight a bear, go down a waterfall in a barrel, and ski while being pulled by a fast moving car. Invariably, they do the stunts just a little wrong and the results are disastrous (and hilarious). (INT/MS)

Peck, Richard. *A Long Way from Chicago.* Joey and Mary Alice go to the country to visit their grandmother, where they are party to the schemes she plans to get even with members of her small community. Their escapades are as funny as they are outlandish. (MS)

Peck, Richard. *A Year Down Under.* In this book, which follows *A Long Way from Chicago,* Mary Alice has to go and stay with her grandmother by herself. Now she not only has to put up with her grandmother's schemes, but she has to attend school in this small town where the kids think she is the rich kid from Chicago. That is far from the truth. (MS)

Pilkey, Dav. *Captain Underpants and the Wrath of the Wicked Wedgie Woman.* In the fifth episode of the saga of the superhero Captain Underpants, our hero has to conquer the bionic-powered Wedgie Woman. In order to succeed he has to overcome his fear of spray starch. (INT/MS)

Pinkwater, Daniel. *Fat Camp Commandos.* Ralph and Sylvia are sent to a fat camp by their parents, but they escape with their new friend Mavis and hide out at her house for the summer. There they start a campaign to change people's attitudes to fat people. (INT/MS)

Rennison, Louise. *Angus, Thongs and Full Frontal Snogging.* Georgia keeps a journal where she writes about the angst of adolescence and her efforts to try to get the "Sex God" she is in love with to notice her, while interspersing everyday events, such as her bedwetting three-year-old sister and her vicious cat. Also by this author: *On the Bright Side, I'm Now the Girlfriend of a Sex God, Knocked Out by My Nunga-Nungas,* and *Running Around in My Nuddy Pants.* (HS)

Sleator, William. *Oddballs.* Dark secrets from the author's childhood are revealed in each hilarious chapter. From vicious car games to bathroom stunts, each event is memorable. (MS/HS)

Snicket, Lemony. *The Bad Beginning.* After the Baudelaire children find out that their parents have died in a fire, they are sent to live with Count Olaf, who is after the family fortune. The three children have to try to outwit him. There are nine books in this series with more to come. (INT/MS)

Spinelli, Jerry. *Who Put That Hair in My Toothbrush?* Between arguments, Megan and her older brother suffer through junior high school. (INT/MS)

Spinelli, Jerry. *Space Station Seventh Grade.* Jason tells all the woes he faces as a typical seventh-grader. (MS)

Spinelli, Jerry. *Crash.* "Crash" has spent years picking on Penn, but it isn't as much fun now that he is in seventh grade. "Crash" is the star of the football team and is popular, while Penn becomes a cheerleader. Still, "Crash" isn't satisfied. (HS)

Strasser, Todd. *How I Spent My Last Night on Earth.* The students of Time Zone High have been told that an asteroid will destroy planet earth in a mere 24 hours. Should they do everything they want during this time, or is it just an untrue rumor that started on the Internet? (HS)

Strasser, Todd. *Girl Gives Birth to Own from Date.* When Nicole needs to find a prom date quickly, she gives her longtime friend Chase a makeover. (HS)

Tashjian, Janet. *The Gospel According to Larry.* Josh, a high school student, starts a Web site where he takes on the persona of the prophet Larry who is against consumerism, particularly the obsession with celebrities. Everyone loves Larry, including Beth, his good friend, but Josh wants her to love the real him. (HS)

Thomas, Rob. *Green Thumb.* Grady has won the National Science Fair for two years and this gets him an offer to do a summer internship in a rain-forest. What the judges don't realize is that Grady is only thirteen. When he arrives, they give him menial jobs, but the more Grady watches and works on his own experiments, the more he is certain that something evil and dangerous is going on. (MS)

Thomas, Rob. *Rats Saw God.* In order to pass English and graduate, Josh has to write a hundred-page essay about his life. He takes the opportunity to look back at what went terribly wrong when he was living with his famous astronaut father in Texas. (HS)

Vande Velde, Vivian. *Never Trust a Dead Man.* Selwyn is falsely accused of murdering a rival suitor for his love's hand and is sentenced to be put in the burial cave until he dies. He's helped by a witch after he promises to be her servant. Unfortunately for them both, the witch tends to make mistakes in her charms. (INT/MS)

Vande Velde, Vivian. *Heir Apparent.* Giannine inadvertently gets stuck in a virtual reality game which the Citizens to Protect Our Children have tampered with. The only way she can get out alive is to win the game. However, she has a limited number of tries, and every time her character dies, she has to start again. (MS)

Wrede, Patricia. *Dealing with Dragons.* In the first of the Enchanted Forest Chronicles, Cimorene, a princess, is bored with all the lessons in the castle and the plans her parents have for her marriage, so she runs away. She ends up being the captive of dragon Kazul. Also by this author: *Calling on Dragons* and *Searching for Dragons.* (MS)

Mysteries

Alphin, Elaine Marie. *Counterfeit Son.* Cameron is always forced to stay in the basement where he reads old files, while his father beats to death the young boys he has kidnapped. After the police finally capture his father, Cameron runs away and knocks on the door of the family he liked the best. He tells them that he is their son. (HS)

Atkins, Catherine. *When Jeff Comes Home.* At age thirteen, Jeff is kidnapped by a pedophile while at a rest stop. Now he is sixteen and back but won't talk about anything that happened to him. (MS)

Avi. *The Man Who Was Poe.* This locked-room mystery takes place in a small town. When a young boy's mother and aunt and sister all disappear, he goes looking for assistance. Edgar Allan Poe agrees to help him solve the mystery. Also by the author: *Wolf Rider.* (MS)

Cooney, Caroline. *The Face on the Milk Carton.* When Jane is having lunch, she recognizes herself as the face on the milk carton. Who is her real family and why have her parents been lying to her? She can't believe that they are kidnappers. (MS)

Cooney, Caroline. *Whatever Happened to Janie?* In this sequel to *The Face on the Milk Carton,* Jane is returned to her real parents and longs to be back where she thinks she belongs. (HS)

Cooney, Caroline. *The Voice on the Radio.* In this sequel Jane goes to visit her boyfriend, who is now in college. She listens to his radio program and is shocked and hurt when she hears all the secrets she had confided to him being told to anyone listening. (HS)

Duncan, Lois. *Killing Mr. Griffin.* Not wanting to take the English final, a group of students kidnap Mr. Griffin, only meaning to scare him. However, Mr. Griffin has a heart condition and dies. Now what should they do? (MS)

Duncan, Lois. *Don't Look Behind You.* April doesn't fully realize why she can't just tell her boyfriend when her family enters the federal witness protection program. (MS)

Duncan, Lois. *Stranger with My Face.* Laurie doesn't know that she was separated at birth from a twin sister who now wants to take over her life. Also by this author: a real-life murder mystery, *Who Killed My Daughter?* (MS)

Duncan, Lois. *The Third Eye.* Karen learns that she has psychic powers, and she uses them to help find missing children. (MS)

Farmer, Nancy. *The Ear, the Eye and the Arm.* Three bungling detectives are hired to find the children of a leader, and in the process get kidnapped themselves. (HS)

Gilmore, Kate. *The Exchange Student.* Nine teenagers from the planet Chelan are sent to earth in what is ostensibly an exchange program, but what they really are there for is quite different. (INT/MS)

Glenn, Mel. *Who Killed Mr. Chippendale?* In this mystery novel in poetry form, Mr. Chippendale, a teacher at Tower High, is running on the track when he is shot and killed. While trying to find the killer, the students examine their feelings. (HS)

Glenn, Mel. *The Taking of Room 114.* In this hostage drama in poems, Mr. Wiedermeyer is tired of all the interruptions while he is teaching, so one day he locks his door and holds his history class hostage. (HS)

Glenn, Mel. *Foreign Exchange.* An exchange program where inner-city high school students visit country students seems like a good idea until a pretty girl with long beautiful blond hair is found murdered. She was last seen in a rowboat with an African-American exchange student, and the police automatically think he is the killer. (HS)

Hoobler, Dorothy. *The Ghost in the Takaido Inn.* When Seikei stays at the Takaido Inn, he sees a legendary ghost stealing a jewel, and from that moment his life changes. (MS)

Konigsburg, E. L. *Silent to the Bone.* Branwell stopped speaking the day his baby sister was injured. Connor, his best friend, knows that Bran could be arrested for the baby's injuries, and he tries to help Branwell. Connor needs to find what really happened. (IIS)

McNeal, Laura, and Tom McNeal. *Crooked.* Ninth-graders Clara and Amos are being terrorized by school bullies. (HS)

McNeal, Laura, and Tom McNeal. *Zipped.* After Mick opens an e-mail for his mother and finds out she is having an affair, he is determined to find out who her lover is. (HS)

McDonald, Joyce. *Swallowing Stones.* When Michael got a rifle for his birthday, he couldn't wait to shoot it, so he went to an undeveloped area and fired off a round. Little did he know that his bullet killed a man working on his roof. (HS)

Myers, Walter Dean. *Monster.* Steve is on trial for murder, but he says he just happened to be standing outside the convenience store where the crime took place. Steve shares his thoughts and feelings through his journal and an excerpt from the trial. (HS)

Nixon, Joan Lowery. *Whispers from the Dead.* After Sarah nearly drowns, she seems haunted by the incident. Her father accepts a transfer, thinking a new surrounding would be good for her, but when Sarah enters the house, she is the only one who knows that a horrible murder has taken place in her new home. (MS)

Nixon, Joan Lowery. *Nobody's There.* Abbie is so upset, even though her parents are divorced, when she sees her father kissing his girlfriend that she throws a rock through the window. She is assigned community service helping Mrs. Merkel. When she finds Mrs. Merkel unconscious from a blow to the head, she tries to find out what is going on. (MS)

Nixon, Joan Lowery. *Secret, Silent Screams.* When Marti's best friend's death is called a suicide, she doesn't believe it and is determined to prove he was murdered. (MS)

Nixon, Joan Lowery. *The Dark and Deadly Pool.* Mary Elizabeth has a great job at a health club one summer, and she loves it until she finds a body in the pool. (MS)

Nixon, Joan Lowery. *The Séance.* When a group of girls are holding a séance they hear a scream. When they put on the lights, Sara is missing. The next morning they find her body. (MS)

Nixon, Joan Lowery. *Playing for Keeps.* Rose goes on a cruise with her aunt and meets Ricky, a Cuban refugee. When he is accused of murder, she tries to help him. (MS)

Nixon, Joan Lowery. *The Other Side of Dark.* Stacy awakens after being in a coma for four years. Will she be able to identify the person who attacked her and killed her mother? (MS)

Plum-Ucci, Carol. *The Body of Christopher Creed.* After being beaten up by bullies, Chris disappears and no one knows if he committed suicide or ran away. (HS)

Qualey, Marsha. *Close to a Killer*. Barrie works in her mother's hair salon, Killer Looks, a good name because all the stylists are convicted murderers. When clients' homes are robbed while their hair is being done, business falls off, but when there are two murders, the shop is in real trouble. (HS)

Sachar, Louis. *Holes*. Stanley is sent to Camp Green Lake after being convicted of stealing a pair of sneakers. When he gets there, he finds himself in the middle of the desert, where every day he and the others go out and dig deep holes. He wants to know why they are digging and what they are really looking for. (MS)

Sweeney, Joyce. *Shadow*. Ever since her cat died, Sarah has been seeing Shadow's ghost. As her twin brother's fighting becomes more and more vicious, she knows her cat is trying to warn her of impending doom. (MS/HS)

Vande Velde, Vivian. *Never Trust a Dead Man*. Selwyn is falsely accused of murder and is sentenced to be entombed alive in a burial cave. A witch comes into the cave and will save him if he will be her servant for the rest of his life. (MS)

Werlin, Nancy. *The Killer's Cousin*. When David is acquitted for the death of his girlfriend, whom he accidentally killed, he goes to live with a cousin to finish his senior year. Some strange things begin to happen, and David becomes very apprehensive about the behavior of his eleven-year-old cousin.(HS)

Werlin, Nancy. *Black Mirror*. When Frances's brother dies of a heroin overdose, she tries to find out what really happened. She joins the charitable organization he was part of looking for answers. (HS)

Werlin, Nancy. *Locked Inside*. Marnie is kidnapped by one of her teachers and thrown into her cellar. The teacher wants her to admit that they share the same mother, Skye, a former famous singer who died. (HS)

White, Robb. *Deathwatch*. Madec is hunting with Ben as his guide; he accidentally shoots a prospector. Madec holds Ben at gunpoint to prevent him from telling the authorities. (MS)

Short Story Collections

Armstrong, Jennifer, ed. *Shattered: Stories of Children and War.* Stories by some of the prominent authors in the field tackle the tough topic of war and how war affects its youngest victims. (MS/HS)

Bauer, Marion Dane, ed. *Am I Blue?* This collection of stories deals with coming to terms with one's sexuality and sexual identity. (HS)

Blume, Judy, ed. *Places I Never Meant to Be.* Stories from writers whose works have been banned and challenged are the focus of this collection. Authors include Norma Fox Mazer, Walter Dean Myers, and Paul Zindel. (MS/HS)

Brooks, Bruce. *All That Remains.* Death and dying tie these short stories together. (MS/HS)

Brooks, Martha. *Paradise Cafe and Other Stories.* The stories in this collection present different aspects of love from the first crush of adolescence, to the love for a dying pet, to unrequited love. (MS/HS)

Cart, Michael, ed. *Love and Sex: Ten Stories of Truth.* This collection runs the gamut from the humorous "Extra Virgin" by Joan Bauer to the more serious exploration of Louise Hawes's "Fine and Dandy." (HS)

Cart, Michael, ed. *Necessary Noise.* Stories about families; all shapes and sizes and types of family form the theme for this collection. (MS/HS)

Cart, Michael, ed. *Tomorrowland.* Cart asked YA authors to imagine what life might be like in the new millennium. This collection is the result of their musings. (MS/HS)

Cart, Michael, ed. *911: The Book of Help.* Contemporary YA authors offer their insights into the tragic events of September 11, 2001, in poetry, essay, and short story formats. (MS/HS)

Cofer, Judith Ortiz. *An Island Like You.* Stories set in the barrio recount the lives of several neighbors, young and old. (HS)

Cormier, Robert. *Eight Plus One.* Nine stories by the master of YA literature provide excellent examples of the genre. (HS)

Coville, Bruce. *Odder Than Ever.* From killer biscuits to stinky princesses, these stories examine many oddities. (INT/MS)

Crutcher, Chris. *Athletic Shorts.* Stories about young men and women involved in a variety of sports form the basis for this collection. (HS)

Dines, Carol. *Talk to Me.* Several short stories and a novella examine how words can drastically affect the lives of others. (MS/HS)

Duncan, Lois, ed. *On the Edge: Stories at the Brink.* Twelve YA novelists share stories of teens who are physically, emotionally, or psychologically on the edge. (MS/HS)

Duncan, Lois, ed. *Trapped: Cages of Body and Mind.* There are many ways one can feel trapped. Acclaimed YA writers examine ways teens might feel caged by circumstances beyond their control. (MS/HS)

Gallo, Donald R., ed. *Sixteen.* Sixteen short stories by noted YA authors are divided into four thematic sections. Discussion questions are provided at the end of the book. Also by this editor: *Connections, Within Reach, Short Circuit,* and *Visions.* (MS/HS)

Gallo, Donald R., ed. *On the Fringe.* Kids who are marginalized in society are the main characters of stories by such noted authors as Joan Bauer, Jack Gantos, and Chris Crutcher. (MS/HS)

Gallo, Donald R., ed. *Destination Unexpected.* Sometimes a trip, even a short one in our own town, can take us places we least expected to go. (MS/HS)

Gallo, Donald R., ed. *Ultimate Sports.* Although sports is the central theme of the collection, these stories are about dealing with all sorts of problems in the world outside the playing fields. (MS/HS)

Gallo, Donald R., ed. *No Easy Answers.* Teens having to make tough choices is the central theme of these stories. (HS)

Gallo, Donald R., ed. *Time Capsule.* Short stories set in each decade of the twentieth century are included in this collection. (MS/HS)

Howe, James, ed. *The Color of Absence.* The major theme explored in this collection is loss. Children and teens deal with a variety of losses in their lives. (MS/HS)

Lynch, Chris. *All the Old Haunts.* Lynch contributes several short stories examining the dark side of a neighborhood. (HS)

Mazer, Harry, ed. *Twelve Shots.* All the stories in this collection deal with the violence and destruction caused by guns, especially guns in the hands of children and teens. (MS/HS)

Paulsen, Gary, ed. *Shelf Life.* This collection, which benefits literacy organizations around the world, centers on the importance of books and reading in the lives of the young characters in the stories. (MS/HS)

Saldana, Rene. *Finding Our Way.* Hispanic young men are the central characters in this collection of stories set in the Rio Grande Valley of Texas. (HS)

Sieruta, Peter. *Heartbeats and Other Stories.* Teens' lives can change in a heartbeat from a life of joy to one of despair. Sieruta captures these shifting emotions in his stories. (MS/HS)

Sleator, William. *Oddballs.* Sleator tells about his adventures and misadventures growing up. (MS)

Weiss, Jerry, and Helen Weiss, ed. *From One Experience to Another.* Contributions from Gordon Korman and Jon Scieszka are just two of the stories that talk about how experiences can change us. Each author talks about how the story came to be written as well. (MS/HS)

Wilson, Budge. *The Leaving and Other Stories.* From a loving English teacher, to parents, to love and friendship, these stories take a look at the lives of adolescents in the midst of conflict. (MS/HS)

Yolen, Jane, ed. *2041.* For this collection, Yolen asked authors in 1991 to project what life might be like for teens fifty years into the future. (MS/HS)

Science Fiction and Fantasy

Armstrong, Jennifer, and Nancy Butcher. *Fire-us #1: The Kindling.* An apocalyptic virus has wiped out the adult population in the United States, leaving children to fend for themselves and make new "families." This is the first in a trilogy. (MS/HS)

Atwater-Rhodes, Amelia. *In the Forests of the Night.* This is the first in a series of books written by a teen that present wonderfully brutal battles among vampires. Other titles include *Demon in My View, Shattered Mirror,* and *Midnight Predator.* (MS)

Barker, Clive. *Abarat.* Candy Quackenbush hates living in Chicken Town. One day, in an attempt to flee from more pain in her life, she finds herself transported to Abarat, a town where things are not what they seem on the surface. (MS/HS)

Barron, T. A. *Tree Girl.* A fantasy about finding one's true place in the world. Anna does not know who her parents are or perhaps were. She feels called to the great willow tree, a place she has been forbidden to visit. (INT/MS)

Barron, T. A. *Lost Years of Merlin.* The saga of Merlin as a boy is told in several volumes. Other titles in this series include *The Fires of Merlin* and *The Seven Songs of Merlin.* (INT/MS)

Bell, Hilari. *A Matter of Profit.* This science fiction thriller also has a nice mystery to be solved. Who are the various beings that make up the T'Chin Empire, and why have they surrendered without a fight? (HS)

Clements, Andrew. *Things Not Seen.* Fifteen-year-old Bobby awakes one morning to discover he is invisible. He manages to inform his parents, but there are bigger problems ahead. (MS)

Dickinson, Peter. *Eva.* When Eva is injured in a near-fatal car accident, her parents give permission for experimental surgery to save her life. Eva wakens with her thoughts and feelings implanted in the brain and body of a chimp. (MS/IIS)

DuPrau, Jeanne. *The City of Ember.* An entire city is built underground to save civilization. Instructions are left behind telling a future generation how to leave the city once it is safe to return to the surface. Those instructions are lost until Lyna and Doon come along. (MS)

Farmer, Nancy. *The House of the Scorpion.* In the future, drug lords clone themselves so that they can harvest organs as they grow older. What happens when one of the clones does not want that to be his fate? (MS/HS)

Gaiman, Neil. *Coraline.* Coraline must rescue her parents and others trapped by evil beings. A cat who speaks might be of some help. (INT/MS)

Gilmore, Kate. *The Exchange Student.* An alien exchange student seems too interested in some of the animal species on Earth. What are his plans for when he returns to his own planet? (INT/MS/HS)

Haddix, Margaret Peterson. *Among the Hidden.* The first in a series of books that examines what happens in a future society where families are limited in the number of children they can have. Luke, one of the forbidden third children, has to find a way to survive. Other titles in the series include *Among the Betrayed* and *Among the Impostors.* (INT/MS)

Hautman, Pete. *Mr. Was.* Why would someone replace a homeless man with an impostor? (HS)

Hesse, Karen. *The Music of Dolphins.* A young girl, raised by dolphins, is rescued and brought to civilization, where she can be studied by a team of scientists. (MS)

Jacques, Brian. *Redwall.* This series of animal fantasies features lots of adventure. Other titles include *Mossflower, Martin of Redwall,* and *Salamandastrom.* (MS)

Jacques, Brian. *The Angel's Command.* Jacques's other series is based on the legend of the Flying Dutchman. (MS)

Kindl, Patrice. *Goose Chase.* Princess Fortunato is imprisoned until she decides which royal she will consent to marry. A flock of geese allow her to escape. Also by this author: *Owl in Love.* (MS).

Klause, Annette Curtis. *Silver Kiss.* Part vampire story, part romance. This novel takes the legend of the vampire to a new level. Also by this author: *Blood and Chocolate.* (HS).

Logue, Mary. *Dancing with an Alien.* Branko has come to Earth looking for a young woman willing to follow him back home. His planet's population has been decimated by a virus, and they need to reestablish the species before it is too late. (HS)

Lowry, Lois. *Gathering Blue.* This companion to *The Giver* shows another side of a seemingly perfect world. Kira, a young woman skilled in embroidery, soon discovers there are dark secrets being kept from her society. (MS/HS)

Napoli, Donna Jo. *Sirena.* The legend of the Sirens is brought to life in this romantic novel. (HS)

Napoli, Donna Jo. *Crazy Jack.* What do the neighbors think when a beanstalk thrusts itself to the sky and Jack begins to climb? (MS)

Napoli, Donna Jo. *Spinners.* The story of Rumpelstiltskin is told in a different light: from the point of view of the man who will come to be known as the "villain" of the story. (HS)

Napoli, Donna Jo. *Zel.* As the title suggests, this is the story of Rapunzel and her romance with the young prince who comes to rescue her. (HS)

Napoli, Donna Jo . *Beast.* Set in Persia, this is the story of Beauty and the Beast. (HS)

Naylor, Phyllis Reynolds. *Jade Green.* Naylor takes on the gothic romance novel in this spooky tale of a young woman forced to take her own life. (MS/HS)

Price, Susan. *The Sterkarm Handshake.* In the future, a company develops a time travel machine. They hope to travel back in time and establish a "resort" of sorts in the unspoiled English countryside. The Sterkarm clan has other plans for the unwelcome visitors. (HS)

Pullman, Philip. *I Was a Rat!* What would happen if one of the rats transformed by Cinderella's fairy godmother remained a boy? (INT/MS)

Pullman, Philip. *The Golden Compass.* This is the first part of the His Dark Materials saga, a series that tells of the quest of Lyra and Will. Other titles include *The Subtle Knife* and *The Amber Spyglass.* (MS)

Rowling, J. K. *Harry Potter and the Sorcerer's Stone.* Is there someone on the planet who does not know this series, which takes Harry Potter from the world of muggles to Hogwarts School of Wizardry? Other titles include: *Harry Potter and the Chamber of Secrets, Harry Potter and the Goblet of Fire, Harry Potter and the Prisoner of Azkaban,* and *Harry Potter and the Order of the Phoenix.* (INT/MS/HS)

Shusterman, Neal. *Downsiders.* There is an entire civilization that dwells underground.

What happens when a Downsider meets a Topsider? (MS)

Skurzynski, Gloria. *Virtual War.* It seems like a perfect solution: instead of actually fighting a war, war is fought in a virtual reality. What could possibly go wrong? (HS)

Sleator, William. *Rewind.* Peter is given a chance to go back to Earth and change his life. It takes him some time to figure out what is leading him to an early death. Also by this author: *The Duplicate, Interstellar Pig, The Boxes, Fingers,* and *Others See Us.* (MS/HS)

Spinner, Stephanie. *Quiver.* This is the retelling of the story of Atalanta, the fastest woman. When her father plans for her arranged marriage, Atalanta asks only that her betrothed be able to beat her in a footrace. (HS)

Stevermer, Caroline. *River Rats.* In a post-Apocalyptic world, a ragtag group of teens travels down the Mississippi à la Mark Twain. (HS)

Vande Velde, Vivian. *Never Trust a Dead Man.* Falsely accused of a crime he did not commit, a young man is sealed in the tomb of his supposed victim. A witch offers to help him, but she is not exactly the answer to his prayers. Also by this author: *Heir Apparent, Curses Inc.,* and *The Rumpelstiltskin Problem.* (MS)

Weaver, Will. *Memory Boy.* In a not-so-distant future, a young man leads his family to the safety of the mountains while crazed looters threaten their existence along the journey. (MS)

Wrede, Patricia. *Dealing with Dragons.* This is the first in a series of books in which Princess Cimorene offers her services to the dragons to avoid marrying someone her parents have selected for her. Also in the series: *Calling on Dragons* and *Searching for Dragons.* (MS)

Nonfiction and Informational Books

Ash, Russell. *Top Ten of Everything.* Annually published, this volume of records relates to everything from popular culture to literature and history. (INT/MS/HS)

Bode, Janet. *Heartbreak and Roses.* Stories of young and troubled love are the focus of this informational book. Some of the stories are told in graphics format. (MS/HS)

Bode, Janet. *New Kids in Town.* The voices of immigrant teens are featured in this examination of how difficult it is to move between cultures. (MS/HS)

Bode, Janet. *Voices of Rape.* Bode interviews teenage victims of sexual assault in this compelling informational book. (HS)

Bode, Janet, and Stan Mack. *For Better, for Worse: A Guide to Surviving Divorce for Preteens and Their Families.* The title pretty much says it all. This is a must-have in the collection. Have multiple copies and urge the public library in the area to stock the shelves as well. (INT/MS/HS)

Bode, Janet, and Stan Mack. *Hard Time.* Bode and her partner, Stan Mack, interviewed teen prisoners, their victims, their families, and the justice system participants to provide an in-depth analysis of juvenile crime. Also by Bode: *Food Fight* (eating disorders), *Trust and Betrayal* (friendship), and *The Colors of Freedom* (children of immigrants). (MS/HS)

Colman, Penny. *Corpses, Coffins and Crypts.* Interested in knowing how death and bur-

ial customs originated? This book provides the background of the ceremonies, superstitions, and customs around the world. (MS/HS)

Crutcher, Chris. *King of the Mild Frontier.* Crutcher's childhood and adolescence are fertile ground for this "ill-advised autobiography." (HS)

Davis, Kenneth C. *Don't Know Much About . . . .* This series presents interesting facts and tidbits about a wide range of subjects. Some of the titles in the series include *Planet Earth, Geography, History, The Solar System,* and *The Fifty States.* (INT/MS)

Fleischman, John. *Phineas Gage.* A true account of a railroad worker whose brain injury led to new ideas about the structures of the brain makes for riveting reading. (MS)

Gantos, Jack. *Hole in My Life.* As a young man, Gantos spent time in a federal prison for his part in running drugs. Here is the honest and riveting recounting of a critical time in his life. (HS)

Gardner, David, and Tom Gardner. *The Motley Fool Investment Guide for Teens.* This how-to guide shows kids how to make wise decisions about investing their money. (HS)

Giblin, James Cross. *Chimney Sweeps.* What was it like to be a sweep many years ago? How do the sweeps of old differ from sweeps today? Giblin uses a "you are there" format to talk about this interesting profession. Also by this author: *The Life and Death of*

Adolf Hitler, Be Seated (about the history of chairs), *From Hand to Mouth* (deals with silverware and table manners) and *When Plague Strikes*. (MS/HS)

Glover, Savion, and Bruce Weber. *Savion! My Life in Tap*. This autobiographical look at the work of Savion Glover jumps with the rhythm of the tap dance that is his life. (MS/HS)

Guinness Book of Records. This is the #1 favorite of kids around the world. (INT/MS/HS)

Harris, Robie. *It's Perfectly Normal*. This informational book tackles the tough topics of sex and sexuality. (MS/HS)

Hoose, Phillip. *It's Our World, Too*. This nonfiction collection examines how ordinary teens changed the life of their communities through social activism. Also by this author: *We Were There, Too! Young People in U.S. History*. (MS/HS)

Kuklin, Susan. *Fighting Back: What Some People Are Doing About AIDS*. Kuklin tells the stories of several AIDS activists. (MS/HS)

Lanier, Shannon, and Jane Feldman. *Jefferson's Children: The Story of One American Family*. Jefferson fathered several children with his slave, Sally Hemmings. Descendants of these children and the descendants of Jefferson by his wife discuss their thoughts and feelings about the revelations only recently confirmed by DNA testing. (HS)

Larson, Gary. *There's a Hair in My Dirt! A Worm's Story*. In a playful cartoon format, Larson discusses how a strand of hair came to be in the dirt being eaten by an earthworm. (MS/HS)

Levine, Ellen. *Freedom's Children*. Levine tells the stories of the children involved in the civil rights movement. She also updates readers on what those children are doing now in their adult lives. (MS/HS)

Lewin, Ted. *I Was a Teenage Professional Wrestler*. As a young man, Lewin wrestled professionally. He sketched and painted many of the famous wrestlers of his day as well. (MS)

Macaulay, David. *Castle*. The building of a fictional castle is outlined in meticulous detail elaborated by intricate illustrations from the author. Also by this author: *Cathedral, Unbuilding*, and *Pyramid*. (INT/MS)

Macaulay, David. *The Way Things Work*. This encyclopedic work details how machines from the simple lever and pulley to the complex inner workings of a computer work. (INT/MS)

Meltzer, Milton. *Langston Hughes*. The life and work of Harlem Renaissance author Hughes is the focus of this biography. Meltzer worked with Hughes on books about African-Americans in the 1960s. Also by this author: *Ain't Gonna Study War No More, There Comes a Time, Ten Queens*, and *The Day the Sky Fell: A History of Terrorism*. (MS/HS)

McKissack, Patricia C., and Fredrick L. McKissack. *Rebels Against Slavery: American Slave Revolts*. How did slave rebellions help lead to the abolition of slavery? Also by these authors: *Red Tail Angels, Black Diamond*, and other topics related to African-American history. (MS)

Murphy, Jim. *Across America on an Emigrant Train*. Murphy recounts what it must have been like to travel from New York across America as a new arrival to this country. Also by this author: *Blizzard: The Storm That Changed America*. (MS/HS)

Myers, Walter Dean. *Bad Boy: A Memoir*. Myers talks about his childhood and adolescence in Harlem. Also by this author: *Amistad: The Long Road to Freedom, The Glory Field*, and *The Greatest: Muhammad Ali*. (MS/HS)

Packer, Alex J. *How Rude! The Teenager's Guide to Good Manners, Proper Behavior and Not Grossing People Out*. The title says it all. This humorous look at all sorts of situations (sex, bathrooms, and in-line skating, to name a few) offers help to teens. (MS/HS)

Stanley, Jerry. *I Am an American*. Using first-person accounts and meticulous research, Stanley tells what life was like for Japanese-Americans after the bombing of Pearl Harbor, when an executive order sent families off to relocation centers. Also by this author: *Digger, Children of the Dust Bowl, Frontier Merchants*, and *Hurry Freedom*. (MS/HS)

Poetry

Carlson, Lori M., ed. *Cool Salsa: Bilingual Poems on Growing up Latino in the United States.* Poems in English and in Spanish and some bilingual recount experiences such as falling in love, going to school, and making new friends. (HS)

Carson, Jo. *Stories I Ain't Told Nobody Yet.* Poems about living in Appalachia form the basis for this collection. (MS/HS)

Dakos, Kalli. *If You're Not Here, Please Raise Your Hand: Poems About School.* This collection of humorous poems skewers some of the situations in which students might find themselves while at school. (INT/MS)

Fletcher, Ralph. *Relatively Speaking: Poems About Family.* Poems deal with topics as familiar with a father who is a comedian and a mom making PB&J for lunch to selections about distant members of the family and how to deal with the death of a family member. (INT/MS)

Franco, Betsy, ed. *You Hear Me? Poems and Writings by Teenage Boys.* Franco solicited poems from adolescent boys across the United States. Their concerns and emotions are remarkably evident in the poems in this collection. (MS/HS)

Franco, Betsy, ed. *Things I Have to Tell You: Poems and Writings by Teenage Girls.* Teenage girls from all over the United States contributed poems for this collection. (MS/HS)

Glenn, Mel. *Class Dismissed.* Poems told from the point of view of a variety of high school students are accompanied by black-and-white photographs. Also in this series of poetry books: *Class Dismissed II* and *Back to Class.* (MS/HS)

Glenn, Mel. *Foreign Exchange.* When a group of kids from Tower High School head off to the country for a visit, they have certain preconceived notions about what they will encounter. Prejudices are challenged until a young woman is found dead under suspicious circumstances. (HS)

Glenn, Mel. *Jump Ball.* A season in the life of a championship basketball team comes to a screeching halt on an ice-slicked highway. Not all the students will survive the bus crash. (HS)

Glenn, Mel. *My Friend's Got This Problem, Mr. Candler.* A day in the life of a high school guidance counselor sets the theme for the poems in this book. (MS)

Glenn, Mel. *The Taking of Room 114.* A social studies teacher takes his class hostage on the last day of school. (HS)

Glenn, Mel. *Who Killed Mr. Chippendale?* When an English teacher is murdered by a sniper on the school grounds, there are many who think they know why. (HS)

Holbrook, Sara. *By Definition: Poems of Feelings.* These poems run the gamut of emotions from elation to pain, from puzzlement to wisdom. (INT/MS)

Holbrook, Sara. *Wham! It's a Poetry Jam.* Performing poetry alone and in groups is the focus of this collection, which includes performance tips along with ideal poems for sharing aloud. (MS)

Janeczko, Paul. *Pocket Poems.* This book, small enough to fit comfortably in a pocket, is a collection of short poems from a wide variety of writers. (MS/HS)

Janeczko, Paul. *Poetspeak.* In this anthology, Janeczko includes photographs of the poets as well as some commentary from the writers about their work. Also by this anthologist and poet: *Brickyard Summer, Stardust 'Otel, Don't Forget to Fly, Postcard Poems, Strings, That Sweet Diamond,* and *Poetry from A to Z.* (INT/MS/HS)

Korman, Gordon, and Bernice Korman. *The D-Poems of Jeremy Bloom.* Jeremy oversleeps and ends up in a poetry class. He makes a rather bad first impression that leads to a truly memorable semester. Also: *The Last Place Sports Poems of Jeremy Bloom.* (MS)

Larrick, Nancy. *Let's Do a Poem.* Lessons on writing various types of poems provide lots of models to use in the classroom. (MS)

Nye, Naomi Shihab. *The Space Between Our Footsteps.* This collection of poems features the words and drawings/paintings of artists from the Middle East. (MS/HS)

Nye, Naomi Shihab. *The Tree Is Older Than You Are.* This collection features works from Mexico in English, Spanish, and bilingual format. (MS/HS)

Nye, Naomi Shihab, and Paul Janeczko. *I Feel a Little Jumpy Around You.* Janeczko and Nye collaborated on this anthology of her and his poems collected in pairs. (MS/HS)

Soto, Gary. *The Fire in My Hands.* Poems can be about many ordinary items, such as an orange that is a "fire in my hands." (MS/HS)

Strauss, Gwen. *Trail of Stones.* Strauss presents an interesting take on some familiar folktales, such as *Cinderella* and *Little Red Riding Hood* in these poems that examine the dark side of the tales. (HS)

Turner, Ann. *Learning to Swim.* This memoir, told in verse, recounts a painful summer in the life of the author. (MS/HS)

Young Adult Literature from Laughter to Tears

19 Varieties of Gazelle: Poems of the Middle East by Naomi Shihab Nye. Nye proves again why she is an acclaimed poet in this collection of poems about people and war and peace. (MS/HS)

33 Snowfish by Adam Rapp. Not for the faint of heart, this story, told from three points of view, deals with the incredibly daunting life of three runaway children. (HS)

Abarat by Clive Barker. Fantasy about a girl's journey to Abarat. (MS)

All American Girl by Meg Cabot. When Samantha Madison saves the life of the President of the United States, it should be a good thing, right? Wrong! (MS/HS)

Almost Home by Nora Raleigh Baskin. Leah is now living with her father and his new wife (she refuses to call her stepmother) and misses her old life with her mother and friends. An unlikely savior in the form of a boy in her class helps Leah to find her way home. (INT/MS)

The Boy Who Saved Baseball by John H. Ritter. Lyrical and lovely, here is a tale that combines baseball and family and community. (MS)

Catalyst by Laurie Halse Anderson. Kate plans to attend her mother's alma mater, MIT. She has no fall-back plan and has to deal with disappointment on the academic and personal front when she is rejected by the school. (HS)

The City of Ember by Jeanne DuPrau. This futuristic novel contains elements of romance, adventure, and suspense, making it an interesting read for a wide variety of audiences. Pair this one with *The Giver* and *Gathering Blue* and other utopian novels. (MS)

Coraline by Neil Gaiman. This chilling tale is perfect for reading aloud. (INT/MS)

Cuba 15 by Nancy Osa. Violet Paz just turned fifteen. Her abuela insists on a quince party. Violet does not much care for this tradition until she is given permission to make this quince her own celebration. (MS/HS)

Dead Girls Don't Write Letters by Gail Giles. Sunny's older sister died in an apartment fire. Now, suddenly, she receives a letter from Jazz telling her she survived and is coming home. (MS/HS)

Fearless Fernie: Hanging Out with Fernie and Me by Gary Soto. This collection of poems details the friendship between two boys. (MS)

Fire-us #1: The Kindling by Jennifer Armstrong and Nancy Butcher. First part of a trilogy about a futuristic world in which only children seem to have survived. (MS/HS)

Friction by E. R. Frank. Alex loves her teacher until a new student begins to accuse Simon of inappropriate behavior. Alex does not know whom to believe: the new kid or Alex's own instincts? (MS)

Getting Away with Murder: The True Story of the Emmett Till Case by Chris Crowe. Emmett Till's true story is credited with beginning some of the protests associated with the civil rights movement. This is a companion to *Mississippi Trial, 1955,* also by Crowe. (MS/HS)

The Glass Café or the Stripper and the State: How My Mother Started a War with the System and Made Us Kind of Rich and a Little Bit Famous by Gary Paulsen. The title says it all. (MS)

Hanging on to Max by Margaret Bechard. Sam's senior year should be a breeze. Baby Max complicates his life more than he could ever have predicted. Can Sam balance school and parenting? (HS)

How Angel Peterson Got His Name, and Other Outrageous Tales About Extreme Sports by Gary Paulsen. Only Paulsen could tell these tall tales and make them seem perfectly believable. Perfect for reluctant readers and for reading aloud. (INT/MS)

If I Were in Charge the Rules Would Be Different! by James Proimos. This collection of poems, reminiscent of Silverstein and Dahl and Prelutsky, will be a welcome addition for intermediate libraries. (INT)

If the Shoe Fits by Laura Whipple. *Cinderella* told in verse from multiple perspectives. (MS/HS)

Jinx by Margaret Wild. When two boyfriends die, Jinx begins to believe she will never be able to seek love again. (HS)

Keeping You a Secret by Julie Anne Peters. When Holland meets Cece, her life is changed forever. However, the two must keep their relationship a secret for fear of what others will think and do in reaction. (HS)

King of the Mild Frontier: An Ill-Advised Autobiography by Chris Crutcher. What can I say? It is vintage Crutcher. Some chapters beg to be read aloud. Some are better read silently. But do read it all. (HS)

Locomotion by Jacqueline Woodson. Novel in verse by a talented writer. Lonnie's teacher is helping him put words about his life on paper. The writing is cathartic and immediate. (MS)

New Rules of High School by Blake Nelson. Max's life seems perfect—good grades, lovely girlfriend. Why, then, is he so unhappy? (HS)

Parallel Universe of Liars by Kathleen Johnson. Robin's life is miserable. Not only does her mother hammer at her about her weight, but her father's new wife is cheating on him with Robin's next-door neighbor. Robin herself is being pulled into Frankie's world, a world where lies appear to be truth. (HS)

Period Pieces: Stories for Girls, edited by Erzsi Deak and Kristin Litchman. Stories about that brink moment when girls become women. (INT/MS)

Phineas Gage: A Gruesome but True Story About Brain Science by John Fleischman. Phineas Gage survives when a piece of iron shoots through his cheek and brain. He becomes a medical marvel. (INT/MS)

Pool Boy by Michael Simmons. Brett is a spoiled rich kid who now has no money. He whines about his status in life, especially about having to find work and help support the family. He is a wonderful example of anti-hero. (HS)

Second Summer of the Sisterhood by Ann Brashares. A fitting sequel to the *Sisterhood of the Traveling Pants* as once again the girls head off for summer adventures. (HS)

Seeing the Blue Between, edited by Paul Janeczko. Poets offer advice and poems for young writers. (MS)

Shakespeare Bats Cleanup by Ron Koertge. A novel in verse tells of a young boy confined to bed rest for mononucleosis. While pining away for baseball, he learns much about poetry and about himself. (MS/HS)

The Silent Boy by Lois Lowry. Historical novel about a girl's befriending a young developmentally challenged boy. This novel sings with lyrical prose. Katy is made real to the reader through meticulous detail. (MS)

Son of the Mob by Gordon Korman. Vince DeLuca's life in high school is made much more difficult because his father is a mob boss. (MS/HS)

Splash: Poems of Our Watery World by Constance Levy. Lovely, lyrical poems and light verse about water in its various states. (INT/MS)

Stand Tall by Joan Bauer. Living between mom's apartment and dad's house proves a bit more than Tree can bear. (MS)

The Steps by Rachel Cohn. Annabel needs a chart to keep track of her various siblings and parental combinations. She is vacationing with her Dad in Australia and hopes to convince him to come back and live in New York so she can be near him. (MS)

Swimming Upstream by Kristine O'Connell George. Subtitled *Middle School Poems,* this collection really hits at the heart of those kids in the middle. (MS)

Tribes by Arthur Slade. Think of high school as an anthropology assignment. (HS)

True Meaning of Cleavage by Mariah Fredericks. One look at the cover, and this book will fly from the shelf. Be happy, for this is the kind of book that speaks volumes to adolescent girls. (MS/HS)

Who the Man by Chris Lynch. Earl Pryor tends to settle any disagreements with his brute strength. After all, that's what a man does, right? Lynch explores the mind of a young man in turmoil, something he does incredibly well. (HS)

Books for Twenty-First Century Teens

Pushing the Format Envelope

Breathing Underwater by Alex Flinn. Sixteen-year-old Nick, convicted of hitting his former girlfriend, is instructed by the judge to write a journal. (HS)

The Brimstone Journals by Ron Koertge. A series of startling and disturbing poems tells of an unforgettable year at Branston High School. (HS)

Captain Underpants and the Wrath of the Wicked Wedgie Woman by Dav Pilkey. Another installment in the crazy Captain Underpants saga. Novel in graphics. (INT/MS)

Echo by Francesca Lia Block. Block employs multiple viewpoints to tell the magical story of a little girl hurtling toward womanhood. (HS)

Empress of the World by Sara Ryan. Nicola's summer at a camp for gifted teens results in some unexpected changes in her life. (HS)

Fat Camp Commandos by Daniel Pinkwater. This novel in graphics looks like a comic book. The zany humor is perfect for middle school readers looking for some light, enjoyable reading. Don't dismiss it too easily, though: there are plenty of tongue-in-cheek jokes for grownup readers, too. (INT)

Fighting Ruben Wolfe by Markus Zusak. Two brothers become involved in a boxing competition in order to help out the family. What happens when they must face each other in the ring? (HS)

For Better, for Worse: A Guide to Surviving Divorce for Preteens and Their Families by Janet Bode and Stan Mack. The title pretty much says it all. This is a must-have in the collection. Have multiple copies and urge the public library in the area to stock the shelves as well. (INT/MS/HS)

Kissing Tennessee and Other Stories from the Stardust Dance by Kathi Appelt. This story collection tells of all the hopes and dreams of an eighth-grade class. (MS)

Love That Dog by Sharon Creech. This slim novel tells the story of Jack and his beloved dog, Sky, in a series of poems. (INT/MS)

On the Bright Side, I Am Now the Girlfriend of a Sex God by Louise Rennison. This is the sequel to the Printz honor medalist *Angus, Thongs and Full Frontal Snogging*. (MS/HS)

The Rumpelstiltskin Problem by Vivian Vande Velde. Here are six alternative versions of the familiar fairy tale. (MS)

Running Back to Ludie by Angela Johnson. A slender novel, told in verse, of a young girl's reunion with a long-absent mother. (MS/HS)

True Believer by Virginia Euwer Wolff. This is a long-awaited sequel to *Make Lemonade*.

More books about LaVaughn are to follow. (MS/HS)

Witness by Karen Hesse. A brilliantly conceived and written novel that uses nine points of view to tell about the Klan's arrival in a New England town in the 1900s. (MS)

Breaking Topic Taboos

All That Remains by Bruce Brooks. This collection of novellas deals with loss. (MS/HS)

All the Old Haunts by Chris Lynch. This story collection demonstrates once again an author at the top of his game. (HS)

Black Angels by Rita Murphy. In the summer of 1961, Celli notices angels no one else can see. Perhaps the angels are in Celli's life for a reason? (MS)

Born Blue by Han Nolan. Leshaya has had a life full of sorrow and tragedy. This life is reflected in the powerful voice she raises in song. (HS)

Darkness Before Dawn by Sharon Draper. Keisha is in her senior year at Hazelwood High School. When the principal's son comes in as a student teacher, he manages to sweep Keisha off her feet and into danger. (HS)

Every Time a Rainbow Dies by Rita Williams-Garcia. From the safety of his rooftop, Thulani watches the world go by. One day he witnesses an event that will change his life forever. (HS)

Give a Boy a Gun by Todd Strasser. It is unthinkable that someone would come to school with a gun intent on killing a classmate. However, as recent events have demonstrated, sometimes the unthinkable occurs. Here is a book to open honest dialogue about bullying and violence. (HS)

The Gypsies Never Came by Stephen Roos. Augie has always felt as if he was accepted by his peers despite the fact that he was born with a stump for a left hand. Now that he is in sixth grade, though, things are changing. Enter the eccentric and fascinating Lydie Rose Meisenheimer. (MS)

Love and Sex, edited by Michael Cart. This story collection is subtitled *Ten Stories of Truth.*

Authors include Joan Bauer, Chris Lynch, Laurie Halse Anderson, and Sonya Sones. (HS)

Of Sound Mind by Jean Ferris. Theo is the only hearing person in his family. As a result, he has been the chief means of communication for his deaf parents and brother. When he meets Ivy, he discovers a friend in a similar situation. (MS/HS)

On the Fringe, edited by Donald R. Gallo. This collection of stories examines what it is like to be a teen pushed to the fringe by bullies. Outstanding stories by Joan Bauer, Jack Gantos, Chris Crutcher, and others. (MS/HS)

Playing for Keeps by Joan Lowery Nixon. Another winning mystery, this time set aboard a cruise ship.

The Rag and Bone Shop by Robert Cormier. This is the final novel of vintage Cormier. Jason is a young man facing a clever police interrogator who will not stop until he secures a confession about a brutal murder. How far are the police willing to go for a conviction? (MS/HS)

Spellbound by Janet McDonald. A teen mother has the opportunity to win a college scholarship. All she has to do is win a spelling contest. (HS)

Whale Talk by Chris Crutcher. Crutcher's long-awaited novel offers a provocative look at how violence begets violence. It also leaves readers knowing that if violence is to end, it is up to them to do something to stop it. (HS)

You Don't Know Me by David Klass. Though the book deals with the serious topic of abuse, the humorous narrative of the protagonist provides much-needed comic relief. (MS/HS)

Distinctive Voices

Anna Casey's Place in the World by Adrian Fogelin. Anna has been shuttled from home to home since the death of her parents. She hopes this next home may become permanent even if it means sharing it with scrawny little Eb. (MS)

Bad Boy: A Memoir by Walter Dean Myers. Myers's childhood was not an easy one. (MS)

Caleb's Story by Patricia MacLachlan. Another of the stories like *Sarah, Plain and Tall*. Here Caleb's journal tells of a mysterious visitor to the farm. (INT/MS)

Cirque Du Freak by Darren Shan. Darren is lured to an abandoned house one evening to see what is billed as a one-of-a-kind freak show. What he sees that night alters the course of his life and of those he loves most. A sequel is *The Vampire's Assistant*. (INT/MS)

The Color of Absence, edited by James Howe. A collection of stories about loss and grief. (MS/HS)

Crazy Loco by David Rice. This collection of stories, set in the Rio Grande Valley, covers the gamut from pets to relatives to school, all with a fresh new outlook.

Dancing in Cadillac Light by Kimberly Willis Holt. Whenever life closes in on Jaynell, she simply climbs inside one of the cars in the local parts junkyard. (MS)

Don't You Know There's a War On? by Avi. As World War II rages overseas, those at home make the necessary adjustments to their lives as well. Howie and his best friend Denny are on the lookout for spies. What they discover instead is a secret about their favorite teacher. (INT/MS)

Freewill by Chris Lynch. Gifted readers will appreciate the almost stream-of-consciousness writing and the delicious symbolism in a story about death and loss and its aftermath. (HS)

A Group of One by Rachna Gilmore. Tara gains new pride in her Indian heritage when she learns of her grandmother's involvement in the Quit India movement. (MS)

Guts by Gary Paulsen. Here are all the true stories behind Paulsen's action-adventure novels. What is it like to eat a raw turtle's egg? How does one survive a moose attack? Those and other answers await readers of

this nonfiction book. (MS)

Hole in the Sky by Pete Hautman. The year is 2028 and most of the population has been wiped out by a flu epidemic. A few have survived the flu; those survivors and the uninfected have formed armed camps. Ceej joins with a Hopi girl to find his sister, Harryette, who has been abducted by a group of Survivors. (MS)

The Island by Gordon Korman. Six kids board a sailing vessel. They have been sent along on this journey in order to learn more about themselves. A sudden storm and a shipwreck cause a handful of teens to face incredible odds. (INT/MS)

Lord of the Deep by Graham Salisbury. Mikey works the fishing boat with his stepfather, Bill. He wants so much to learn the ropes, to become a good fisherman. Wrestling with giant marlin and other sport fish makes for adventure and danger. (MS)

Memory Boy by Will Weaver. The year is 2008 and volcanic eruptions have altered the environment of the Pacific Northwest. Volcanic ash has affected crops, and the hoarding has begun. Violence is soon to follow as homeless, hungry people scavenge for food. Miles and his family must leave the city and find safety elsewhere. (MS)

No More Dead Dogs by Gordon Korman. Wallace has vowed that he will read no more books in which a dog dies. When his teacher requires a book report on *Old Shep, My Pal*, Wallace responds with his honest appraisal. The results are utterly unpredictable and utterly hilarious. (MS)

Pray Hard by Pamela Walker. When Amelia's father is killed in a plane crash, she blames herself for the accident. A mysterious visitor, Brother Mustard Seed, may have the answer to her prayers. (INT/MS)

Princess in the Spotlight by Meg Cabot. This is the sequel to *The Princess Diaries*. Forget the movie; read the book. (MS/HS)

Rooster by Beth Nixon Weaver. Kady is ashamed of her shabby house and hand-me-down clothes now that Jon is showering attention on her. (MS)

Sights by Susanna Nance. Baby Girl can see the future. Her talent is sometimes more of a curse than a blessing, especially when it comes to the people she loves most. (MS)

Sisterhood of the Traveling Pants by Ann Brashares. One pair of pants and four friends make for a memorable summer in this quirky coming-of-age story. (MS/HS)

6-321 by Michael Laser. For Mark, sixth grade is a time of great changes and challenges. (INT/MS)

Slap Your Sides by M. E. Kerr. It's tough when all the young men around you are enlisting to fight in World War II and you remain a conscientious objector. (MS/HS)

Stuck in Neutral by Terry Trueman. The main character is a young man stricken with cerebral palsy. This unusual narrator faces a unique situation as well. He believes his father plans to kill him. (HS)

Tough Books for Tough Times

Here are books for the more mature YA reader. Most are excellent for use in high school classes, especially as independent reading material. The topics tackled in these books are often controversial. By sharing books such as these with our students, we allow them the opportunity to express opinions about the ills of society (both adult and teen). More important, we provide them with a safe environment in which to work through their positions about topics with which they will deal in life.

Brashares, Ann. *Sisterhood of the Traveling Pants.* One pair of pants and four friends make for a memorable summer in this quirky coming-of-age story. (MS/HS)

Cart, Michael, ed. *Love and Sex: Ten Stories of Truth.* These stories deal with love of all kinds. Authors include Joan Bauer, Chris Lynch, Laurie Halse Anderson, and Sonya Sones. (HS)

Cormier, Robert. *The Rag and Bone Shop.* This is the final novel of vintage Cormier. Jason is a young man facing a clever police interrogator who will not stop until he secures a confession about a brutal murder. How far are the police willing to go for a conviction? (MS/HS)

Crutcher, Chris. *Whale Talk.* Crutcher's long-awaited novel offers a provocative look at how violence begets violence. It also leaves readers knowing that if violence is to end, it is up to them to do something to stop it. (HS)

Flinn, Alex. *Breathing Underwater.* Sixteen-year-old Nick, convicted of hitting his former girlfriend, is instructed by the judge to write a journal chronicling the events that led him to become abusive. (HS)

Gallo, Donald R., ed. *On the Fringe.* This collection of stories examines what it is like to be a teen pushed to the fringe by bullies. Outstanding stories by Joan Bauer, Jack Gantos, Chris Crutcher, and others. (MS/HS)

Gantos, Jack. *Hole in My Life.* Gantos spent part of his life in prison for running drugs. This slice-of-life autobiography tells of his experiences. (MS/HS)

Garcia, Rita Williams. *Every Time a Rainbow Dies.* From the safety of his rooftop, Thulani watches the world go by. One day he witnesses an event that will change his life forever. When Thulani sees the rape of a teenage girl, he knows he must do something to help. (HS)

Giles, Gail. *Shattering Glass.* Remarkable first novel tells how peer pressure can cause teens to act outside their comfort zone. When a group of teens decides to make an outcast the toast of the school, they will stop at nothing to achieve their goal. (HS)

Howe, James, ed. *The Color of Absence: Stories About Loss and Hope*. Twelve stories about loss and grief by some of the best YA authors. Included in the collection are Avi, Naomi Nye, Angela Johnson, and Chris Lynch. (MS/HS)

Howe, James. *The Misfits*. Sticks and stone may break my bones, but names will break my spirit. This book examines how name-calling changes the lives of a group of friends. (MS)

Kelzer, Garret. *God of Beer*. A group of high school students are determined to prove that drinking as an act of civil disobedience can make some changes in their community. (HS)

Kerr, M. E. *Slap Your Sides*. It's tough when all the young men around you are enlisting to fight in World War II and you remain a conscientious objector. (MS/HS)

Klass, David. *You Don't Know Me*. Though the book deals with the serious topic of abuse, the humorous narrative of the protagonist provides much-needed comic relief. (MS/HS)

Koertge, Ron. *Brimstone Journals*. A series of startling and disturbing poems tells of an unforgettable year at Branston High School. (HS)

Lynch, Chris. *Freewill*. Gifted readers will appreciate the almost stream-of-consciousness writing and the symbolism in a story about death and loss and their aftermath. (HS)

McDonald, Janet. *Spellbound*. A teen mother has the opportunity to win a college scholarship. (HS)

Oates, Joyce Carol. *Big Mouth and Ugly Girl*. Big Mouth stands accused of threatening to bring a gun to school. He is innocent, but no one seems willing to vouch for him. An unusual friendship sparks when Ugly Girl stands up for what is right. (MS/HS)

Spinelli, Jerry. *Loser*. Zinkoff has always been a loser at school. However, being a loser does not seem to bother him much. (INT/MS)

Zusak, Markus. *Fighting Ruben Wolfe*. Two brothers become involved in a boxing competition in order to help out the family. What happens when they must face each other in the ring? (HS)

Multicultural Literature for Young Adults

Alvarez, Julia. *Before We Were Free.* Anita doesn't realize what a dictatorship really is until she finds out her father and her uncles are in a plot to kill the leader. (HS)

Alvarez, Julia. *How Tia Lola Came to (Visit) Stay.* Miguel is embarrassed when his Tia Lola comes to visit. Tia is flamboyant. Miguel prefers to remain anonymous. (MS)

Baskin, Nora Raleigh. *Almost Home.* Leah is now living with her father and his new wife (she refuses to call her stepmother) and misses her old life with her mother and friends. An unlikely savior in the form of a boy in her class helps Leah to find her way home. (INT/MS)

Bauer, Joan. *Stand Tall.* Living between mom's apartment and dad's house proves a bit more than Tree can bear. (MS)

Bauer, Marion Dane, ed. *Am I Blue?* This collection of stories deals with coming to terms with one's sexuality and sexual identity. (HS)

Beals, Melba Patillo. *Warriors Don't Cry.* This memoir tells what happened when Melba Patillo and a group of her friends were the first to integrate Central High in Little Rock, Arkansas. (MS/HS)

Bechard, Margaret. *Hanging on to Max.* Sam's senior year should be a breeze. Baby Max complicates his life more than he could ever have predicted. Can Sam balance school and parenting? (HS)

Bertrand, Diane Gonzalez. *Sweet Fifteen.* Stephanie's quince celebration will be soon, but she can't really enjoy the preparations because she still is so upset that her father died. (MS/HS)

Carlson, Lori. *Cool Salsa.* This collection of bilingual poems covers traditional poetry, street poetry, and everything in between. (MS/HS)

Cart, Michael, ed. *Love and Sex: Ten Stories of Truth.* This collection runs the gamut from the humorous "Extra Virgin" by Joan Bauer to the more serious exploration of Louise Hawes's "Fine and Dandy."

Cart, Michael. *Necessary Noise.* Stories about families, all shapes and sizes and types of family form the theme for this collection. (MS/HS)

Cisneros, Sandra. *Woman Hollering Creek and Other Stories.* The everyday lives of Hispanics are revealed in stories that deal with friendship, superstition, religion, and love. (MS/HS)

Cisneros, Sandra. *The House on Mango Street.* Esperanza talks about her experiences living on Mango Street. (HS)

Cohn, Rachel. *Gingerbread* After being kicked out of boarding school, Cyd stays with her mother for six months and then is shipped to her biological father. She just can't find a place she thinks she belongs. (HS)

Cohn, Rachel. *The Steps*. Annabel needs a chart to keep track of her various siblings and parental combinations. She is vacationing with her Dad in Australia and hopes to convince him to come back. (MS)

Cole, Brock. *Goats*. Howie and Laura are the goats at camp. As the ultimate joke they are stripped naked and put on an island. They decide to fight back, and when the counselors come to get them the next morning, they are gone. (MS)

Crowe, Chris. *Mississippi Trial, 1955*. In 1955 a black boy dared to speak to a white woman and was murdered. Hiram, who is visiting his grandfather for the summer, cannot understand how this can happen and is worried about what part his grandfather might have played in the incident. (MS/HS)

Crowe, Chris. *Getting Away with Murder*. This is the true account that was fictionalized in *Mississippi Trial, 1955*. The Emmett Till murder trial drew attention to the dearth of justice for African-Americans, especially in the South. (MS/HS)

Crutcher, Chris. *Whale Talk*. T. J. forms a swim team with the misfits of the school so that they too will be able to win letter jackets like the elite athletes. (HS)

Curtis, Christopher Paul. *The Watsons Go to Birmingham—1963*. Kenny watches his older brother make one wrong decision after another until his parents say that is it. The family piles into the car and goes from Flint, Michigan, to Birmingham, Alabama. Soon, the family is embroiled in one of the most tragic events of the civil rights movement. (INT/MS)

Curtis, Christopher Paul. *Bud, Not Buddy*. Bud runs away from an orphanage in search of a standup bass player he is sure is his father. (INT/MS)

Desai Hidier, Tanuja. *Born Confused*. Dimple Lala doesn't fit in. She isn't Indian enough nor American enough and is trying to find her place. (HS)

Draper, Sharon. *Tears of a Tiger*. Alex is filled with guilt because his best friend is killed while he is driving under the influence. The loss of this student affects the entire school. (MS/HS)

Draper, Sharon. *Double Dutch*. While preparing for the big national double-dutch jumping contest, two members of the team try to hide their secrets. Delia, an eighth-grade student, can't read; Randy is living alone because his father has disappeared. (MS)

Draper, Sharon. *Darkness Before Dawn*. Keisha likes the attention that she is getting from the new student teacher, who is good looking and smart and is interested in her. When she foolishly goes to his apartment, she is not prepared for his advances. (HS)

Draper, Sharon. *Forged by Fire*. Gerald has been with a relative because his mother is sent to prison for child neglect. Her sentence is up, and she wants Gerald to live with her. He vehemently says no until he realizes that his stepfather has been abusing his little half-sister. (MS/HS)

Ellis, Deborah. *Parvana's Journey*. After the death of her father, Parvana wanders through Afghanistan looking for any other family member that might be alive. (HS)

Flake, Sharon. *The Skin I'm In*. Maleeka doesn't like the way she looks; she thinks her skin is too dark. Things are made worse when a classmate makes fun of her. (MS/HS)

Flake, Sharon. *Money Hungry*. Ever since Raspberry Hill has lived on the streets, she saves every penny she can get her hands on in the hopes that she and her mother will be able to move out of the projects into a nice place. Also by this author: *Begging for Change*. (MS/HS)

Frank, E. R. *America*. After America tries to commit suicide, he is sent to a resident facility to get the help he so desperately needs and to find out who he is. (HS)

Gantos, Jack. *Joey Pigza Swallowed the Key*. Joey is out of control in school and often at home because his medication doesn't work to control his attention deficit/hyperactivity disorder. (MS)

Gaskins, Pearl Fuyo, ed. *What Are You? Voices of Mixed-Race Young People.* Forty young adults, through either poetry or prose, tell what it is like living as a mixed-race person. (HS)

Grimes, Nikki. *Bronx Masquerade.* During open mike in English class, seniors recite their poetry or just talk about how they feel. (HS)

Hamilton, Virginia. *A White Romance.* Talley and her friends have a hard time adjusting when their all-black high school is integrated. (HS)

Hamilton, Virginia. *M. C. Higgins the Great.* M. C.'s home, which has been in his family since his great-great-grandmother ran away from her owner, is about to be destroyed by strip mining. (MS)

Hoose, Phillip. *It's Our World, Too.* This nonfiction collection examines how ordinary teens changed the life of their communities through social activism. (MS/HS)

Jimenez, Francisco. *The Circuit.* This autobiography is broken into stories where the author talks about what it was like being a child of migrant worker parents and the packing, the moving, the new schools, and many other things he went through. Also by this author: *Breaking Through.* (MS/HS)

Johnson, Angela. *The Other Side.* Through poetry and photographs, Angela Johnson revisits her past. (MS)

Johnson, Angela. *The First Part Last.* This prequel to *Heaven* tells the back story of a young father raising his daughter on his own. (HS)

Johnson, Angela. *Heaven.* When the church burns down, Marley needs new baptismal papers and she learns her parents are really her aunt and uncle and her "uncle" Jack is really her father. (MS)

Johnson, Angela. *Toning the Sweep.* When Emily goes with her mother to help move her sick grandmother in with them, she takes a video camera and films her grandmother's friend so their thoughts and memories would stay alive. (HS)

Johnson, Angela. *Humming Whispers.* No matter what she is doing or where she is, Sophie cannot forget her sister, who has schizophrenia. (HS)

Lester, Julius. *When Dad Killed Mom.* Jeremy and his younger sister Jenna try to understand why their father killed their mother. (MS/HS)

Lester, Julius. *Othello.* Shakespeare's play is retold with some important changes: the story is set in England, and Iago and his wife are both African-American. (HS)

Lowry. Lois. *The Silent Boy.* Historical novel about a girl's befriending of a young developmentally challenged boy. This novel sings with lyrical prose. Katy is made real to the reader through meticulous detail. (MS)

McDonald, Janet. *Spellbound.* Raven wants to win the spelling contest because if she does, she will be able to enter a college prep program and get a full scholarship in the fall. (HS)

McDonald, Janet. *Chill Wind.* Aisha, a high school dropout who is nineteen and has two children, has reached her five-year limit on welfare and needs to get a job. (HS)

McKissack, Patricia, and Frederick McKissack. *Christmas in the Big House, Christmas in the Quarters.* In 1859, on a plantation in Virginia, the slaves get the master's house and their own ready for Christmas. Also by these authors: *Red-Tailed Angels, Black Hands, White Sails, Black Diamond,* and *Rebels Against Slavery.* (MS/HS)

Meyer, Carolyn. *Drummers of Jericho.* When a Jewish student refuses to participate in the marching band's formation of a cross, she comes under much criticism from others in the community. (MS)

Meyer, Carolyn. *Rio Grande Stories.* A class begins to write stories about their ancestors and the history of their town. (MS)

Myers, Walter Dean. *Bad Boy.* This memoir vividly portrays the life and times of Myers growing up in Harlem. (MS/HS)

Myers, Walter Dean. *Fallen Angels*. A gripping story about the violence and death in Vietnam is related by Perry, a young African-American soldier. (HS)

Myers, Walter Dean. *Scorpions*. When his brother goes to jail, Jamal takes over the responsibilities for the family, but when his brother asks him to take over his gang, Jamal has second thoughts, particularly when his brother's friend gives him a gun. (HS)

Na, An. *A Step from Heaven*. It isn't easy when Young Ju's family leaves Korea for America, and her parents have a hard time getting jobs. Her father drinks more and more, and beats her mother, until Young Ju takes some action. (MS/HS)

Nye, Naomi Shihab. *19 Varieties of Gazelle*. This collection of poems about the Middle East was a National Book Award finalist. Also by this author: *Space Between Our Footsteps, The Tree Is Older Than You Are,* and *Habibi.* (MS/HS)

Osa, Nancy. *Cuba 15*. Violet Paz just turned fifteen. Her abuela insists on a quince party. Violet does not much care for this tradition until she is given permission to make this quince her own celebration. (MS/HS)

Park, Linda Sue. *A Single Shard*. Tree Ear works for an artist who makes ceramic ware to repay the artist for breaking some. He has the chance to redeem himself by taking special vases to the palace in hopes that a royal commission will be secured. He is attacked and the vases are thrown over a cliff, but Tree Ear manages to save a single shard. (MS)

Park, Linda Sue. *When My Name Was Keoko*. When South Korea is occupied by the Japanese, Sun-hee needs to adjust. (HS)

Paulsen, Gary. *Harris and Me*. What happens when a naive city boy spends a summer on the farm with his cousin Harris? (MS)

Peters, Julie Anne. *Keeping You a Secret*. When Holland meets Cece, her life is changed forever. However, the two must keep their relationship a secret for fear of what others will think and do in reaction. (HS)

Peters, Julie Anne. *Define "Normal."* Antonia is assigned as a peer counselor to Jazz, who looks like a "druggie," but it is really Antonia who needs the help. (HS)

Rapp, Adam. *33 Snowfish*. Not for the faint of heart, this story, told from three points of view, deals with the incredibly daunting life of three runaway children. (HS)

Rice, David. *Crazy Loco*. Short stories about Mexican-Americans who live in the Rio Grande Valley in Texas. (MS/HS)

Ritter, John H. *The Boy Who Saved Baseball*. Lyrical and lovely, here is a tale that combines baseball and family and community. (MS)

Saldana, Rene. *Jumping Tree*. Rey lives near the border, and his family is close, both in America and across the border. He plays with his friends, and they like to challenge each other. One day Rey breaks his wrist. Also by this author: *Finding Our Way.* (MS)

Soto, Gary. *Buried Onions*. Eddie views life as the onions he always smells, with all different layers. He wants to be away from gangs and poverty so he gets a job with a landscaper in a wealthy neighborhood. Things change when his boss's truck is stolen. Also by this author: *Baseball in April, Local News.* (HS)

Trueman, Terry. *Stuck in Neutral*. Shawn has suffered from cerebral palsy and he can no longer move or talk, but he can think, even though no one suspects that his mind is sharp. Shawn realizes that his father is planning to kill him. (MS/HS)

Werlin, Nancy. *Black Mirror*. When Frances's brother dies of a heroin overdose, she tries to find out what really happened. She joins the charitable organization he was part of, looking for answers. (HS)

Williams, Lori Aurelia. *When Kambia Elaine Flew in from Neptune*. Kambia is the new girl in town and whenever she is asked about her personal life she tells a fairy tale and warns her good friend Shayla to watch out for the wolves in the wallpaper. (MS/HS)

Williams, Lori Aurelia. *Shayla's Double Brown Baby Blues.* In this sequel to *When Kambia Elaine Flew in from Neptune,* Kambia is now living with a wonderful family but has started to have nightmares and to withdraw. Her friend Shayla starts to worry about her. (MS/HS)

Williams-Garcia, Rita. *Like Sisters on the Homefront.* Gayle is sent to live with relatives in Georgia when it is learned that she is pregnant. She is fourteen and very resentful at this move. (HS)

Winnick, Judd. *Pedro and Me.* This novel in graphics tells about Pedro Zamora, who was on MTV's Real World, and his struggle with AIDS and wanting to educate others about the disease.(HS)

Woodson, Jacqueline. *Hush.* Toswiah and her family have to enter the witness protection program after her father testifies that he saw two white policeman shooting a black man. Things don't go very well for the family. Also by this author: *If You Come Softly, Locomotion, Maizon of Blue Hill,* and *From the Notebooks of Melanin Sun.* (MS/HS)

Books to Accompany Havighurst's Developmental Tasks

Getting Along with Peers

The Adventures of the Blue Avenger by Norma Howe (HS)

All American Girl by Meg Cabot (HS)

Boys Lie by John Neufeld (MS)

Breaking Point by Alex Flinn (HS)

Crews by Maria Hinojosa (HS)

Crooked by Laura McNeal and Tom McNeal (HS)

Define "Normal" by Julie Anne Peters. (MS)

Freak the Mighty by Rodman Philbrick (INT/MS)

The Friends by Kazumi Yumoto (MS)

Hanging on to Max by Margaret Bechard (HS)

Hoot by Carl Hiaasen (MS)

House of the Scorpions by Nancy Farmer (MS/HS)

Letters from the Inside by John Marsden (HS)

On the Fringe, edited by Donald R. Gallo (MS/HS)

Pictures of Hollis Wood by Patricia Reilly Giff (MS)

The Princess Diaries by Meg Cabot (HS)

The Revelation of St. Bruce by Tres Seymour (HS)

Simon Says by Elaine Marie Alphin (HS)

Speak by Laurie Halse Anderson (MS/HS)

Split Image by Mel Glenn (MS/HS)

Welcome to the Ark by Stephanie Tolan (MS/HS)

Whistling Toilets by Randy Powell (HS)

Changing Relationships with Parents

3 NBs of Julian Drew by James Deem (HS)

The Birthday Room by Kevin Henkes (INT/MS)

Born Blue by Han Nolan (HS)

Bruises by Anke De Vries (HS)

Claws by Will Weaver (HS)

Conditions of Love by Ruth Pennebaker (MS)

A Face in Every Window by Han Nolan (MS)

Gingerbread by Rachel Cohn (HS)

Gypsy Davey by Chris Lynch (HS)

Memory Boy by Will Weaver (MS)

Of Sound Mind by Jean Ferris (MS)

Sometimes I Think I Hear My Name by Avi (MS)

Son of the Mob by Gordon Korman (MS)

Walk Two Moons by Sharon Creech (MS)

What Hearts by Bruce Brooks (MS)

What My Mother Doesn't Know by Sonya Sones (MS)

What Would Joey Do? by Jack Gantos (MS)

When Dad Killed Mom by Julius Lester (MS)

Zero at the Bone by Michael Cadnum (HS)

Easy Relationship with the Opposite Sex

The Adventures of the Blue Avenger by Norma Howe (HS)

Big Mouth and Ugly Girl by Joyce Carol Oates (HS)

Blue Avenger Cracks the Code by Norma Howe (HS)

Caleb's Story by Patricia MacLachlan (MS)

Catalyst by Laurie Halse Anderson (HS)

Dancing in Cadillac Light by Kimberly Willis Holt (MS)

Echo by Francesca Lia Block (HS)
Harmony by Rita Murphy (HS)
Hoot by Carl Hiaasen (MS)
The Misfits by James Howe (MS)
Of Sound Mind by Jean Ferris (MS)
Running Back to Ludie by Angela Johnson (MS)
Say Yes by Audrey Couloumbis (MS)
Slap Your Sides by M. E. Kerr (MS/HS)
Stand Tall by Joan Bauer (MS)
You Don't Know Me by David Klass (MS/HS)

Developing Morals and Values

Ash: A Novel by Linda Faustino (MS)
Becoming Joe Dimaggio by Maria Testa (MS)
Behaving Bradley by Perry Nodelman (HS)
Boys Lie by John Neufeld (MS/HS)
Conditions of Love by Ruth Pennebaker (MS/HS)
The Cure by Sonia Levitin (MS/HS)
Fighting Ruben Wolfe by Markus Zusak (HS)
God of Beer by Garret Kelzer (HS)
The Gospel According to Larry by Janet Tashjian (HS)
A Group of One by Rachna Gilmore (MS)
Leaving Fishers by Margaret Peterson Haddix (MS)
Mississippi Trial, 1955 by Chris Crowe (MS/HS)
The Revelation of St. Bruce by Tres Seymour (HS)
Rooster by Beth Nixon Weaver (MS)
Shattering Glass by Gail Giles (HS)
Slap Your Sides by M. E. Kerr (HS)
Witness by Karen Hesse (MS)

Adapting to Their Physical Bodies

Blubber by Judy Blume (MS)
Cut by Patricia McCormick (HS)
Deenie by Judy Blume (MS)
Extreme Elvin by Chris Lynch (MS)
Freak the Mighty by Rodman Philbrick (MS)
Harmony by Rita Murphy (HS)
Life in the Fat Lane by Cherie Bennett (MS)
Mind's Eye by Paul Fleischman (HS)
The Misfits by James Howe (MS)
One Fat Summer by Robert Lipsyte (MS)
Stand Tall by Joan Bauer (MS)
Staying Fat for Sarah Byrnes by Chris Crutcher (MS/HS)
Who the Man by Chris Lynch (HS)

Defining Appropriate Sex Roles

Big Mouth and Ugly Girl by Joyce Carol Oates (HS)
Crash by Jerry Spinelli (MS)
Eight Seconds by Jean Ferris (HS)
Empress of the World by Sara Ryan (HS)
Just Ella by Margaret Peterson Haddix (MS)
Love That Dog by Sharon Creech (MS)
Priscilla and the Wimps by Richard Peck (MS)
Rainbow Boys by Alex Sanchez (HS)
Rat by Jan Cheripko (MS)
Rewind by William Sleator (MS)
Stand Tall by Joan Bauer (MS)

Working for Pay

Handbook for Boys: A Novel by Walter Dean Myers (MS/HS)
Hope Was Here by Joan Bauer (MS/HS)
Lord of the Deep by Graham Salisbury (MS)
No Coins, Please by Gordon Korman (MS)
One Fat Summer by Robert Lipsyte (MS)
Pool Boy by Michael Simmons (HS)
Razzle by Ellen Wittlinger (HS)
Rules of the Road by Joan Bauer (MS/HS)
Sisterhood of the Traveling Pants by Anne Brashares (HS)
True Believer by Virginia Euwer Wolff (MS)

Finding a Vocation or Career

Backwater by Joan Bauer (MS/HS)
Bad Boy by Walter Dean Myers (MS/HS)
Gathering Blue by Lois Lowry (MS/HS)
The Giver by Lois Lowry (MS/HS)
The Midwife's Apprentice by Karen Cushman (MS)
Rules of the Road by Joan Bauer (MS/HS)
Second Summer of the Sisterhood by Anne Brashares (HS)
The Silent Boy by Lois Lowry (MS)
Spellbound by Janet McDonald (HS)

Twenty Young Adult Books Often Challenged

Annie on My Mind by Nancy Garden (HS)

Athletic Shorts by Chris Crutcher (HS)

Bridge to Terabithia by Katherine Paterson (INT/MS)

Catcher in the Rye by J. D. Salinger (HS)

The Chocolate War by Robert Cormier (HS)

The Face on the Milk Carton by Caroline B. Cooney (MS/HS)

Fallen Angels by Walter Dean Myers (HS)

Forever by Judy Bloome (HS)

The Giver by Lois Lowry (MS)

Go Ask Alice, edited by Beatrice Sparks (MS/HS)

It's Perfectly Normal by Robie H. Harris (MS/HS)

Killing Mr. Griffin by Lois Duncan (HS)

The Outsiders by S. E. Hinton (MS/HS)

The Perks of Being a Wallflower by Stephen Chbosky (HS)

The Pigman by Paul Zindel (MS/HS)

Running Loose by Chris Crutcher (HS)

Speak by Laurie Halse Anderson (HS)

Stotan! by Chris Crutcher (HS)

We All Fall Down by Robert Cormier (HS)

A Wrinkle in Time by Madeleine L'Engle (INT/MS)

Alternatives to Book Reports

A Author study or author report

B Booktalk

C Commercial to sell the book

D Diorama

E Evaluative criteria for the genre applied

F Footsteps showing the path taken by a character

G Game based on the book

H Hanger mobile

I Imagine yourself in the story and write a scene

J Journey map for one of the characters/ journal entries for characters

K Key events of story on key mobile

L Lyrics of songs that would fit moods of story

M Make it into a movie and cast the roles

N New blurbs for back of book

O Outline of character filled in with adjectives describing character

P Poster with new cover

Q Quilt book report or classroom novel quilt

R Reading log

S Summarize the plot

T Title change suggestions

U Undercover police report on actions of a character

V Verses created from a chapter in the book

W Word find

X X-ray of main character's heart

Y "You Are There" report

Z Zero to ten scale rating

Print and Online Resources

ALAN Review. Journal of the Assembly on Literature for Adolescents, National Council of Teachers of English. Contains reviews of YA titles. www.alan-ya.org/.

Allen, Janet. 2000. *Yellow Brick Roads.* Portland, ME: Stenhouse.

Allen, Janet, and Kyle Gonzalez. 1997. *There's Room for Me Here.* Portland, ME: Stenhouse.

Beers, Kylene. 2002. *When Kids Can't Read, What Teachers Can Do.* Portsmouth, NH: Heinemann.

Beers, Kylene, and Teri S. Lesesne, eds. 2001. *Books for You: An Annotated Booklist for Senior High Students.* Urbana, IL: National Council of Teachers of English.

Beers, Kylene, and Barbara Samuels, eds. 1998. *Into Focus: Understanding and Creating Middle School Readers.* Norwood, MA: Christopher-Gordon.

Bodart, Joni Richards. 2000. *The World's Best Thin Books, or What to Read When Your Book Report Is Due Tomorrow.* Lanham, MD: Scarecrow Press.

Book Lists for Young Adults on the Web. www.seemore.mi.org/.

Booklist. Review journal of the American Library Association.

Books for the Teen Age. Annual. New York: New York Public Library.

Carlsen, G. Robert. 1980. *Books and the Teen-Age Reader.* 2d ed. New York: Harper and Row.

Cart, Michael. 1996. *From Romance to Realism: 50 Years of Growth and Change in Young Adult Literature.* New York: HarperCollins.

Carter, Betty. 2000. *Best Book for Young Adults: The Selections, the History, the Romance.* 2d ed. Chicago: American Library Association.

Carter, Betty, and Richard F. Abrahamson. 1990. *Nonfiction for Young Adults: From Delight to Wisdom.* Westport, CT: Oryx Press.

Dresang, Eliza T. 1999. *Radical Change: Books for Youth in a Digital Age.* New York: H. W. Wilson.

Early, Margaret. 1960. "Stages of Growth in Literary Appreciation." *English Journal* 49 (March): 161–167.

English Journal. NCTE Journal for secondary English teachers.

Gallo, Donald R., ed. 1990. *Speaking for Ourselves: Autobiographical Sketches by Notable Authors of Books for Young Adults.* Urbana, IL: National Council of Teachers of English.

———. 1993. *Speaking for Ourselves, Too: More Autobiographical Sketches by Notable Authors of Books for Young Adults.* Urbana, IL: National Council of Teachers of English.

Gallo, Donald R., and Sarah Herz. 1996. *From Hinton to Hamlet: Building Bridges Between Young Adult Literature and the Classics.* Westport, CT: Greenwood.

Hipple, Ted. 1997. *Writers for Young Adults.* 3 vols. New York: Scribner's.

International Reading Association www.reading.org/.

Jones, Patrick. 1998. *Connecting Young Adults and Libraries: A How-to-Do It Manual.* 2d ed. New York: Neal-Schuman.

Journal of Adolescent and Adult Literacy. Membership journal of the International Reading Association.

Kaywell, Joan. 1993–2000. *Adolescent Literature as a Complement to the Classics.* 4 vols. Norwood, MA: Christopher-Gordon.

Kutzer, M. Daphne. 1996. *Writers of Multicultural Fiction for Young Adults.* Westport, CT: Greenwood.

Lesesne, Teri S., and Rosemary Chance. 2002 *Hit List for Young Adults: 2: Frequently Challenged Books.* Chicago: American Library Association.

National Council for the Social Studies booklist. www.socialstudies.org/resources/notable/.

National Council of Teachers of English. www.ncte.org.

Reading Rants! Site maintained by Jennifer Huber. tln.lib.mi.us/~amutch/jen/.

Richie's Picks: Great Books for Children and Young Adults. richiespicks.com/.

Schon, Isabel. 1993. *Books in Spanish for Children and Young Adults.* Series VI. Lanham, MD: Scarecrow Press.

School Library Journal. Review journal. slg.reviewnews.com/.

Sherman, Gale W., and Bette D. Ammon. 1993. *Rip-Roaring Reads for Reluctant Teen Readers.* Westport, CT: Libraries Unlimited.

Spencer, Pam. 1997–2001. *What Do Young Adults Read Next? A Reader's Guide to Fiction for Young Adults.* 4 vols. Farmington Hills, MI: Gale.

Teacher Librarian: The Journal for School Library Professionals. Contains review columns. www.teacherlibrarian.com/.

Voice of Youth Advocates (VOYA). Review journal for YA materials. www.voya.com/.

Voices from the Middle. Journal for middle-level teachers. Urbana, IL: National Council of Teachers of English.

Webb, Anne, ed. 1993. *Your Reading: A Booklist for Junior High and Middle School.* 9th ed. Urbana, IL: National Council of Teachers of English.

Young Adult Library Services Association (YALSA). www.ala.org/yalsa/.

Zvirin, Stephanie. 1996. *The Best Years of Their Lives: A Resource Guide for Teenagers in Crisis.* Chicago: American Library Association.

Selected Awards for Young Adult and Children's Books

ALAN Award

Given by the Assembly on Literature for Adolescents (ALAN) of the National Council of Teachers of English (NCTE), this award recognizes significant contributions to the field of YA literature. Past recipients include Mildred Taylor, S. E. Hinton, Robert Lipsyte, M. E. Kerr, Patty Campbell, and Paul Zindel. www.alan-ya.org/.

Alex Awards

Given by the Young Adult Library Services Association (YALSA) of the American Library Association (ALA), these awards honor ten adult books each year that are appropriate for YA readers. www.ala.org/.

Best Books for Young Adults

Given by the Young Adult Library Services Association (YALSA) of the American Library Association (ALA), these awards honor the best YA book each year as judged by a committee of YALSA members. www.ala.org/.

Best of the Best Books for Young Adults

Every few years, a group of YALSA members meets to discuss past BBYA lists. From those lists are culled the books the group believes represent the best of the BBYA lists of the past thirty years.

Caldecott Medal

Given by the Association for Library Service to Children (ALSC) of ALA, this award is presented annually to the illustrator of the most distinguished U.S. picture book for children. The committee may also present up to five honor awards. Many of these stunning picture books are appropriate for YA readers. A list of picture books for older readers is in Appendix H. www.ala.org/.

Children's Choices

This joint project of the International Reading Association (IRA) and the Children's Book Council (CBC) results in a list of approximately one hundred books a year voted as favorites of children in Pre-K to eighth grade. A list of winners is published annually in the October issue of *The Reading Teacher*. www.reading.org/. www.cbcbooks.org/.

Coretta Scott King Award

Given by ALSC of ALA, this award honors distinguished work by an African-American author and an African-American illustrator whose books promote positive images of African-

Americans. Named in honor of the widow of Martin Luther King, Jr., the award is given annually. As many as five books may also be named as honor award winners in both the text and illustration categories. www.ala.org/.

Margaret A. Edwards Award

Given by YALSA, this award, established in 1988, honors an author's lifetime achievement for writing books that have been popular over a period of time. Past winners include Chris Crutcher, Nancy Garden, Richard Peck, Paul Zindel, and Gary Paulsen. www.ala.org/.

Michael L. Printz Award

Given by YALSA, this award recognizes distinguished contributions to literature for young adults. The Printz Committee names one winner and may select up to five honor books annually. Past recipients of the award include *A Step from Heaven, Monster, Postcards from No Man's Land,* and *Kit's Wilderness.* www.ala.org/.

NCTE Award for Excellence in Poetry for Children

Presented by the National Council of Teachers of English, this award is presented every three years to a living poet for a body of work. Past winners include Mary Ann Hoberman, X. J. Kennedy, Barbara Esbensen, and Eloise Greenfield. www.ncte.org/.

Newbery Medal

Given by ALSC of ALA, this award is presented to the author of the most distinguished contribution to literature for children. As many as five books may be designated as honor medalists each year as well. www.ala.org/.

Notable Books

An ALSC committee compiles a list of these notable books. Categories include Younger Readers, Middle Readers, Older Readers, and All Ages. www.ala.org/.

Notable Social Studies Books for Young People

A joint project of the National Council for the Social Studies (NCSS) and the Children's Book Council, this bibliography features over 150 K–8 annotated titles grouped by subject, including biography; contemporary concerns; environment; energy and ecology; folktales; geography; peoples and places; history, life, and culture in the Americas; social interaction and relationships; and world history and culture. www.cbcbooks.org/.

Orbis Pictus

Given by NCTE, this relatively recent award (it was first given in 1990) honors nonfiction for children. It is given annually. www.ncte.org/.

Outstanding Science Books for Students K–12

A joint project of the National Science Teachers Association (NSTA) and the Children's Book Council, this annotated bibliography features K–8 titles selected by a book review committee appointed by the National Science Teachers Association. Categories include life and earth science, environment, and archaeology. www.cbcbooks.org/.

Pura Belpre

Presented jointly by ALSC and REFORMA every two years, this award honors contributions to the text and illustration of books by Latino/Hispanic artists. Along with the Coretta Scott King Award, it is a good place to begin when developing your multicultural collection. www.ala.org/.

Quick Picks for Reluctant Readers

Given by YALSA, this list is for reluctant readers ages 12–18. It is intended as a motivational list, not for remediation. www.ala.org/.

Robert Sibert Award

Given by ALSC, this award honors contributions to informational books for children. Up to
five additional books may receive honor medal
awards. This is one of the newest awards given
for children's literature. www.ala.org/.

Teachers' Choices

This joint project of the International Reading
Association (IRA) and the Children's Book
Council (CBC) results in a list of approximately
thirty books a year voted as favorites of teachers
working in Pre-K to eighth grade. A list of winners is published annually in a fall issue of *The
Reading Teacher*. www.reading.org/. and
www.cbcbooks.org/.

Young Adults' Choices

This joint project of the International Reading
Association (IRA) and the Children's Book
Council (CBC) results in a list of approximately
thirty books a year voted as favorites of children in grades 7–12. A list of winners is published annually in the November issue of
Journal of Adolescent and Adult Literacy.
www.reading.org/. and www.cbcbooks.org/.

FAQ—Frequently Asked Questions

What is the single best piece of advice you can give me for motivating kids to read?

I begin with the easiest question. In order to best motivate kids to read, you must be a reader yourself. If I wanted to have someone teach me about tennis, I would look for someone who plays on a regular basis. When I took my motorcycle class, we spent most of the time actually riding the bike and not discussing the theory of riding. In order to motivate students to read, we have to read ourselves. We have to read widely, outside of what is our "comfort zone." We have to read all kinds of books because we have such a wide variety of kids with a wide range of experiences and backgrounds in our classrooms. So, unless we are practicing, we'd best not be preaching. Kids can spot a phony a mile away. They will know if we are readers or not.

What are some resources I could use for developing my classroom library?

Here is one suggestion from Nancy Patterson, a former middle school teacher and now an assistant professor at Grand Valley State University, Allendale, Michigan:

> *I built the classroom library in my room a couple of different ways. In the beginning, I offered ten M&Ms for any book that was donated to the library and accepted. If the book was chewed on by unknown teeth, I declined to accept. And if it was too old (meaning the cover was so out-of-date no kid would touch it), I declined. Or if it was geared to too old (mature) an audience or too young, I declined. Kids brought bags of books in. Sometimes parents would come to school with bags of books. It was great!*
>
> *Also, I had book club contests and lent money to kids so they could buy books from Scholastic's Tab. They were pretty good about paying me back. I used the bonus points to get books. I also haunted the sale tables*

at bookstores and spent my own money. And I used curriculum money to buy books, especially Lit Circle titles.

I would add the following:

- Volunteer to clean out lockers at the end of the school year with the provision that any book not belonging to the library becomes yours for the classroom library.
- Visit the publishers' booths at professional conferences. Often some books are given away. Generally, on the final day of the conference, most books are sold at deep discounts.
- Locate a book jobber in your area who will give you a large discount. Do not settle for a measly 10 percent from bookstores. I work with someone who provides a 30 percent discount and offers me books tax-exempt as well.
- Ask parents to donate books to the library in honor of a special occasion such as a child's birthday.
- Volunteer to participate in some of the national book selection programs such as Teachers Choices, YA Choices, and Children's Choices, all joint ventures of the International Reading Association and the Children's Book Council. The schools who worked with me in the past on these projects added hundreds of books to the classroom and school libraries.
- Seek small grants for buying books.

What are some sources for funding for research and for books from classroom libraries?

ALAN, the Assembly on Literature for Adolescents, of NCTE offers research grants each year to its members for research into YA literature. Grant application forms are available at www.alan-ya.org/.

The American Library Association and its divisions also support research through a variety of grants. The Frances Henne/YALSA/VOYA grant is designated for research into improving services to young adults in libraries. Why not collaborate with your school librarian on a project of interest to you both?

Cooperative ventures with universities in the area are another good source of funding. Frequently, professors are encouraged to form partnerships with local schools and districts for the purpose of research. Sam Houston State University provided the seed money for the first computers I used in my electronic mentoring project many years ago. Additional grants have been received from library professional organizations, from the state English and reading groups, from ALAN, and from YALSA over the past ten years.

Businesses in the community surrounding the school often offer grants and funds to teachers. Our local Target and Wal-Mart stores were pleased to offer us discounts when we purchased cassette players and headphones for our audiobook project. In addition, the audiobook company with which we did business was happy to offer a substantial discount as well.

Censorship—What do you do?
As in football and other sports, the best defense is a good offense. Check with your school librarian to see what the school's policy is for selecting materials and for handling challenges that might arise. Most schools have a selection policy for the collection that requires positive reviews of the materials added to the shelves. English departments would do well to follow suit.

Make certain that you have a rationale on hand for any potentially objectionable materials. Sample rationales are available from NCTE and from ALA. A rationale basically makes the case for why you might use a book in the classroom, what awards the book has received, and positive reviews of the material as well.

Do not restrict choice to one book for the entire class. If you give several choices, there is seldom a reason for an objection to be made in the first place. If you do want to use a class novel, be sure to have some alternative selections available just in case.

Never remove a challenged book from the shelf or from a student until the proper process is followed. If someone challenges a book, follow the policy for your school district to the letter. It has been my experience that most challenges from a parent can be handled in a conference. What the parent wants is someone to listen to her or his concerns. You can be that person as long as you remain calm and follow the procedure.

Be familiar with which books are being targeted (see Appendix U). Check the American Library Association's Office of Intellectual Freedom Web site to see the top 10 or top 100 Challenged Books each year. There are very few books that are completely "safe." Remember, *Charlotte's Web* is on the list each year, as are other childhood classics.

Have a copy of *Hit List for Young Adults* (available from ALA Editions) in the professional collection in the school library for reference as well as *Hit List for Children* (ALA) and *Rationales for Commonly Taught Challenged Books* (NCTE).

How can I stay current?

More than five thousand books were published for kids last year. I am always behind in my reading. However, I do not despair. I belong to several listservs that discuss books, such as ncte-middle, yalsa-bk, and child_lit. When a book gets a lot of favorable buzz, and I have not read it yet, it moves to the top of my pile. I read the starred reviews in *School Library Journal, Horn Book,* and *Booklist* as well as the books reviewed by VOYA with high ratings. This also helps me keep up with the books I think I need to know. Of course, I read books by my favorite authors or in my favorite genres as well.

I also take advantage of the booklists that are handed out at conferences and posted at the Web sites of the professional organizations to which I belong. I visit exhibits of publishers at the conferences to see what books are being featured. The best way to stay current is to make the time to read every day, if only for a few minutes. My secret: I have books everywhere. I have bathroom books (poetry and story collections work well for those short reads) and books in the car (in case of gridlock). I always take books when I have any kind of appointment. I know how many pages I can read while my hair is being highlighted. It all adds up.

What about those canned programs that promise to make kids into readers?

That is a subject for an entire book, I think. However, let me point out some of the inherent flaws in such programs.

- There is no reputable research that indicates that a program in and of itself leads to any increases they may claim. The research they send out in their packets is not really about the program results; it is about motivation. Some new research indicates that these programs do not achieve the results they promise. See Linda Pavonetti's piece in the December 2002/January 2003 issue of *Journal of Adolescent and Adult Literacy.* Another fine article is Betty Carter's "Hold the Applause: Do Accelerated Reader and Electronic Bookshelf Send the Right Message?", *School Library Journal,* October 1996. Stephen Krashen has an area at his Web site devoted to a meta-analysis of the research into such programs. Take a look there before you decide to let a company dictate your reading program. www.sdkrashen.com/articles/does_accelerated_reader_work/ index.html.

- The reading lists from these programs are quite restricted. Unless you have all the disks, (and even if you do) there are many fine titles missing. Of course, new books are slow to have test disks made. My granddaughter had to wait for the Harry Potter disk and the Newbery disk for this year's winners. The company will tell you that tests can be made at the school level. However, it is time-consuming at best.

- These programs force kids to read books in their "zone," a misapplication of Vygotsky. That means they cannot read easy or tough books; they need to stay in a range. That range sometimes results in some interesting and appropriate books' being missing from a child's list of books he or she can read. We all know that there is a world of difference between reading levels and interest levels. Here are a few examples. *Nightjohn* by Gary Paulsen, the story of a young slave girl who defies her master and learns to read, is given a level between third and fourth grade by some of the programs. *Speak* by Laurie Halse Anderson, which tells of the aftermath of a rape, is also at a similar level. If a child has to read within her or his level, imagine the consequences of kids' checking out books well beyond them developmentally.

- Many programs offer a "one size fits all" curriculum—this program is good for every kid in every grade, according to its proponents, which is definitely not the case. I know of many good readers and many poor readers who hate these programs.

- Cheating is possible. (Heck, face up to it—it happens a lot.)

- The tests from these companies check at the lowest levels of thought; there are closed-ended questions with discrete answers. Basically, if you are good at remembering details, you can do well on the test. If you read for big ideas, too bad. Also, if you cannot take the test right away, chances are you will not do well. Most tests are limited to ten questions. Imagine a ten-item test on Harry Potter.

- These programs are now driving the library collections in many schools. That means funds are being spent for program books and not necessarily for the best new books.

- Kids cannot reread books for points. Since these programs are now showing up at lower levels (kindergarten, for example), this is a drawback. Rereading is something we all do and enjoy.

- Costs are hidden. Initial setup is not so bad, but add on new disks all the time and training for teachers, and you have spent a ton of dollars better spent in bringing in authors, buying new books in multiple copies, and so on.

- Decisions about such programs are coming from the top down. These companies market to administrators, promising increased test scores, and then teachers are told to adopt them.

Finally, be aware that reading aloud, having free choice of books, getting time in school to read, and the other elements of these programs are tested and do increase reading and, generally, test scores. It is not the test that is doing the trick. The elements of a good literacy program cause the effects.

How do I go about arranging an author visit?
First, decide on your budget. If you have $500, there will be certain restrictions. Author fees range widely, but many authors have honoraria between $1,000 and $3,000 per day plus travel and accommodations. If you do not have that kind of financial support, you should consider using someone local (eliminates travel and accommodations) or perhaps having a storyteller instead.

Once you know you can afford an author visit, contact the publisher. Many authors have agents who book their appearances; the publishers will know whom to put you in contact with to make arrangements.

Make arrangements well in advance and have several dates as options. Some authors book speaking engagements up to twenty-four months in advance. You need to be flexible about the date in order to accommodate the author's schedule.

Sometimes it is helpful to have several schools in the same area who will share an author over the course of several days or a week. This means splitting travel expenses and can work to your advantage.

Once times and dates and budgets are confirmed, put it all in a written contract and have a signed one for your files. It does not have to be a legal document, just one that states who will do what.

There are hundreds of details that will follow the contract. For guidance, see Sharron McElmeel's *ABCs of an Author/Illustrator Visit* (2001).

What if I can't afford to bring an author to my school?
Here are some alternatives, although there is no substitute for actually having an author in front of the kids:

- Arrange a telephone conference.
- Arrange a video conference.
- Visit the author's Web site.
- Show kids videos made about the authors.
- Read interviews with the authors. One of the best sites for this is Don Gallo's authors4teens.com.

Contributors' Works

This bibliography lists works by the eighteen authors who contributed memories of their youthful reading experiences to this book. After students have read those short selections, you may wish to encourage them to read books by these authors.

Appelt, K. 1995. *Bayou Lullaby*. New York: Morrow.
———. 1996a. *Red Wagon Year*. San Diego: Harcourt Brace Jovanovich.
———. 1996b. *Thunderherd*. New York: Morrow.
———. 1996c. *Watermelon Year*. New York: Henry Holt and Co.
———. 1997a. *Elephants Aloft*. San Diego: Harcourt Brace Jovanovich.
———. 1997b. *I See the Moon*. Grand Rapids, MI: William B. Erdmans.
———. 1997c. *Just People: Paper/Pen/Poem*. Houston, TX: Absey and Co.
———. 1998. *Bat Jamboree*. New York: Scott Foresman.
———. 1999a. *Bats on Parade*. New York: Morrow.
———. 1999b. *Cowboy Dreams*. New York: HarperCollins.
———. 2000a. *Bats Around the Clock*. New York: HarperCollins.
———. 2000b. *Kissing Tennessee and Other Stories from the Stardust Dance*. San Diego: Harcourt Brace Jovanovich.
———. 2000c. *Oh My Baby, Little One*. San Diego: Harcourt Brace Jovanovich.
———. 2001a. *Bubbles, Bubbles*. New York: HarperCollins.
———. 2001b. *Down Cut Shin Creek: The Pack Horse Librarians of Kentucky*. New York: HarperCollins.
———. 2002a. *Bubba and Beau, Best Friends*. San Diego: Harcourt Brace Jovanovich.
———. 2002b. *Poems from Homeroom: A Writer's Place to Start*. New York: Henry Holt and Co.
———. 2003a. *The Best Kind of Gift*. New York: HarperCollins.
———. 2003b. *Bubba and Beau Go Night-Night*. San Diego: Harcourt Brace Jovanovich.
———. 2003a. *Incredible Me!* New York: HarperCollins.
Barron, T. A. 1990. *Heartlight*. New York: Philomel Books.
———. 1992. *The Ancient One*. New York: Philomel Books.
———. 1993. *To Walk in Wilderness: A Rocky Mountain Journal*. Englewood, CO: Westcliffe.

———. 1994. *The Merlin Effect.* New York: Philomel Books.

———. 1996. *The Lost Years of Merlin.* New York: Philomel Books.

———. 1997. *The Seven Songs of Merlin.* New York: Philomel Books.

———. 1998. *The Fires of Merlin.* New York: Philomel Books.

———. 1999. *The Mirror of Merlin.* New York: Philomel Books.

———. 2000a. *Where Is Grandpa?* New York: Philomel Books.

———. 2000b. *The Wings of Merlin.* New York: Philomel Books.

———. 2001. *Tree Girl.* New York: Philomel Books.

———. 2002. *The Hero's Trail: A Guide for a Heroic Life.* New York: Philomel Books.

Cart, Michael. 1995a. *Presenting Robert Lipsyte.* New York: Twayne.

———. 1995b. *What's So Funny? Wit and Humor in American Children's Literature.* New York: HarperCollins.

———. 1996a. *From Romance to Realism: 50 Years of Growth and Change in Young Adult Literature.* New York: HarperCollins.

———. 1996b. *My Father's Scar: A Novel.* New York: Simon and Schuster Books for Young Readers.

———. 1999. *Tomorrowland: Ten Stories About the Future.* New York: Scholastic.

Cart, Michael, ed. 2001. *Love and Sex: Ten Stories of Truth.* New York: Simon and Schuster Books for Young Readers.

———. 2002a. *911: The Book of Help.* Chicago: Cricket Books.

———. 2002b. *In the Stacks: Short Stories About Libraries and Librarians.* New York: Overlook.

———. 2003. *Necessary Noise.* New York: Simon and Schuster.

Creech, Sharon. 1994. *Walk Two Moons.* New York: HarperCollins.

———. 1995. *Absolutely Normal Chaos.* New York: HarperCollins.

———. 1996. *Pleasing the Ghost.* New York: HarperCollins.

———. 1997. *Chasing Redbird.* New York: HarperCollins.

———. 1998. *Bloomability.* New York: HarperCollins.

———. 2000a. *Fishing in the Air.* New York: Joanna Cotler Books.

———. 2000b. *The Wanderer.* New York: HarperCollins.

———. 2001a. *A Fine, Fine School.* New York: Joanna Cotler Books.

———. 2001b. *Love That Dog.* New York: HarperCollins.

———. 2002. *Ruby Holler.* New York: Joanna Cotler Books.

———. 2003. *Granny Torrelli Makes Soup.* New York: Joanna Cotler Books.

Crowe, Chris. 1994. *Two Roads.* Salt Lake City, UT: Bookcraft.

———. 1995. *Fatherhood, Football and Turning Forty.* Salt Lake City, UT: Bookcraft.

———. 1997. *For the Strength of You.* Salt Lake City, UT: Bookcraft.

———. 1999. *Presenting Mildred D. Taylor.* New York: Twayne.

———. 2002. *Mississippi Trial, 1955.* New York: P. Fogelman Books.

———. 2003. *Getting Away with Murder: The True Story of the Emmett Till Case.* New York: P. Fogelman Books.

Crowe, Chris, ed. 1998. *From the Outside Looking In: Short Stories for LDS Teenagers.* Salt Lake City, UT: Bookcraft.

Crutcher, Chris. 1983. *Running Loose.* New York: Greenwillow Books.

———. 1986. *Stotan!* New York: Greenwillow Books.

———. 1987. *The Crazy Horse Electric Game.* New York: Greenwillow Books.

———. 1989. *Chinese Handcuffs.* New York: Greenwillow Books.

———. 1991. *Athletic Shorts: Six Short Stories.* New York: Greenwillow Books.

———. 1992. *The Deep End: A Novel of Suspense.* New York: W. Morrow and Co.

———. 1993. *Staying Fat for Sarah Byrnes.* New York: Greenwillow Books.

———. 1995. *Ironman: A Novel.* New York: Greenwillow Books.

———. 2001. *Whale Talk.* New York: Greenwillow Books.

———. 2003. *King of the Mild Frontier: An Ill-Advised Autobiography.* New York: Greenwillow Books.

Gantos, Jack. 1976a. *Rotten Ralph.* Boston: Houghton Mifflin.

———. 1976b. *Sleepy Ronald.* Boston: Houghton Mifflin.

———. 1977. *Fair-Weather Friends.* Boston: Houghton Mifflin.

———. 1978a. *Aunt Bernice.* Boston: Houghton Mifflin.

———. 1978b. *Worse Than Rotten Ralph.* Boston: Houghton Mifflin.

———. 1980a. *Swampy Alligator.* New York: Windmill/Wanderer Books.

———. 1980b. *The Werewolf Family.* Boston: Houghton Mifflin.

———. 1980c. *Willy's Raiders.* New York: Parents Magazine Press.

———. 1984. *Rotten Ralph's Rotten Christmas.* Boston: Houghton Mifflin.

———. 1986. *Rotten Ralph's Trick or Treat!* Boston: Houghton Mifflin.

———. 1989. *Rotten Ralph's Show and Tell.* Boston: Houghton Mifflin.

———. 1990. *Happy Birthday Rotten Ralph.* Boston: Houghton Mifflin.

———. 1994a. *Heads or Tails: Stories from the Sixth Grade.* New York: Farrar, Straus and Giroux.

———. 1994b. *Not So Rotten Ralph.* Boston: Houghton Mifflin.

———. 1995. *Jack's New Power: Stories from a Caribbean Year.* New York: Farrar, Straus and Giroux.

———. 1996. *Zip Six: A Novel.* Bridgehampton, NY: Bridge Works Publishing. Distributed in the U.S. by National Book Network.

———. 1997a. *Desire Lines.* New York: Farrar, Straus and Giroux.

———. 1997b. *Jack's Black Book.* New York: Farrar, Straus and Giroux.

———. 1997c. *Rotten Ralph's Rotten Romance.* Boston : Houghton Mifflin.

———. 1998a. *Back to School for Rotten Ralph.* New York: HarperCollins.

———. 1998b. *The Christmas Spirit Strikes Rotten Ralph.* New York: HarperFestival.

———. 1998c. *Joey Pigza Swallowed the Key.* New York: Farrar, Straus and Giroux.

———. 1998d. *Rotten Ralph's Halloween Howl.* New York: HarperFestival.

———. 1999a. *Jack on the Tracks: Four Seasons of Fifth Grade.* New York: Farrar, Straus and Giroux.

———. 1999b. *Rotten Ralph's Thanksgiving Wish.* New York: HarperFestival.

———. 1999c. *Wedding Bells for Rotten Ralph.* New York: HarperCollins.

———. 2000. *Joey Pigza Loses Control.* New York: Farrar, Straus and Giroux.

———. 2001. *Rotten Ralph Helps Out.* New York: Farrar, Straus and Giroux.

———. 2002a. *Hole In My Life.* New York: Farrar, Straus and Giroux.

———. 2002b. *Practice Makes Perfect for Rotten Ralph.* New York: Farrar, Straus and Giroux.

———. 2002c. *What Would Joey Do?* New York: Farrar, Straus and Giroux.

———. 2003. *Jack Adrift: Fourth Grade Without a Clue.* New York: Farrar, Straus and Giroux.

Glenn, Mel. 1982. *Class Dismissed! High School Poems.* New York: Clarion Books.

———. 1984. *One Order to Go.* New York: Clarion Books.

———. 1986a. *Class Dismissed II: More High School Poems.* New York: Clarion Books.

———. 1986b. *Play-by-Play.* New York: Clarion Books.

———. 1988. *Back to Class.* New York: Clarion Books.

———. 1989. *Squeeze Play: A Baseball Story.* New York: Clarion Books.

———. 1991. *My Friend's Got This Problem, Mr. Candler: High School Poems.* New York: Clarion Books.

———. 1996. *Who Killed Mr. Chippendale? A Mystery in Poems.* New York: Lodestar Books.

———. 1997a. *Jump Ball: A Basketball Season in Poems.* New York: Lodestar Books.

———. 1997b. *The Taking of Room 114: A Hostage Drama in Poems.* New York: Lodestar Books.

———. 1999. *Foreign Exchange: A Mystery in Poems.* New York: Morrow Junior Books.

———. 2000. *Split Image: A Story in Poems.* New York: HarperCollins.

Holt, Kimberly Willis. 1998a. *Mister and Me.* New York: Putnam.

———. 1998b. *My Louisiana Sky.* New York: Henry Holt and Co.

———. 1999. *When Zachary Beaver Came to Town.* New York: Henry Holt and Co.

———. 2001. *Dancing in Cadillac Light.* New York: Putnam.

———. 2003. *Keeper of the Night.* New York: Henry Holt and Co.

Hopkins, Lee Bennett. 1975. *Do You Know What Day Tomorrow Is? A Teacher's Almanac.* New York: Citation.

———. 1976. *I Loved Rose Ann.* New York: Knopf.

———. 1979. *Wonder Wheels: A Novel.* New York: Knopf.

———. 1980. *The Best of Book Bonanza.* New York: Holt, Rinehart and Winston.

———. 1983. *How Do You Make an Elephant Float? and Other Delicious Riddles.* Chicago: A. Whitman.

———. 1989a. *Animals from Mother Goose: A Question Book.* San Diego: Harcourt Brace Jovanovich.

———. 1989b. *People from Mother Goose: A Question Book.* San Diego: Harcourt Brace Jovanovich.

———. 1992. *Let Them Be Themselves.* New York: HarperCollins.

———. 1993. *The Writing Bug.* Katonah, NY: R. C. Owen.

———. 1995a. *Been to Yesterdays: Poems of a Life.* Honesdale, PA: Wordsong/Boyds Mills Press.

———. 1995b. *Good Rhymes, Good Times: Original Poems.* New York: HarperCollins.

———. 1998. *Pass the Poetry, Please!* New York: HarperCollins.

———. 1999. *Mother Goose and Her Children.* New York: Sadlier-Oxford.

———. 2000a. *Mama.* Honesdale, PA: Boyds Mills Press.

———. 2000b. *Mama and Her Boys.* Honesdale, PA: Boyds Mills Press.

———. 2003. *Alphathoughts.* Honesdale, PA: Wordsong/Boyds Mills Press.

Hopkins, Lee Bennett, comp. 1976. *Good Morning to You, Valentine: Poems.* San Diego: Harcourt Brace Jovanovich.

———. 1977a. *A-Haunting We Will Go: Ghostly Stories and Poems.* Chicago: A Whitman.

———. 1977b. *Beat the Drum, Independence Day Has Come Poems.* San Diego: Harcourt Brace Jovanovich.

———. 1977c. *Monsters, Ghoulies, and Creepy Creatures: Fantastic Stories and Poems.* Chicago: A. Whitman.

————. 1977d. *Witching Time: Mischievous Stories and Poems.* Chicago: A. Whitman.

————. 1978a. *Merrily Comes Our Harvest In: Poems for Thanksgiving.* San Diego: Harcourt Brace Jovanovich.

————. 1978b. *To Look at Any Thing: Poems.* San Diego: Harcourt Brace Jovanovich.

————. 1979a. *Easter Buds Are Springing: Poems for Easter.* San Diego: Harcourt Brace Jovanovich.

————. 1979b. *Go to Bed! A Book of Bedtime Poems.* New York: Knopf.

————. 1979c. *Kits, Cats, Lions, and Tigers: Stories, Poems, and Verse.* Chicago: A. Whitman.

————. 1979d. *Merely Players: An Anthology of Life Poems.* New York: Elsevier/Nelson.

————. 1979e. *My Mane Catches the Wind: Poems About Horses.* San Diego: Harcourt Brace Jovanovich.

————. 1979f. *Pups, Dogs, Foxes, and Wolves: Stories, Poems, and Verse.* Chicago: A. Whitman.

————. 1980a. *By Myself: Poems.* New York: Crowell.

————. 1980b. *Elves, Fairies and Gnomes: Poems.* New York: Knopf.

————. 1980c. *Moments.* San Diego: Harcourt Brace Jovanovich.

————. 1980d. *Morning, Noon, and Nighttime, Too: Poems.* New York: Harper and Row.

————. 1981. *I Am the Cat: Poems.* San Diego: Harcourt Brace Jovanovich.

————. 1982a. *And God Bless Me: Prayers, Lullabies, and Dream-Poems.* New York: Knopf.

————. 1982b. *Circus! Circus!: Poems.* New York: Knopf.

————. 1983a. *A Dog's Life: Poems.* San Diego: Harcourt Brace Jovanovich.

————. 1983b. *The Sky Is Full of Song.* New York: Harper and Row.

————. 1983c. *A Song in Stone: City Poems.* New York: Crowell.

————. 1984a. *Love and Kisses: Poems.* Boston: Houghton Mifflin.

————. 1984b. *Surprises.* New York: Harper and Row.

————. 1985a. *Creatures: Poems.* San Diego: Harcourt Brace Jovanovich.

————. 1985b. *Munching: Poems About Eating.* Boston: Little, Brown.

————. 1986a. *Best Friends: Poems.* New York: Harper and Row.

————. 1986b. *The Sea Is Calling Me: Poems.* San Diego: Harcourt Brace Jovanovich.

————. 1987a. *Dinosaurs: Poems.* San Diego: Harcourt Brace Jovanovich.

————. 1987b. *More Surprises.* New York: Harper and Row.

————. 1988. *Side by Side: Poems to Read Together.* New York: Simon and Schuster Books for Young Readers.

————. 1989. *Still as a Star: A Book of Nighttime Poems.* Boston: Little, Brown.

————. 1990. *Good Books, Good Times!* New York: Harper and Row.

————. 1991a. *Happy Birthday: Poems.* New York: Simon and Schuster Books for Young Readers.

————. 1991b. *On the Farm.* Boston: Little, Brown.

————. 1992a. *Flit, Flutter, Fly! Poems About Bugs and Other Crawly Creatures.* New York: Doubleday Books for Young Readers.

————. 1992b. *Pterodactyls and Pizza: A Trumpet Club Book of Poetry.* New York: Trumpet Club.

————. 1992c. *Questions: Poems.* New York: HarperCollins.

————. 1992d. *Ring Out, Wild Bells: Poems About Holidays and Seasons.* San Diego: Harcourt Brace Jovanovich.

————. 1992e. *Through Our Eyes: Poems and Pictures About Growing Up.* Boston: Little, Brown.

————. 1992f. *To the Zoo: Animal Poems.* Boston: Little, Brown.

————. 1993a. *Extra Innings: Baseball Poems.* San Diego: Harcourt Brace Jovanovich.

————. 1993b. *It's About Time: Poems.* New York: Simon and Schuster Books for Young Readers.

————. 1993c. *Ragged Shadows: Poems of Halloween Night.* Boston: Little, Brown.

————. 1994a. *April, Bubbles, Chocolate: An ABC of Poetry.* New York: Simon and Schuster Books for Young Readers.

————. 1994b. *Hand in Hand: An American History Through Poetry.* New York: Simon and Schuster.

————. 1994c. *Weather.* New York: HarperCollins.

————. 1995a. *Blast Off! Poems About Space.* New York: HarperCollins.

————. 1995b. *Small Talk: A Book of Short Poems.* San Diego: Harcourt Brace Jovanovich.

————. 1996a. *Opening Days: Sports Poems.* San Diego: Harcourt Brace Jovanovich.

————. 1996b. *School Supplies: A Book of Poems.* New York: Simon and Schuster Books for Young Readers.

————. 1997a. *Marvelous Math: A Book of Poems.* New York: Simon and Schuster Books for Young Readers.

————. 1997b. *Song and Dance: Poems.* New York: Simon and Schuster Books for Young Readers.

————. 1998a. *All God's Children: A Book of Prayers.* San Diego: Harcourt Brace Jovanovich.

————. 1998b. *Climb into My Lap: First Poems to Read Together.* New York: Simon and Schuster Books for Young Readers.

————. 1999a. *Dino-Roars.* New York: Golden Books.

————. 1999b. *Lives: Poems About Famous Americans.* New York: HarperCollins.

————. 1999c. *Spectacular Science: A Book of Poems.* New York: Simon and Schuster Books for Young Readers.

————. 1999d. *Sports! Sports! Sports! A Poetry Collection.* New York: HarperCollins.

————. 2000a. *My America: A Poetry Atlas of the United States.* New York: Simon and Schuster Books for Young Readers.

————. 2000b. *Yummy! Eating Through a Day: Poems.* New York: Simon and Schuster Books for Young Readers.

————. 2002. *Home to Me: Poems Across America.* New York: Orchard Books.

————. 2003. *A Pet for Me: Poems.* New York: HarperCollins.

Hopkins, Lee Bennett, ed. 2002. *Hoofbeats, Claws and Rippled Fins: Creature Poems.* New York: HarperCollins.

Ingold, Jeanette. 1998. *Pictures, 1918.* San Diego: Harcourt Brace Jovanovich.

————. 1999. *Airfield.* San Diego: Harcourt Brace Jovanovich.

————. 2002. *The Big Burn.* San Diego: Harcourt Brace Jovanovich.

————. 2003. *The Window.* San Diego: Harcourt Brace Jovanovich.

Janeczko, Paul B. 1984. *Loads of Codes and Secret Ciphers.* New York: Macmillan.

————. 1986. *Bridges to Cross.* New York: Macmillan.

————. 1989. *Brickyard Summer: Poems.* New York: Orchard Books.

————. 1993. *Stardust Hotel: Poems.* New York: Orchard Books.

———. 1998. *That Sweet Diamond: Baseball Poems*. New York: Atheneum Books for Young Readers.

———. 1999. *How to Write Poetry*. New York: Scholastic Reference.

Janeczko, Paul, comp. 1981. *Don't Forget to Fly: A Cycle of Modern Poems*. Scarsdale, NY: Bradbury.

———. 1983. *Poetspeak: In Their Work, About Their Work: A Selection*. Scarsdale, NY: Bradbury.

———. 1984. *Strings: A Gathering of Family Poems*. Scarsdale, NY: Bradbury.

———. 1985. *Pocket Poems*. Scarsdale, NY: Bradbury.

———. 1987a. *Going Over to Your Place: Poems for Each Other*. Scarsdale, NY: Bradbury.

———. 1987b. *This Delicious Day: 65 Poems*. New York: Orchard Books.

———. 1988. *The Music of What Happens: Poems That Tell Stories*. New York: Orchard Books.

———. 1990. *The Place My Words Are Looking For: What Poets Say About and Through Their Work*. Scarsdale, NY: Bradbury.

———. 1991. *Preposterous: Poems of Youth*. New York: Orchard Books.

———. 1993. *Looking for Your Name: A Collection of Contemporary Poems*. New York: Orchard Books.

———. 1994. *Poetry from A to Z: A Guide for Young Writers*. Scarsdale, NY: Bradbury.

———. 1995. *Wherever Home Begins: 100 Contemporary Poems*. New York: Orchard Books.

———. 1997. *Home on the Range: Cowboy Poetry*. New York: Dial Books.

———. 1999. *Very Best (Almost) Friends: Poems of Friendship*. Cambridge, MA: Candlewick.

———. 2000. *Stone Bench in an Empty Park*. New York: Orchard Books.

———. 2001a. *Dirty Laundry Pile: Poems in Different Voices*. New York: HarperCollins.

———. 2001b. *A Poke in the I*. Cambridge, MA: Candlewick.

———. 2002. *Seeing the Blue Between: Advice and Inspiration for Young Poets*. Cambridge, MA: Candlewick.

———. 2003. *Opening a Door*. New York: Scholastic.

Janeczko, Paul, ed. 1979. *Postcard Poems: A Collection of Poetry for Sharing*. Scarsdale, NY: Bradbury.

Meyer, Carolyn. 1976a. *Amish People: Plain Living in a Complex World*. New York: Atheneum.

———. 1976b. *Coconut, the Tree of Life*. New York: Morrow.

———. 1976c. *Lots and Lots of Candy*. San Diego: Harcourt Brace Jovanovich.

———. 1977. *Being Beautiful: The Story of Cosmetics from Ancient Art to Modern Science*. New York: Morrow.

———. 1978a. *C.C. Poindexter*. New York: Atheneum.

———. 1978b. *Mask Magic*. San Diego: Harcourt Brace Jovanovich.

———. 1979. *The Center: From a Troubled Past to a New Life*. New York: Atheneum.

———. 1980. *Rock Band: Big Men in a Great Big Town*. New York: Atheneum.

———. 1982. *Eulalia's Island*. New York: Atheneum.

———. 1983. *The Summer I Learned About Life*. New York: Atheneum.

———. 1984. *The Luck of Texas McCoy*. New York: Atheneum.

———. 1986a. *Elliott and Win*. New York: Atheneum.

———. 1986b. *Voices of South Africa: Growing Up in a Troubled Land.* San Diego: Harcourt Brace Jovanovich.

———. 1987a. *Denny's Tapes.* New York: M. K. McElderry Books.

———. 1987b. *Voices of Northern Ireland: Growing Up in a Troubled Land.* San Diego: Harcourt Brace Jovanovich.

———. 1988. *A Voice from Japan: An Outsider Looks In.* San Diego: Harcourt Brace Jovanovich.

———. 1989. *Wild Rover.* New York: M. K. McElderry Books.

———. 1990. *Killing the Kudu.* New York: M. K. McElderry Books.

———. 1992. *Where the Broken Heart Still Beats: The Story of Cynthia Ann Parker.* San Diego: Harcourt Brace Jovanovich.

———. 1993. *White Lilacs.* San Diego: Harcourt Brace Jovanovich.

———. 1995. *Drummers of Jericho.* San Diego: Harcourt Brace Jovanovich.

———. 1996. *Gideon's People.* San Diego: Harcourt Brace Jovanovich.

———. 1997. *Jubilee Journey.* San Diego: Harcourt Brace Jovanovich.

———. 1999. *Mary, Bloody Mary.* San Diego: Harcourt Brace Jovanovich.

———. 2000a. *Anastasia, the Last Grand Duchess.* New York: Scholastic.

———. 2000b. *Isabel: Jewel of Castilla.* New York: Scholastic.

———. 2001. *Beware, Princess Elizabeth.* San Diego: Harcourt Brace Jovanovich.

———. 2002. *Doomed Queen Anne.* San Diego: Harcourt Brace Jovanovich.

———. 2003. *Brown Eyes Blue: A Novel.* Bridgehampton, NY: Bridge Works Publishing.

Meyer, Carolyn, comp. 1994. *Rio Grande Stories.* San Diego: Harcourt Brace Jovanovich.

Nixon, Joan Lowery. 1976. *The Mysterious Prowler.* San Diego: Harcourt Brace Jovanovich.

———. 1977. *Writing Mysteries for Young People.* Boston: The Writer.

———. 1978a. *The Boy Who Could Find Anything.* San Diego: Harcourt Brace Jovanovich.

———. 1978b. *Danger in Dinosaur Valley.* New York: Putnam.

———. 1978c. *Muffie Mouse and the Busy Birthday.* New York: Seabury.

———. 1978d. *When God Listens.* Huntington, IN: Our Sunday Visitor.

———. 1978e. *When God Speaks.* Huntington, IN: Our Sunday Visitor.

———. 1979a. *Bigfoot Makes a Movie.* New York: Putnam.

———. 1979b. *The Grandmother's Book.* Nashville: Abingdon.

———. 1979c. *The Halloween Mystery.* Chicago: A. Whitman.

———. 1979d. *The Kidnapping of Christina Lattimore.* San Diego: Harcourt Brace Jovanovich.

———. 1979e. *The New Year's Mystery.* Chicago: A. Whitman.

———. 1979f. *The Valentine Mystery.* Chicago: A. Whitman.

———. 1980a. *The April Fool Mystery.* Chicago: A. Whitman.

———. 1980b. *Casey and the Great Idea.* New York: Dutton.

———. 1980c. *Gloria Chipmunk, Star!* Boston: Houghton Mifflin/Clarion Books.

———. 1980d. *The Happy Birthday Mystery.* Chicago: A. Whitman.

———. 1980e. *If You Say So, Claude.* New York: F. Warne.

———. 1980f. *The Séance.* San Diego: Harcourt Brace Jovanovich.

———. 1980g. *The Thanksgiving Mystery.* Chicago: A. Whitman.

———. 1981a. *The Christmas Eve Mystery.* Chicago: A. Whitman.

———. 1981b. *The Easter Mystery.* Chicago: A. Whitman.

———. 1981c. *Mysterious Queen of Magic.* Champaign, IL: Garrard Publishing.

———. 1981d. *Mystery Dolls from Planet Urd.* Champaign, IL: Garrard Publishing.

———. 1982. *The Specter.* New York: Delacorte.

———. 1983a. *Days of Fear.* New York: Dutton.

———. 1983b. *A Deadly Game of Magic.* San Diego: Harcourt Brace Jovanovich.

———. 1983c. *The Gift.* New York: Macmillan.

———. 1983d. *Magnolia's Mixed-Up Magic.* New York: Putnam.

———. 1984. *The Ghosts of Now.* New York: Delacorte.

———. 1985a. *The Horror.* New York: Scholastic.

———. 1985b. *Maggie, Too.* San Diego: Harcourt Brace Jovanovich.

———. 1985c. *The Stalker.* New York: Delacorte.

———. 1986a. *Beats Me, Claude.* New York: Viking Kestrel.

———. 1986b. *And Maggie Makes Three.* San Diego: Harcourt Brace Jovanovich.

———. 1986c. *The Other Side of Dark.* New York: Delacorte.

———. 1987a. *The Dark and Deadly Pool.* New York: Delacorte.

———. 1987b. *Fat Chance, Claude.* New York: Viking Kestrel.

———. 1987c. *Maggie Forevermore.* San Diego: Harcourt Brace Jovanovich.

———. 1988a. *If You Were a Writer.* New York: Four Winds.

———. 1988b. *Secret, Silent Screams.* New York: Delacorte.

———. 1989a. *Star Baby.* New York: Bantam Books.

———. 1989b. *You Bet Your Britches, Claude.* New York: Viking Kestrel.

———. 1990a. *Encore.* New York: Bantam Books.

———. 1990b. *Overnight Sensation.* New York: Bantam Books.

———. 1991. *A Candidate for Murder.* New York: Delacorte.

———. 1992a. *A Deadly Promise.* New York: Bantam Books.

———. 1992b. *That's the Spirit, Claude.* New York: Viking.

———. 1992c. *The Weekend Was Murder!* New York: Delacorte.

———. 1993. *The Name of the Game Was Murder.* New York: Delacorte.

———. 1994a. *A Dangerous Promise.* New York: Delacorte.

———. 1994b. *Shadowmaker.* New York: Delacorte.

———. 1994c. *When I Am Eight.* New York: Dial Books for Young Readers.

———. 1994d. *Will You Give Me a Dream?* New York: Four Winds.

———. 1995a. *Backstage with a Ghost.* New York: Disney.

———. 1995b. *Check in to Danger.* New York: Disney.

———. 1995c. *John's Story, 1775.* New York: Delacorte.

———. 1995d. *Keeping Secrets.* New York: Delacorte.

———. 1995e. *The Legend of Deadman's Mine.* New York: Disney.

———. 1995f. *Spirit Seeker.* New York: Delacorte.

———. 1995g. *The Statue Walks at Night.* New York: Disney.

———. 1996a. *Beware the Pirate Ghost.* New York: Disney.

———. 1996b. *Catch a Crooked Clown.* New York: Disney.

———. 1996c. *Don't Scream.* New York: Delacorte.

———. 1996d. *Fear Stalks Grizzly Hill.* New York: Disney.

———. 1996e. *The House Has Eyes.* New York: Disney.

———. 1996f. *Sabotage on the Set.* New York: Disney.

———. 1996g. *Search for the Shadowman*. New York: Delacorte.

———. 1996h. *Secret of the Time Capsule*. New York: Disney.

———. 1997a. *Bait for a Burglar*. New York: Disney.

———. 1997b. *Circle of Love*. New York: Delacorte.

———. 1997c. *The Internet Escapade*. New York: Disney.

———. 1997d. *Murdered, My Sweet*. New York: Delacorte.

———. 1998a. *Aggie's Home*. New York: Delacorte.

———. 1998b. *Champagne with a Corpse*. Lincolnwood, IL: Contemporary Books.

———. 1998c. *Champagne at the Murder*. Lincolnwood, IL: Contemporary Books.

———. 1998d. *Champagne at Risk*. Lincolnwood, IL: Contemporary Books.

———. 1998e. *David's Search*. New York: Delacorte.

———. 1998f. *The Haunting*. New York: Delacorte.

———. 1998g. *Lucy's Wish*. New York: Delacorte.

———. 1998h. *Will's Choice*. New York: Delacorte.

———. 1999. *Who Are You?* New York: Delacorte.

———. 2000a. *Ann's Story, 1747*. New York: Delacorte.

———. 2000b. *Caesar's Story, 1759*. New York: Delacorte.

———. 2000c. *Caught in the Act*. Milwaukee, WI: Gareth Stevens Publishing.

———. 2000d. *In the Face of Danger*. Milwaukee, WI: Gareth Stevens Publishing.

———. 2000e. *A Family Apart*. Milwaukee, WI: Gareth Stevens Publishing.

———. 2000f. *Ghost Town: Seven Ghostly Stories*. New York: Delacorte.

———. 2000g. *Nancy's Story, 1765*. New York: Delacorte.

———. 2000h. *Nobody's There*. New York: Delacorte.

———. 2000i. *A Place to Belong*. Milwaukee, WI: Gareth Stevens Publishing.

———. 2000j. *Over the Wall*. New York: Philomel Books.

———. 2001a. *Gus and Gertie and the Lucky Charms*. New York: SeaStar Books.

———. 2001b. *Land of Dreams*. Milwaukee, WI: Gareth Stevens Publishing.

———. 2001c. *Land of Hope*. Milwaukee, WI: Gareth Stevens Publishing.

———. 2001d. *Land of Promise*. Milwaukee, WI: Gareth Stevens Publishing.

———. 2001e. *Maria's Story, 1773*. New York: Delacorte.

———. 2001f. *Playing for Keeps*. New York: Delacorte.

———. 2001g. *Will's Story, 1771*. New York: Delacorte.

———. 2002a. *The Making of a Writer*. New York: Delacorte.

———. 2002b. *The Trap*. New York: Delacorte.

Ritter, John H. 1998. *Choosing Up Sides*. New York: Philomel Books.

———. 2001. *Over the Wall*. New York: Putnam.

———. 2003. *The Boy Who Saved Baseball*. New York: Philomel Books.

Smith, Cynthia Leitich. 2000. *Jingle Dancer*. New York: Morrow Junior Books.

———. 2001. *Rain Is Not My Indian Name*. New York: HarperCollins.

———. 2002. *Indian Shoes*. New York: HarperCollins.

Sones, Sonya. 1999. *Stop Pretending: What Happened When My Big Sister Went Crazy*. New York: HarperCollins.

———. 2001. *What My Mother Doesn't Know*. New York: Simon and Schuster Books for Young Readers.

Williams, Lori Aurelia. 2000. *When Kambia Elaine Flew in from Neptune*. New York: Simon and Schuster.

———. 2001. *Shayla's Double Brown Baby Blues*. New York: Simon and Schuster.

Professional Works Cited

Allen Janet. 1999. *Words, Words, Words: Teaching Vocabulary in Grades 4–12.* Portland, ME: Stenhouse.

———. 2001. *Yellow Brick Road: Shared and Guided Paths to Independent Reading, 4–12.* Portland, ME: Stenhouse.

Atwell, Nancie. 1987. *In the Middle: Writing, Reading, and Learning with Adolescents.* Portsmouth, NH: Heinemann.

Becoming a Nation of Readers: The Report of the Commission on Reading. 1985. Champaign, IL: Center for the Study of Reading, University of Illinois.

Beers, Kylene. 1990. Choosing Not to Read: An Ethnographic Study of Seventh-Grade Aliterate Students. Unpublished doctoral diss. University of Houston, TX.

———. 2002. *When Kids Can't Read, What Teachers Can Do.* Portsmouth, NH: Heinemann.

Beers, Kylene, and Barbara Samuels, eds. 1998. *Into Focus: Understanding and Creating Middle School Readers.* Norwood, MA: Christopher-Gordon.

Brown, Jean, and Elaine Stevens. 1995. *Teaching Young Adult Literature: Sharing the Connection.* Belmont, CA: Wadsworth.

Bushman, John, and Kay Parks Bushman. 1997. *Using Young Adult Literature in the English Classroom.* Columbus, OH: Merrill.

Carlsen, G. Robert. 1967. *Books and the Teenage Reader.* New York: Harper.

———. 1974. "Literature Is . . . ." *English Journal* 63: 23–27.

Carlsen, G. Robert, and Anne Sherrill. 1988. *Voices of Readers: How We Come to Love Books.* Urbana, IL: National Council of Teachers of English.

Carter, Betty, and Richard F. Abrahamson. 1990. *Nonfiction for Young Adults: From Delight to Wisdom.* Phoenix, AZ: Oryx Press.

Daniels, Harvey. 2002. *Literature Circles: Voice and Choice in Book Clubs and Reading Groups.* 2d ed. Portland, ME: Stenhouse.

Donelson, Kenneth, and Aileen Pace Nilsen. 1999. *Literature for Today's Young Adults.* Glenview, IL: Scott Foresman.

Early, Margaret. 1960. "Stages in Growth in Literary Appreciation." *English Journal* 49: 161–167.

Estes, Thomas. 1971. "A Scale to Measure Attitude Toward Reading." *Journal of Reading* 15: 135–138.

Fox, Mem. 2001. *Reading Magic: Why Reading Aloud to Our Children Will Change Their Lives Forever.* San Diego: Harcourt Brace Jovanovich.

Gallo, Donald R. 1985. "Are Kids Reading or Aren't They?" *ALAN Review* (Winter): 46–50.

Hahn, Mary Lee. 2002. *Reconsidering Read-Aloud.* Portland, ME: Stenhouse.

Havighurst, Richard. 1972. *Developmental Tasks and Education.* New York: David McKay.

Hipple, Ted. 1991. "What Are the Qualities of a Good Book for Young Adults?" Speech at the Sam Houston State University Young Adult conference. November 1, 1991, Huntsville, TX.

Janeczko, Paul. 2003. *Opening a Door: Reading Poetry in the Middle School Classroom.* New York: Scholastic.

Kohlberg, Lawrence. 1976. "Moral Stages and Moralization." In *Moral Development and Behavior,* ed. T. Lickona. New York: Harper and Row.

———. 1987. *Child Psychology and Childhood Education.* New York: Longman.

Kutiper, Karen. 1985. A Survey of Adolescent Poetry Preferences of Seventh-, Eighth-, and Ninth-Graders. Unpublished doctoral diss. University of Houston, Houston, TX.

Livaudais, Mary. 1986. A Survey of Secondary Students' Attitudes Toward Reading Motivation Activities. Unpublished doctoral dissertation, University of Houston, Houston, TX.

Ley, Terry C. 1979a. "Getting Kids into Books: The Importance of Individualized Reading." *Media & Methods* 15: 22–25.

———. 1979b. "How to Set Up and Evaluate a DIR Program." *Media & Methods* 15: 21–25.

Maslow, Abraham. 1982. *Toward a Psychology of Being.* New York: Van Nostrand Reinhold.

McElmeel, Sharron. 2001. *ABCs of an Author/Illustrator Visit.* 2d ed. Worthington, OH: Linworth.

Norton, Donna. 2003. *Through the Eyes of a Child.* Upper Saddle River, NJ: Prentice Hall.

Peck, Richard. 1978. "Questions to Ask About a Novel." *ALAN Review* 5: 1, 7.

Piaget, Jean. 1969. *The Psychology of the Child.* New York: Basic Books.

———. 1971. *Science of Education and the Psychology of the Child.* New York: Viking.

Piaget, Jean, and Barbel Inhelder. 1969. *The Psychology of the Child.* New York: Basic Books.

Rief, Linda. 1992. *Seeking Diversity: Language Arts with Adolescents.* Portsmouth, NH: Heinemann.

Ross, Catherine S. 1995. "If They Read Nancy Drew, So What?: Series Book Readers Talk Back." *Library and Information Science Research* 17 (3): 201–236. Recipient of the 1995 Jesse Shera Award for Research.

Smith, Frank. 1997. *Reading Without Nonsense.* New York: Teachers College Press.

Sullivan, Edward T. 2002. *Reaching Reluctant Young Adult Readers: A Practical Handbook for Librarians and Teachers.* Lanham, MD: Scarecrow.

Terry, C. Ann. 1974. *Children's Poetry Preferences: A National Survey of the Upper Elementary Grades.* Urbana, IL: National Council of Teachers of English.

Trelease, Jim. 2002. *The New Read-Aloud Handbook.* 4th ed. New York: Penguin Putnam.